Time Lords and Star Cops

Manchester University Press

Time Lords and Star Cops

British science fiction television in the 1970s–1980s

Philip Braithwaite

MANCHESTER UNIVERSITY PRESS

Copyright © Philip Braithwaite 2023

The right of Philip Braithwaite to be identified as the author of this work has been asserted in accordance with the Copyright, Designs and Patents Act 1988.

Published by Manchester University Press
Oxford Road, Manchester M13 9PL

www.manchesteruniversitypress.co.uk

British Library Cataloguing-in-Publication Data
A catalogue record for this book is available from the British Library

ISBN 978 1 5261 6337 0 hardback
ISBN 978 1 5261 8729 1 paperback

First published 2023
Paperback published 2025

The publisher has no responsibility for the persistence or accuracy of URLs for any external or third-party internet websites referred to in this book, and does not guarantee that any content on such websites is, or will remain, accurate or appropriate.

EU authorised representative for GPSR:
Easy Access System Europe – Mustamäe tee 50, 10621 Tallinn, Estonia, gpsr.requests@easproject.com

Typeset
by Cheshire Typesetting Ltd, Cuddington, Cheshire

Contents

Acknowledgements	*page* vi
Introduction	1
1 British science fiction television in the consensus era: authority and paternalism	20
2 'Wealth is the only reality': *Blake's 7* and Thatcherism	63
3 *Sapphire & Steel*: the illusion of independence	87
4 Rewriting the Doctor: *Doctor Who* in the late Thatcher era	116
5 'A precarious existence': science fiction television adaptations of the 1980s	147
6 'It Won't be Easy': original science fiction series of the 1980s	175
Conclusion	206
Television programmes discussed	217
Bibliography	221
Index	234

Acknowledgements

The inspiration for this book – and much of its contents – grew out of my PhD thesis, so I'd like to thank my supervisors for that project: Associate Professors Luke Goode and Neal Curtis at the University of Auckland. Both of them gave me valuable advice and shaped my thinking in ways that they will recognise in the pages of this book.

I'd also like to thank the BBC Written Archives Centre in Reading, who provided me with endless documents to pore over.

Thanks to Matthew Frost and the team at Manchester University Press, who made the process easy and enjoyable. The final stages of this book were completed during a sabbatical, so I want to thank my colleagues at the University of Central Lancashire for allowing me the time to finish this work.

Finally, to my wife Jennifer, for her endless faith, patience and encouragement.

Introduction

One evening when I was a small child, my parents took me to a dinner with their friends. I didn't want to go: I wanted to stay at home and watch the final episode of *Blake's 7*. Fortunately, my parents' friends allowed me to watch it in a bedroom, on a tiny television set. There I witnessed a massacre: all the heroes of the series fall into a trap engineered by the evil Galactic Federation, and one by one they are slaughtered. In the final frame, Avon, the Machiavellian alpha male of the crew of rebels, is surrounded by Federation troopers. He has no means of escape. He raises his weapon slowly, while facing the camera and smiling enigmatically. The screen cuts to the closing credits as the sounds of gunshots are heard.

It wasn't until 2007 that I saw a comparable ending in television, and it came by way of David Chase's celebrated series, *The Sopranos* (1999–2007). In the final scene of that series, mob boss Tony Soprano and his family are in a diner. Tony's crew has just come out of a mob war. Tony has survived, but Tony is always a marked man. He selects a song on the mini-jukebox: Journey's 'Don't Stop Believin''. As his daughter Meadow walks into the diner, we cut to Tony's face looking up at her, and then the screen sharply cuts to black, with the chorus of the song ringing out, 'Don't stop ...'. There has been much interpretation of that final moment: was it merely a statement that 'life goes on', with the ending serving as an arbitrary cut-off point? Or, as the more popular theory suggests (and Chase himself has seemingly confirmed), was Tony shot, with the blackness an indication that he had ceased to 'see' anything? Perhaps if it is the latter then Journey's song is treated ironically.

In any case, though it is a completely different genre, in its ambiguity and fatalism the ending of *The Sopranos* reminded me of the ending of *Blake's 7*. Both end by killing most or all of the protagonist's crew and hinting at the death of the protagonist himself. In the case of *Blake's 7*, Avon's ironic look to the camera indicates perhaps a resignation, a cynical confirmation of his fear – or his conviction – that the struggle was futile from the start. Or could it be intended to indicate his knowledge that the struggle will continue even if he and his crew are dead, remembered as martyrs? Perhaps then his smile is a rueful acknowledgement that resistance is not about the individual, but the movement.

The Sopranos, and the series following it which to some extent derive from its storytelling techniques (*Breaking Bad*, *Mad Men*, *Deadwood*, *Fargo* and others) are considered a fresh approach to televisual storytelling, and to the treatment of character. Indeed they apply a complexity of character and story that sometimes borders on Shakespearian tragedy. Blurring the binaries of 'good' and 'evil', they present the 'anti-hero' as the protagonist: a morally compromised character, suspended in a liminal space between altruism and cruelty, responsibility and selfishness; between 'moral' and 'immoral' behaviour. Yet the ending of *Blake's 7*, originally broadcast in 1981, shocked and fascinated me as a child because of the same basic ambiguities and tensions. It was the first example of science fiction television – or any genre television – I had seen which refused to reassure its audience of a simplistic morality: that good triumphs over evil. Instead, it blurred the distinctions between 'good' and 'evil' in a manner that forced me to question my own understanding of the categories.

Though *Blake's 7* and contemporaneous British science fiction television series are enjoyable and have garnered cult followings, they are not generally regarded as exemplars of great film-making, and they seldom make significant aesthetic contributions to their genre. *Blake's 7* (1978–81), *Sapphire & Steel* (1979–82) and late-era *Doctor Who* (1963–89) in the Thatcher era, as well as shorter and less successful series like *The Tripods* (1984–85), *Star Cops* (1987) and *Knights of God* (1987), are mostly made cheaply: the 'special effects' are often embarrassing; the costumes, makeup, sets, sometimes even the acting, are poor quality. Studies have been written that re-evaluate the aesthetic and technical sides of these productions, and these will be mentioned where relevant, but I am less interested in the visual effects or cinematography. The point I want to make is that these series, despite their limitations, are cultural artefacts, no less significant as descriptors of their time than any other. And they are more than that. As the 1970s and 1980s progress, the most salient of these series become, in a small way, radical: they depart significantly from the traditions built around generic science fiction television (the word 'generic' is used in this book only to refer to the genre to which they all belong, not to diminish them or suggest a formulaic approach). They depict dystopian worlds plagued by authoritarianism. They problematise binaries of good and evil; they become a site where 'virtuous' characteristics – courage, heroism, loyalty – clash uncomfortably with selfishness and greed. The characters no longer offer certainties, they no longer reassure; instead they estrange us in a way that is unique to their era. In short, they describe, critique and problematise the transition to Thatcherite neoliberalism.

The change was not without precedent. As this book will highlight, the earlier 1970s series such as *UFO* (1970), *Space: 1999* (1975–77) and *Survivors* (1975–77) pave the way for this mentality. The worlds they present are still governed by different – and more traditional – forces. They possess a kind of optimism and teleology, a faith in technology as the driving force of future enlightenment. The protagonists in these series are often scientists or military men, with an authority that is basically undisputed. People always invest great trust in them and they usually deliver. But there is a creeping change – a Realpolitik attitude, a more compromised character – beginning to emerge. The series of the 1980s capitalise on this darker character and bring it to the fore.

My contention is that these 1980s series – in many ways markedly different from the generic science fiction television series that preceded them – are wrestling with a new set of cultural and political ideas in the real-world environment in which they were produced. Replacing the optimism and teleology of the 1970s series is a cynicism and futility unique to the 1980s. Replacing the hopeful, rational and morally centred characters of the 1970s are cynical, Machiavellian and ironic 'heroes'. The utopian dream has become a dystopian nightmare. These ideas were tentatively and sporadically emerging in the early and mid-1970s, and were cemented by way of Britain's decisive restructure of 1979: the beginning of Thatcherism, and even more significantly, the beginning of neoliberal economics, which will be discussed throughout the book. As a result, the series reveal a great deal about this restructure, and provide a window into understanding the way that popular culture negotiated with this change. This is especially so for science fiction because of its special capacity to imagine distant, new, or alternative worlds in which to play out contemporary anxieties.

Other writers have, to some extent, explored the area of British science fiction television and its relation to Thatcherism, though the list is relatively short. Wright (2006, 2009) has written the most extensively on the subject of *Sapphire & Steel* and Thatcherism, and my analysis of *Sapphire & Steel* in Chapter 3 owes a great deal to Wright's assessment of the series. Some writers have also hinted at the connection between Thatcherism and *Blake's 7*. Bignell and O'Day (2004), Bould (2008) and Cornea (2011) have discussed the connection between Servalan, the female president of the fictional Terran Federation in *Blake's 7*, and Thatcher, noting the subversion of traditionally feminine roles in both cases (leading to very different outcomes). McCormack (2006) mentions some of the political situations that may have inspired the series. Geraghty (2011) discusses the short-lived science fiction series *The Tripods* (1984–85), making comparisons to Thatcher's regime. This book draws together a discussion on the many ways the series challenge the then-emerging common sense of Thatcherism, and expands on work already done, offering comprehensive analyses of the impact of the neoliberal era and Thatcherism on individual science fiction series that in some cases were overlooked or undervalued.

Neoliberalism, Thatcherism, and British science fiction television

In order to understand the many ways in which these tensions were playing out within the series, it is necessary to briefly situate the Thatcher era in its context. This will lead to a discussion of neoliberalism, which is the most significant factor of change in the narrative of these series, but it is tempered by a Thatcherite sensibility which uses language that could be described as mythical. I will briefly examine the change that Thatcherism brought about and how it impacted television, and then connect it to the series.

A basic understanding of Thatcherism rests on two pillars: economic liberalism and social conservatism. Though Thatcherism did not 'come into its own' politically and economically until after the Falklands victory in 1982, the seeds of this 'revolution' were in evidence long before. The cultural theorist Stuart Hall begins the 'Thatcherite project' in 1975, which he calls the

> climacteric in British politics. First of all, the oil hike. Secondly, the onset of the capitalist crisis. Thirdly, the transformation of modern Conservatism by the accession of the Thatcherite leadership. (1988: 166)

In 1977, two years before her premiership, Thatcher said:

> I believe you won't get political freedom unless you also have economic freedom, which means that you must have a large part of free enterprise in your whole economy. (*Firing Line*, 1977)

This 'economic freedom' had been an undercurrent in British, American and European thought for some time. Filby notes that the right-wing Institute of Economic Affairs in Britain was set up in 1955 (2015: 90), and even earlier – in 1947 – economists such as Hayek, Friedman and others were meeting in private to discuss their ideas about the 'neoliberal turn'. Neoliberalism is an economic system which favours lower taxes, deregulation of industry and privatisation of state assets. But it is more than that: in Thatcher's reasoning, it is a highly *moral* system. Thatcher once claimed, 'Economics are the method; the object is to change the heart and soul' (1981a: para 3). Through selling state-owned assets and removing regulations, competition among private entrepreneurs is encouraged, allowing wealth creation, taking responsibility for welfare and other services away from the government and delivering it to the private citizen. The citizen then has greater control over their own finances and, Thatcher believed, they are then 'free'. However, when most of the traditional restrictions and obligations on workers and employers are lifted, it leaves them free to pursue the profit margin more aggressively. This can lead to cost-cutting measures that make the position of vulnerable employees precarious. It can also lead to a fragmented working environment, where priorities are constantly rearranged, and there is very little stability. Therefore, despite Thatcher's insistence on the moral nature of the system, in practice it could and did lead to a range of behaviours, including those that can be considered selfish and Machiavellian.

Technically distinct from economic radicalism, Thatcher used what she considered the Victorian ideal to explicate her vision of an ideal social structure (a point made by many scholars, as this book will show). In 1983, she said: 'The essence of Victorian times, they said, yes, they said there is a dark side, now let's tackle it. I don't know of any time when the tackling got faster' (1983b: sec. 2, para 76). This vision of tackling social wrongs matched with the virtue of work, would ultimately lead her to express her vision of a neoliberal economic system through the lens of personal, individual effort, rather than reliance on the State to solve one's problems.

When placed together, economic liberalism and Victorian social conservatism reveal a contradiction. On the one hand the free market allows the consumer to decide on issues of 'decency' and 'taste', which can easily lead to amoral outcomes. On the other hand Thatcher resorts to a Victorian morality for her guiding principles. This contradiction is, to some extent, reconciled in Thatcherism through what Antonio Gramsci (Hoare and Nowell Smith, 1999) would call 'common sense'. Rather than the 'practical wisdom' that people normally think of when the phrase is used, Gramsci thought of common sense as a collection of disparate and often contradictory ideas that people generally hold as coherent (traditional Christian beliefs and Darwinian evolution might be one example) (see Harvey, 2005: 39). Hall interprets Thatcherism through a Gramscian lens when he asks:

> How do we make sense of an ideology which is not coherent, which speaks now, in one ear, with the voice of free-wheeling, utilitarian, market-man, and in the other ear, with the voice of respectable,

bourgeois, patriarchal man? How do these two repertoires operate together? We are all perplexed by the contradictory nature of Thatcherism. (1988: 236)

He goes on to say that Thatcherism and its contradictions form a '"unity" out of difference' (236). This 'unity' is one he later characterises as 'marching towards the future clad in the armour of the past' (713). Thatcher worked very hard to reconcile the two poles by expressing one (economic 'freedom') in terms of the other (the Victorian emphasis on hard work and self-reliance), but the tension between these two ideological positions remained and bled into the science fiction television analysed in this book.

Thatcher also found a unique means of delivering her ideas. A tool for understanding the power of Thatcherite rhetoric, to which this book will occasionally return, is Roland Barthes's concept of 'mythologies' from his eponymous 1957 book. Barthes's central argument in *Mythologies* is that bourgeois society uses its ideological positions to 'turn history into nature' (Allen, 2003: 36) The bourgeois class uses its positions to de-historicise the bourgeois view of reality and focus on a mythological 'universality' of human nature.

Barthes discusses the idea that society is composed of 'essential types' (1991: 156) – characters with an archetypal quality – which are identified by the bourgeois class to impose a hierarchy of values. Some qualities are considered by the bourgeois class as 'good', and others 'bad'. This usually necessitates a kind of erasure of 'true' history, with all its vicissitudes, collapsed into a mythical grand narrative, describing the 'natural' development of essentialist ideas. Barthes provides an example of these concepts in the oft-cited representation of the French soldier, which Barthes came across on the cover of the magazine *Paris Match*. The soldier is black, saluting the French flag. As Barthes relates, 'I see very well what it signifies to me: that France is a great Empire, that all her sons, without any colour discrimination, faithfully serve under her flag' (114). The ideological connotations made of that are clear – the collapsing of history into timelessness by way of a denial of the history of colonialism and all its complications; the acceptance without nuance of a French imperial superiority. Mythology, then, in Barthes's view, takes what is a constructed set of events – history – and makes them seem inevitable, self-evidently correct and 'timeless'. This concept will be discussed and elaborated on throughout the book with references to various television series.

In a speech she gave at the University of Zurich, Switzerland, in 1977, Thatcher used a 'common-sense' approach to combine economic freedom with social conservatism in a way that was to become a rhetorical signature:

> In our philosophy the purpose of the life of the individual is not to be the servant of the State and its objectives, but to make the best of his talents and qualities. The sense of being self-reliant, of playing a role within the family, of owning one's own property, of paying one's own way, are all part of the spiritual ballast which maintains responsible citizenship, and provides the solid foundation from which people look around to see what more they might do, for others and for themselves. That is what we mean by a moral society; not a society where the State is responsible for everything, and no one is responsible for the State. (sec. 2, para 65)

Here, Thatcher uses words such as 'spiritual' and 'moral' and aligns them with an economic system, which has the effect of naturalising that economic system, and implicitly painting socialism as the moral enemy.

The Thatcherite 'common sense' was brought to bear on many sectors of society which were traditionally reliant on public funds, including television. To take the example of the BBC, debate had raged for decades about the political leanings of the network, with many politicians accusing it of being too left wing. Thatcher herself interfered in much of the BBC's workings and made herself unpopular among the management (discussed further in later chapters). Because of her social conservatism, Thatcher was in favour of the network and its 'traditional' values insofar as they had been preserved, and where they had been eroded in her estimation, she sought to redress the balance, appointing her own ministers and colleagues to the Board of Governors. Then, in the opposite direction, neoliberal economics dictated that the BBC would operate more efficiently under a commercial model, dislodging it from its public service roots and launching it into the choppy waters of market forces. To this end the Peacock Committee was established in 1985 to investigate whether the BBC should be privatised in the long term. The Thatcherite common sense as applied to the BBC was not wholly successful – she didn't manage to fully commercialise the network – but she and her government did manage to introduce competitive measures that severely inhibited the broadcaster's ability to take artistic risks, which affected the process of funding television programmes – especially science fiction – in the 1980s.

The science fiction television series studied in this book grapple with the Thatcherite 'mythologies' by various means as they contend with the emerging world of Thatcherism. *Blake's 7* and *Sapphire & Steel* begin their run early in the Thatcher era, and present morally and ethically compromised characters who, for the sake of personal enrichment, are persuaded to take various measures that might have horrified their generic predecessors. Those two series, as we will see in later chapters, anticipate the change through their presentations of characters with Machiavellian, cynical attitudes, highlighting the new emphasis on wealth and individualism and the loss of collectivism. *Blake's 7* begins to explore a kind of Realpolitik pragmatism, using the central character of Avon to argue (as Thatcher did) for wealth as the only guarantee of freedom; *Sapphire & Steel* is both a lament for a 'lost' Britain, already mythologised, and a right-wing dream of progress while entombed in an indeterminate and inert present; *Doctor Who*, already in production since 1963, emerges from its complacency into a fragmented and uncertain world, and in the 1980s the series approaches Thatcherism from a position of (broadly left-wing) dissent, yet buckles in opposition to it. Though outspoken in its disavowal of Thatcherism, the series nonetheless mimics the uncertainty and contradictions of that system in its structure, with the central character of the Doctor presented as a duplicitous, and ultimately authoritarian, figure, no longer worthy of complete trust. The 1981 adaptation of John Wyndham's *The Day of the Triffids* critiques Thatcherism in a representation of a Britain abandoned by a rapacious government while people riot in the streets (Geraghty, 2011: 106). This image of Britain also appears in the final *Quatermass* serial, broadcast in 1979. *The Tripods*, broadcast in 1984–85, presents a post-apocalyptic Britain ravaged by giant alien machines. Its regressive vision of a future bucolic idyll setting is reminiscent of Thatcher's Victorian dream (Geraghty, 2011: 105). All the series wrestle with the contradictory tropes of Thatcherism, and become somewhat contradictory in their own messaging.

A 'constellation' of theories

This book will deploy two different methods to analyse the ways science fiction television reflected the neoliberal change in the Thatcher years. The first, where relevant, is from an institutional standpoint – the way television was structured, the debates around television production at the time. The second, and much more substantial, is from the perspective of content – the ways in which the television series themselves encoded ruminations on the society they existed within. The two are intertwined. Television is a populist medium, and as such it relies on large quantities of money, and needs to provide for public taste. So the two are connected by means of the political economy. Both point to the same idea: that neoliberalism and the authoritarianism of the Thatcher government changed the landscape of television.

Television, as a populist medium, is potentially more powerful than literature as a means of reaching a wide range of people. This was particularly so in the era before streaming and cable services. In the 1950s and 1960s, this power was keenly felt. Caughie comments that many of his contemporaries in the 1950s 'came out of university with the idea that culture mattered, and that television as a popular form was an arena in which a difference might be made' (2000: 61). Much of this idealism has been eroded in the intervening decades, but television remains a politically potent form of entertainment and subject of academic study.

Turnock notes that television's '"multifarious" nature' demands a multidisciplinary approach when studying its impact on society' (2007: 7). The concepts discussed in this book are informed by such an approach, and together form what Adorno would call a 'constellation' of theories and theoretical structures:

there is no step-by-step progression from the concepts to a more general cover concept. Instead, the concepts enter into a constellation. (2004: 162)

The 'constellation of theories' in this book sits at the crossroads between science fiction studies, television studies and British cultural studies. These three sets of discourse are applied to the works studied in an interdisciplinary manner because their themes and concerns are all interconnected. The arrangement of theories I am using shares some of the same theoretical underpinnings, combining textual analysis with cultural analysis, allowing us to explore the connection between Thatcherism and science fiction television from different (but complementary) angles. From this position I will present the case that the science fiction television series that appeared just before and during the Thatcher era slowly changed from representing a world of moral certainty, social cohesion and taken-for-granted authority, to a fractured world of individualism, amorality and duplicity: a reaction to the emerging hegemony of what became Thatcherism.

For the major series studied, an authoritarianism was often coupled with a cynicism and Machiavellian world view, markedly different from the series of the early 1970s. Individualism is critiqued – sometimes passionately adhered to, sometimes rejected. In the minor series, which I look at in the last two chapters, the Machiavellianism and cynicism of the protagonists have receded, but the dread of authoritarianism is present, sometimes even intensified, and neoliberal practices are often at the forefront.

To determine how much of this was 'intentional' is always already complicated in a medium like television because of the nature of its collaborative process. Some television producers in this era were clearly anti-Thatcher. Andrew Cartmel (script editor for *Doctor Who* in 1988–89) and his writers (and even Sylvester McCoy, the actor who played the Doctor in that era), are on record voicing their opposition to Thatcher and outlining how that opposition found its way into the series. Chris Boucher, who became the driving force behind *Blake's 7*, based the characters on revolutionaries like Che Guevara, pointing to a left-wing and therefore anti-Thatcher stance. But to claim any consistent and unified political stance across the series of this era (or any era) is problematic. Television production is the result of many creative minds, as well as logistical concerns. Kracauer reminds us that 'films are never the product of an individual', citing the Russian film director Pudovkin, who emphasises 'the collective character of film production by identifying it with industrial production' (1946: 5). The same can be said for television production. Mimi White adds to this notion by writing that television is

> a mass industrial medium involving a variety of texts, produced by many different groups (and individuals), and aimed at a broad and heterogeneous set of audiences. It thus becomes difficult to talk about a single set of beliefs or ideas that are carried by television in any simple or immediate sense. (1992: 164)

To that end, it is too reductive to focus only on the intended meaning of one 'auteur'.

Further to this point, Bignell and O'Day write that the 'authorial intent' of Terry Nation, creator of both *Survivors* and *Blake's 7*, 'is dissimilar in principle to the network of interpretations that audiences in fact create when watching the programme' (2004: 176). This approach finds resonance in Barthes's contention that any text is a 'fabric of quotations' (1989: 148): the author is born into language and merely shapes it as they write. The language used has many more connotations and possible meanings than the author intended or was aware of, which are decoded by the audience according to their own experiences, personal biographies and social status. Therefore, even if the claim could be made that any text has a sole author or 'auteur', nonetheless the author is not the sole shaper of meaning. This position is further problematised within the multi-author format of television. For these reasons it is sometimes necessary to employ a degree of speculation and interpretation, concordant with discourses around television studies, cultural studies and other disciplines.

With all this in mind, there are nonetheless enough changes in the 1970s, and enough internal changes especially within the BBC in particular, that limit the range of interpretations possible. Scholars of television such as Stuart Hall (2006), John Fiske (1980), Alan McKee (2001), Ted Nanicelli (2017) and Matt Hills (2018) discuss in different ways the flow of meanings written into the televisual text, and the process of audience interpretation. Hall labels this process 'encoding/decoding' and contends that there is a 'preferred meaning' that the writers and producers 'encode' into televisual texts, but they are 'decoded' in ways that are sometimes oppositional to those preferred readings (2006: 35). Televisual texts are polysemous – having many possible meanings and readings – and for Nannicelli (2017), this is a problem because of what he dubs 'ontological constructivism' – which Hills describes as texts taking on 'a heterogeneous range of different meanings for different audiences' (2018: 172). Hills discusses Sandvoss (2004) and his similar term 'neutrosemy', which claims that the text is so open-ended that it functions 'as a blank screen on which fans' self-image is reflected' (2018: 172). However, Hills stresses that televisual interpretation and audience readings 'remain grounded in available cultural discourses and textual ambiguities, so this is never an interpretive free-for-all' (2018: 172). This is congruent with my argument that the televisual text, while 'open' to an extent, also exists within a finite range of readings, and it has been my task to 'decode' these meanings in a specific light – the series' connection to the emerging Thatcherite world of neoliberal economics.

Television is a product of its era, uniquely 'time-tied' according to Ellis (2007: 18). It is reflective of its social and cultural milieu, and attentive to the concerns of the era in which it is produced. Across both networks, television series before and during Thatcher's administration were, of course, making social commentary relevant to the contemporary moment, sometimes more directly than science fiction series. Comedy series *The Good Life* (1975–78) presents a protagonist tired of his career as a graphic designer, designing meaningless consumer objects. *Me & My Girl* (1984–88), a saccharine comedy about a single father and his daughter, portrays the protagonist Simon as the co-director of an advertising agency. Martin, the highly strung protagonist in the sitcom *Ever Decreasing Circles* (1984–89) becomes dismayed when he discovers his wife may be active in left-wing student politics. All three depict a new world of corporatism which was absent in sitcoms of the 1960s, and their politics are largely conservative.

By contrast, drama series *Boys from the Blackstuff* (1980–82), *Edge of Darkness* (1985), *The Singing Detective* (1986), and even the absurd comedy of *The Young Ones* (1982–84) appear to make pointed criticisms of the emerging and evolving Thatcherite milieu, expressing more radical political positions. But science fiction is particularly useful as social commentary because of its ability to create distance between the reality of the moment, and its own fictional world: in the middle ground is a fertile subtext. Many movies and television series speak to their time, but science fiction does so in a specific way. Science fiction pulls us out of our milieu, complicating our social, political and psychological expectations, and relocating us in an unfamiliar terrain: a different time, place and society.

Darko Suvin calls this 'new place' the 'novum'. Drawn from the work of Ernst Bloch (1995 [1954]), the novum refers to 'newness', and relates to the presence of a new thing – machine, device, place or characteristic – in the story that allows us to imagine a different ordering of our world. This has the effect of distancing us from the present moment, and reflecting back on it. Suvin contends that:

> An SF narration is a fiction in which the SF element or aspect, the novum, is hegemonic, that is, so central and significant that it determines the whole narrative logic – or at least the overriding narrative logic – regardless of any impurities that might be present. (1979: 75)

It can explore new ways of behaving and being, governed by a logic that is, for Suvin, cognitively derived. This means that, for Suvin, science fiction is always based on science, and the logic of the science fiction world is always based on scientific principles, rather than magic or myth.

Suvin describes a 'feedback oscillation' (1979: 73) that reverberates back and forth between the science fiction setting and the reader's and writer's present time. In this constant reverberation or 'oscillation' of familiar and unfamiliar, we are estranged, and therefore afforded a distance to reflect on our present society and notice the differences, as well as the similarities. This gives rise to his famous 'cognitive estrangement', with which we are able to see afresh the ideological constructs in our current time that may otherwise remain unconscious. Ryan and Kellner present a similar concept, which they call 'temporal displacement', writing, 'Fantasies of the future may simply be ways of putting quotation marks around the present' (1990: 254), suggesting that the future in science fiction texts is often an extrapolation of present concerns, and through engaging with these future scenarios, we are able to reflect on our own time with more clarity. This forces us to reflect on our own context, perhaps enabling us to view our own era as a part of an ever-changing historical landscape, rather than merely the 'natural' state of being.

Suvin contends that when he first wrote on science fiction, he imagined a more 'utopian' future, informed by his Marxist leanings. In 1979 he comments, 'As a minimum, we must demand from SF that it be wiser than the world it speaks to' (36). Since then he has developed a more dystopian view of recent history. He attributes this dystopian trend in large part to the rise of neoliberal economics, commenting in 2010:

> The central shift of horizons ... is that up to 1991 I was still confident that the antifascist impetus and achievements of my youth could be carried on – with whatever modifications towards a New Left and whatever huge difficulties in finding a way between capitalism and Stalinism. (2)

In 2014 he notes that from his earliest writings:

> I presupposed the tide of history was flowing, even if with regrettable eddies, towards socialism or democratic communism, and concentrated on the problems of understanding, pleasure, and form within that tide. Thus, I seem to have felt I could freeze or even freeze out history, as all pursuits of aesthetics do: transcending the moment. I was wrong. (sec. 5, para 2)

For these reasons Suvin transitioned from a more optimistic or utopian vision of humanity's future to a more dystopian one. Generic television science fiction has traditionally explored these two different future scenarios. The most obvious example of utopian science fiction is the *Star Trek* franchise (1966–present), which presents, in all its iterations, a galaxy where all (or at least most) peoples are united in a kind of galactic version of the UN. Most other science fiction series have, to some extent, blended the two. The major series studied in this book, however, are largely or wholly dystopian in their implications.

Suvin concedes that much science fiction writing has shifted towards the dystopian, and, as Wegner comments, he lays much of the blame on writers:

> too readily conceding to the central Thatcher/Reagan-era doctrine dubbed TINA ('There is no alternative') ... In such a view, Suvin argues, the global neo-liberal free market order is presented as 'inevitable and unchangeable,' and the primary concern becomes how one might survive within it. (2010: xxii)

The series studied in this book, most obviously *Blake's 7*, are examinations within generic television science fiction appearing in the Thatcherite landscape of a kind of concession to this emerging system, and 'how one might survive within it'. The series anticipate the rise of this system and one of its architects – Thatcher herself.

Studies more relevant to televisual and filmic science fiction have emerged, expanding on Suvin's work, and much of it situates the genre within the format of television. Catherine Johnston 'borrows' the term 'telefantasy' from fan discourse. It is not a term that is used in TV production, but is useful in describing the way television uses elements of science fiction and other influences. It's probable that all the series discussed in this book fit into what Johnson and others describe as telefantasy, which is a way to bring together fantasy, science fiction and horror television programmes. Indeed, the format of television is flexible enough that it can and does incorporate any number of influences. Bignell and O'Day comment, 'While programmes are assimilated into a dominant genre, all texts necessarily participate in several genres simultaneously and this extends the boundaries of authorship (2004: 74). This is particularly common in television programmes. *Sapphire & Steel* contains elements of detective fiction and ghost stories. *Doctor Who* scavenges its sources very widely indeed, from any number of generic influences. But all are subordinated into the genre of science fiction.

I will also draw from Utopian studies, particularly Tom Moylan's (2000) notion of the 'critical dystopia'. Moylan sees the critical dystopian texts as those which open up traditional dystopian narrative to name a utopian elsewhere that resists becoming filled in by a determinate content that would compromise or shut down its own most radical gesture to a future that is not yet achieved. (2000: 189)

With its tendency to revolution, *Blake's 7* fits into this category. *Doctor Who* also uses this concept in some of the worlds the Doctor visits.

All of these areas together – television studies, cultural studies and science fiction studies – will contribute to a composite understanding of the television series studied in this book and the ways in which they discuss and critique the Thatcherite administration and its neoliberal system.

Structure and rationale

The series selected for this book are all examples of science fiction television in the era designed to reach a broad audience – the 'family' or 'adult' demographic, rather than strictly for children. The study also avoids comedy series (because they follow a different logic which is outside of the scope of this book to explore), and uses only live-action series as examples. Even then, it is not possible to comment on every series or serial made in this era, and some are inevitably left out. I have endeavoured to select the most salient and representative series of the era, with the most to say (on a consistent basis) about the political state of the nation.

Chapter 1: 'British science fiction television in the consensus era: authority and paternalism' looks at the 1970s – the last decade of the consensus era – and analyses the science fiction television produced in that era, including ITV series *UFO* (1970) and *Space: 1999* (1975–77). These series were produced by the impresario Lew Grade, who looked to the American market, and negotiated the production styles of both British and American television. This resulted in a hybridised product. Alongside this are BBC series *Survivors* (1975–77), *Moonbase 3* (1973) and the 1970s incarnations of *Doctor Who* (1963–89). Changes from the 1950s/1960s were detectable, but my contention is that this era still retains many of the characteristics of the consensus era, including optimism – faith in technology – a strong belief in the authority of the male protagonist, and a conservative trust in the efficacy and reliability of the government.

Over the following chapters – 2, 3 and 4 – I examine the major series to have appeared during the Thatcher years: *Blake's 7* (1978–81), *Sapphire & Steel* (1979–82) and late *Doctor Who* (focusing on the era 1983–89). Each of these series presents a different critique of Thatcherism, whether from a conservative perspective (*Sapphire & Steel*, though its conservatism is the subject of debate in the chapter) or a more radical one. Much criticism has been directed at them for not living up to contemporaneous American science fiction television, and this will be examined. These series present in many ways a negation of many of the positions of the consensus era. Where the early 1970s series at least exhibited faith – in technology, or authority – the series in this middle-ground often present inertia, paralysis and a loss of meaning. *Blake's 7* never presents any nostalgia, nor any future vision; *Sapphire & Steel*, which is forever entombed in the non-specific present, remains pessimistic about progress. *Doctor Who* in the Thatcher era presents a breakdown of trust in most political systems, and even in the Doctor himself.

Chapters 5 and 6 discuss the less successful science fiction series of the 1980s. Chapter 5, '"A precarious existence": science fiction television adaptations of the 1980s', looks at the 1981 adaptation of *The Day of the Triffids*, and the 1984–85 adaptation of *The Tripods* series. Most of the focus of the chapter is on *The Tripods*, because of the many connections it makes with the neoliberal era, and the logic of authoritarianism. Chapter 6, '"It Won't be Easy": original science fiction series of the 1980s', looks at the only two science fiction television series of the 1980s written directly for television: *Knights of God* and *Star Cops*, both broadcast in 1987. The two series are radically different, but both are anchored in the neoliberal world. We will see that the series are slowly 'colonised' by these new ideas – of market liberalism, of Machiavellian behaviour brought about by the offering of individual 'freedom', though offering as many forms of resistance along the way. In the 1970s they operate similarly to the series before them – reflecting their social issues for sure, but also being somewhat content with the status quo.

Neoliberalism has now become the dominant economic system in the Western world, and at the present time this system is in crisis. Recent years have produced crises such as the global financial crisis of 2007–08 and the subsequent Wall Street crash, and now we are in the midst of a new oil and gas crisis. Yet the system continues. We are in a potential period of deformation and possible reformation of this system. There are attempts by identitarian groups from all sides of the political spectrum to mobilise the crisis, and despite attempts, there are no obvious answers as to what should or could solve the current dilemma. This book explores the beginning of that economic system in Britain and looks at some of the science fiction texts that emerged within it, negotiating and challenging its basic axioms.

1

British science fiction television in the consensus era: authority and paternalism

The political and economic tensions of 'consensus-era Britain', beginning at the end of the Second World War and ending in 1979 with Thatcher's election, reached a crisis point in the 1970s. This era saw a focus on state ownership of assets and a governmental commitment to social welfare, housing, education, employment, labour unions and public health, but fell apart under its own weight. It reached its final disaster in 1979 when the Callaghan-led Labour government, in an attempt to control inflation, imposed sanctions on trade unions, resulting in strikes. These strikes caused blackouts in what was the coldest winter in sixteen years, the so-called 'Winter of Discontent'. This crisis strengthened the Thatcher-led Conservative Party in the year that they won the general election and began to point to the alternative of a market-led economy.

This chapter focuses on the content of some of the science fiction series produced in the last decade of the 'consensus' era, situated in their cultural and political context. An analysis of these series allows a counterpoint to the way the themes are explored, and subverted, in the Thatcher era. Through analysis of the emerging themes of these series, it will become apparent how the later series in the Thatcher era represent a strong departure from the series that preceded them, despite exhibiting some similar themes and generic traditions. It is the work of this chapter to highlight these themes: where they differ, and where they prefigure elements of the later series. To that end, I have selected the series that most clearly function as the forerunners of Thatcher-era series, exhibiting in nascent form many of the themes either amplified or indeed reversed in the

Thatcher era. Though they are not intended to represent *all* the science fiction television produced in the era, they carry stylistic traits and themes that are indicative of the majority. With the exception of the *Quatermass* serials (1953–79, 2005) sketched out here because of their seminal place in British science fiction televisual history and their influence on later series, the chapter is limited to selected science fiction television series that were produced in the 1970s and intended for a wide audience. In these 1970s series people work together in groups, and the individual is not so prominent. The social-democratic society's hierarchical order is largely upheld. The class system is somewhat stratified, and this gives rise to the mythical 'hero figure' of the day. Within these fictional narratives the scientist, the military leader, the 'alpha male', all operate according to a moral duty. That duty is based in what Hutchings calls a 'Churchillian stoicism', which demands 'that relentless sacrifice is required in the conflict with the aliens' (2011: 95). This also draws influence from the American Western, which will be discussed. The alpha male and the military are at times in conflict, but they are nonetheless all 'heroes' in these narratives because of their shared devotion to duty.

Forster considers that the scientist is a 'mythologised figure' (2009: 77) in this era. His moral allegiance is to reason and rationality. The military leader too has fidelity to his crew or the units under his command, and ultimately to his country (or, in the case of *UFO*, his planet). They are all middle-class white men with authority. This man uses technology and rational thinking as his primary means of solving problems. He exhibits a moral attitude of duty to a political and civic system, whether governmental or military. He is almost always a traditional heroic figure: courageous, stoic, strong and intelligent. If necessary, he is prepared to sacrifice himself. Where there is moral deviation (taking the form of sacrificing someone else) it is an aberration, an exception to prove the rule, and it is executed only in the service of duty. All subordinates to this man place their faith and trust in him. This quite different set of ideas at play in these pre-Thatcher series work to naturalise certain ideological positions – the patriarchal system, the prevalence of rational thought over 'superstition', the waning of religious faith, the structure of authority, and the necessity of moderation and self-control. Later we will see more clearly the stark differences between them and the concerns of the Thatcher-era series.

Some writers have claimed an anxiety and discontent in the 1970s series, attributable to the very real political turmoil in the era. Forster writes that there is a 'mistrust of authority' in these series, which 'is keenly pertinent to the feeling of Britain in the 1970s' (2009: 82). Hutchings believes this era is 'characterised by economic troubles and political and social unrest' (2011: 87). Equally, Vohlidka claims, in a discussion of 1970s *Doctor Who*, that 'Britain was in a state of social turmoil: tensions over Northern Ireland, economic recession and immigration resulted in a more jaded society' (2013: 119). It is of course true that there was an erosion of trust in governmental authority in 1970s British society dating back to the Suez Crisis in 1956 and the Profumo affair in the 1960s, and the series do exhibit anxiety around issues like immigration, race, the environment, and other politically charged issues. But the challenges to political certainties, if they are that, seldom work as a challenge to the moral authority naturalised in the series, or to the *institution* of British democracy, at least in the abstract. Bureaucrats may be insufferable, government representatives tedious and unimaginative, but nonetheless the *idea* of British democracy is not subject to serious debate or dispute: its merits are considered self-evident. This all breaks down in the Thatcher era, where governmental authority, morality and faith are unshackled from their comfortable certainties, mainly by way of a deep cynicism and lack of trust in leaders. In the Thatcher era, authority is loathed, challenged, and threatened.

While it is true that these series grapple with forms of social and political discontent, I will argue that the 1970s series selected for this chapter take as almost axiomatic this version of the traditional male hero authority figure with all the associated attributes discussed, and many assumptions – about the role of women, the military, technological progress – are naturalised within that. The 1970s series may display stylistic differences between series and between networks, but their attitude to patriarchal values is very similar. Drawing many of their themes from science fiction novels – the BBC series borrow liberally from the work of H. G. Wells, also drawing from John Wyndham's *The Day of the Triffids* (1951), and Arthur C. Clarke's *Childhood's End* (1953) – they construct attributes of a certain British character: stoic, scientific, duty-bound, but with an occasional hint of the kind of Realpolitik and duplicitous behaviour that would be emphasised in the Thatcher era. Despite ITV and the BBC's somewhat competing agendas, the values of the paternalistic consensus era permeate across both networks. Arguably, the discontent with authority should've been more prominent on ITV because it contained 'Americanised' elements theoretically more associated with disaffected youth, but in practice it often endorsed officially sanctioned structures of authority more stridently than the BBC. The traditional pillars of the British Establishment are either treated uncritically, or are outwardly celebrated.

ITV: hybridity and Americanisation

The idea of 'Americanisation' was emerging as a discourse in the 1950s, when the growing affluence of Britons brought about a growth in consumerism, and this carried with it an interest in popular culture and, more specifically, American popular culture (Fiske, 2009: 263). According to Fiske, this culture was taken up by the working-class youth who

> found in its flashy streamlining a way to articulate their new class confidence and consciousness. Such symbolisations of their identity were simply not available in 'British' culture which appeared to offer two equally unacceptable sets of alternatives – the one a romanticised cloth-cap image of an 'authentic' traditional working-class culture, the other a restrained, tasteful, BBC-produced inflection of popular culture. (qtd in Johnston, 2009: 143)

Fiske goes on to comment how the commodities that American culture produced were seen as scandalous to the British Establishment (see Johnston, 2009: 143–4). This Establishment dislike of American culture reflected a more general fear of Americanisation: American cultural imports were typically seen as 'vulgar'. This 'mass culture' of consumerism came to a head in some aspects of ITV, the 'independent' network begun in 1955. Series like *Danger Man*

(ITV 1960–68) and *The Saint* (ITV 1962–69) were made to exploit American styles of storytelling overlaid with a British sensibility.

The word 'Americanisation' then, applies to a set of cultural values: a 'crude' nationalism, a certain superficiality, and advertising mass market products designed to appeal to the 'lowest common denominator'. As Bignell writes, 'America stood for commerce, and thus not only vigour, entrepreneurialism and progress, but also venality, greed and exploitation' (2005: 62). Loss of cultural specificity was also of great concern for the British Establishment, and the arrival of ITV signalled fears of a more fractured society (Turnock, 2007: 50), though Raymond Williams, a pioneer in television studies, claimed that British society was never as monolithic as the elites depicted it. Rodman notes of Williams that 'a truly democratic society cannot be built around the elitist assumption that "the masses" possess nothing more than a watered-down version of "real" culture' (2010: 154). Nonetheless, behind this notion of fragmentation was an Establishment fear that society would lose its values. There was a great deal of paternalism in these fears: the Establishment saw the BBC as 'the elder statesman, and "true" advocate of public service broadcasting' (Johnson and Turnock, 2005: 2), whereas ITV was 'less of a "Cinderella" institution and more of an "ugly sister"' (Johnson and Turnock, 2005: 2). This became apparent in the eventual differences in programming between the BBC and ITV, though it was not clear from the start.

All of these concerns, about the vulgarities and 'Americanisms' brought with the advent of advertising, and the 'lowered tone' of ITV programmes, came to a head in the person of Lew Grade. Grade was a symbol of the perceived threat, but also managed, if not to reconcile these two positions of free-market enterprise and public service, at least to complicate the whole process. Bignell comments:

> the adventure series associated with Grade were uncertainly poised in the perceptions of contemporaneous commentators as both high and low quality, as both British and American in character, so Grade's own role could be mobilised in conflicting and ambiguous ways. (2005: 60)

Grade was an impresario and show-business mogul. Originally from Ukraine, he came to Britain as a boy. Grade's company, the Incorporated Television Company (ITC), successfully made various television series under ITV, including those created by Gerry and Sylvia Anderson, most famously *Thunderbirds* (1964–66). Grade's operating methods were much more entrepreneurial in nature than anything previously witnessed in British public service broadcasting, and this led to a hybridisation of British and American styles and values, both on screen and off – Grade frequently made deals with American networks in order to broadcast the series his company made on American stations. He also encouraged co-productions between America and Britain, as well as for American productions to be made in Britain, such as *The Muppet Show* (1976–81). In a way, Grade's forays into the marketplace exemplified everything that the British Establishment feared about Americanisation. Bignell explains, '[America] stood for modernity, youth and opportunity, but also disrespect for tradition, loss of national specificity and cultural colonisation' (2005: 62). This all worked as a direct threat to the Establishment's British identity.

Not all cultural specificity is lost, however. *UFO* (1970), for instance, is still grounded in a recognisably 1960s/1970s London (despite being set in 1980). In a sense, these series are an answer to what later became the paradoxical approach of the Thatcher regime: how to retain 'British values' while at the same time exploiting the demands of the marketplace. But it is also important to mention that these series were not popular: *UFO* only lasted one season, while *Space: 1999* only made it to a second season after an extensive image overhaul. Some semblance of that British sense of culture can also be seen in these programmes – the 1970s aesthetic of *UFO*; the emphasis on characterisation and dialogue over action (though this changed in the second season of *Space: 1999*) – yet both are also generic and Americanised action-adventure programmes.

Within this framework, these series are carefully tailored to appeal to Americans and American values, and therefore the effect is that they become neither culturally specific nor completely generic, but somewhere in between. Turnock argues:

these genres were appropriated, reinterpreted and synthesised with cultural elements drawn from Britain and continental Europe. The end product was something that looked very British, yet there is an explicit connection with consumer culture here (2007: 156–7).

As Telotte (2008) noted, these series display a heavy reliance on technology, and mythologise it in various ways. Woodhead writes that in the consensus era, especially the 1960s, 'the Church ceased to offer a credible cultural and moral framework' (2016: sec. 1, para 19). This faith in technology, stemming from an Enlightenment faith in reason and science, came to replace religious faith as a dominant social discourse. The myth of forward-looking modernity and technology had been on the rise starting around the 1960s. Cornea notes, 'the 1960s was a time when science fiction and science fact became remarkably intertwined, sometimes blurred, particularly within the context of an American national preoccupation with the story of the Space Race' (2007: 79). In this era people were facing up to the implications of technology – the moon landings, jet technology in the development of Concorde in Britain and France, and architecture, where high-rise buildings were becoming a feature of the landscape (explored by J. G. Ballard in his 1975 novel *High-Rise*, later considered by O'Day as an influence on the *Doctor Who* story, 'Paradise Towers', which will be discussed in Chapter 4). Soon after, the impact of computer technology became prominent. By the 1970s, when Britain was facing economic and social troubles, faith in technology began to wane, but not to ebb away completely. There are times when technology is broadly mistrusted, or it leads to moral dilemmas, but the series are nonetheless driven by a teleology grounded in technological development. By contrast, the Thatcher-era series present a kind of technological inertia which Fisher, when writing of *Sapphire & Steel*, characterises as 'the slow cancellation of the future' (2014: 3), wherein time collapses on itself, and it seems there is no way forward, and nothing recognisable about 'now' to place it in a definite present. Some form of that inertia is apparent in all three of the major series studied, but absent here.

The series

The two Grade-produced ITC series discussed here: *UFO* (1970) and *Space: 1999* (1975–77), were both created and developed by Gerry and Sylvia Anderson, who are most associated with marionette series – most notably *Thunderbirds* (1964–66). Bould claims, 'Gerry Anderson's science fiction series consistently depict a utopian future benefiting from world government, high technology, ethnic diversity, and a generally positive sense of Americanisation' (2008: 219). This is very similar in tone to the utopian values of *Star Trek* (1966–69), and indeed the producer Fred Freiberger, who worked on the last season of *Star Trek*, was called upon to oversee the second season of *Space: 1999*. Despite this utopianism, Osgerby claims that the ITC productions were 'characterised by a sense of unease and insecurity ... the productions of the late Sixties and Seventies dramatised at a symbolic level the wider sense of crisis and the collapse of social and political certainties' (2000: 135). However, if this is true it is far less apparent than in the BBC series. These ITC series display a commercial American sensibility, driven more by the action/adventure genre, favouring entertainment over social commentary, even if they do engage in small measure with social problems such as nuclear weapons and the threat of nuclear war, xenophobia and racism.

UFO (1970), created by Gerry and Sylvia Anderson, is a flashy, stylistically bold series – its colourful format concealing some of its darker undertones. The title sequence boldly signals that this is going to be a series that foregrounds action, adventure and sex appeal. The music is fast and upbeat, and the barrage of images fly at the viewer in a series of quick cuts. They depict the bright, psychedelic colours of Moonbase – the women with purple hair and body-hugging silver outfits seemingly made of tinsel – and the high-energy sequences of military vehicles – submarines, rockets, tanks – flying, shooting lasers, and exploding. *UFO* announces itself as an Americanised product, designed for a youth market. Its upbeat title sequence matches its optimistic vision of a technological future. This future is anchored in a 1960s/1970s milieu which Cook connects with the hippie movement of the era, promising a 'positive future of idealism, enlightenment and an altogether more rational, empirical attitude towards dealing with the problems besetting the planet' (2006: 94).

The series is about a secret organisation called SHADO whose job is to detect UFOs and shield the general public from knowledge of their existence. At the helm of SHADO is Commander Ed Straker. Straker is burdened by emotional trauma: his marriage has broken up, and his personal life is in tatters. Yet through it all he displays the highest commitment to duty, even when it forces him to make personally devastating decisions. Straker's decisions occasionally edge towards the morally compromised, but they are always based on duty, and not the kind of cynical amorality expressed in the characters of the Thatcher-era series. Straker is not a 'hero' in any conventional sense, but his motives are not ambiguous, nor are they selfish, as compared to later characters such as Avon from *Blake's 7*, or (in a sense) the Seventh Doctor. Rather, Straker is a kind of 'hard boiled' film noir detective: a character whose home life is a disaster, meaning that work is his only home, to which he is entirely devoted. In the episode 'A Question of Priorities', Alec Freeman (the Colonel of SHADO and Straker's second-in-command) suggests to Straker that he goes home. Straker replies, 'What home?' Straker is an anti-hero, but one who is stridently devoted to his duty.

In the same episode, Straker must face a near-impossible moral dilemma. His son has been hit by a car and requires immediate medical attention. His only hope is a drug that can be imported from America. Straker directs one of SHADO's planes to retrieve the drug and bring it to England. But in a sub-plot, a UFO has appeared in Ireland. In order to quickly send someone there, Freeman diverts the plane that Straker ordered to be sent with the drug for his son. When Freeman explains this, Straker says nothing. Consequently, his son dies. This is a particularly knotted moral dilemma for a character from a generic science fiction television series to face. His decision reflects a kind of civic virtue in which he places public over private interests, and could be seen as roughly utilitarian, using Bentham's 'fundamental axiom', that 'it is the greatest happiness of the greatest number that is the measure of right and wrong' (Burns, 2005: 47). Straker serves as an interesting prototype for the kinds of anti-heroes that emerge in the Thatcher-era series, in which we see this dilemma played out on a larger scale.

In *Blake's 7*, Blake must make the decision to destroy Star One, the mainframe computer that is the source of power for his enemy, the corrupt Federation, at the cost of the lives of millions of (presumably innocent) people who rely on it. In *Sapphire & Steel*, the protagonists (usually Steel) often make the choice to sacrifice someone for the good of others. In *Doctor Who* the Seventh Doctor uses his own companion, Ace, as a kind of sacrifice – not allowing her to die, but to be emotionally broken down – in the service of what he considers the 'greater good'. The difference, however, is that the characters in these Thatcher-era series are usually either anti-authority (as in the case of *Blake's 7* and *Doctor Who*) or simply independent of authority (as in *Sapphire & Steel*), and indeed these characters are edging closer to a Machiavellian mindset, positioning them as authoritarian in themselves, which intensifies as each series goes on. Straker's actions, while in some ways a forerunner of these Thatcher-era characters, are consistent with an essentially morally straightforward character, and they come at great personal cost. In all his dealings, Straker emphasises Hutchings's 'Churchillian stoicism' (2011: 95). This contrasts with the more arbitrary moral decisions of Avon in *Blake's 7*, or the detached and even glib moral decisions of the Sixth and Seventh Doctors in *Doctor Who*, when dealing with similar situations.

Within *UFO*'s conservative structure, showcasing a military hierarchy, some 'darker' and more politically provocative themes are occasionally explored. These include domestic issues like drug use and marriage breakdown, and political issues such as racism and (to a lesser extent) xenophobia. Forster comments on these pre-Thatcher series that, 'What it meant to be British became ... contested through anxieties over immigration and nationhood' (2009: 75–6). The vague parallels to xenophobia are found in the aliens that invade, but there is little beyond these very loose (and generic) metaphors with which to engage. Outside of this, *UFO* may highlight 'social unrest', but it does little to critique the naturalised patriarchal system.

UFO was broadcast two years after Conservative politician Enoch Powell's notorious and incendiary 'Rivers of Blood' speech, in which he warned against black immigration, claiming, 'In this country in fifteen or twenty years' time the black man will have the whip hand over the white man' (2007: para 6). Hall and others (chapters in Durham and Kellner, 2006) discuss the emergence of subcultures since the 1950s, and the way they created 'moral panics'. This led to the construction of 'folk devils' (Procter, 2004: 76) – those the media and politicians tend to vilify. In the 1970s, because of ethnic violence, these folk devils became black Britons, most of whom were immigrants or children of immigrants – many from the Windrush generation, with all its attendant injustices. Seemingly as a response to Powell's sentiments, and the general unrest over immigration, the episode 'Computer Affair' has Doctor Shroeder carrying out a series of tests on the black Lieutenant Bradley. He says to Bradley, 'I've no liking for you blacks ... you ever heard that or something similar on Moonbase?' Bradley replies that he has never heard anything like it, and assumes the doctor must not mean what he says, which indeed he doesn't – it was merely a psychological test to ensure that Moonbase is harmonious. This (albeit slight) discussion of racial tolerance hints at a 'wiser world' (Suvin, 1979: 36) than aspects of Britain of the time, but there are very few examples of similar political impact.

Whereas there is a sense of inertia in the Thatcher-era series, there is an optimistic, somewhat utopian, sense of teleological forward motion in *UFO*. Cook considers the series an expression of 'the imminent technological utopia to come' (2006: 87). Technology is not always trusted in *UFO*, but it is always relied upon, and there is a general sense of 'loving attention to technology and organisational efficiency' (Hutchings, 2011: 86). Sometimes this is questioned within the series. In 'Computer Affair', a group of pilots are subjected to psychological tests, from which a computer determines their fitness for work. The computer (and the philosophy behind it) is criticised in this episode, firstly by Freeman, who disapprovingly tells Straker, 'You make all your decisions based on cold logic – computer predictions.' Later, at a restaurant with a colleague, Lieutenant Bradley says, 'I wonder what it'll be like in twenty years' time. Will the computers take over completely? ... We build them, programme them, and they tell us what we're going to think before we know it ourselves.' However, this suspicion of technology is minor, and the series generally aligns its faith with technological progress.

But in other ways, notably feminism, the series is regressive, or at least ambiguous, about women's roles. Cook comments:

> If, on one level, the series depicts a future world of gender equality, where women work alongside men in positions of authority, it is nevertheless frequently the commander's physical attributes that the show chooses to foreground ... Hence, while this is a depicted future of greater freedom and equality between the sexes, it is also a veritable sexual playground ... ultimately a late-1960s male liberatory fantasy. (2006: 105–6)

The women on Moonbase, while entrusted with positions of responsibility, are also clearly positioned to titillate male viewers, with their figure-hugging outfits, and shots of them changing clothes. They work alongside men in authoritative positions as Cook asserts, but only in the most limited way. Straker's (and to a lesser extent Freeman's) authority is absolute. Alec Freeman, at least in the first episode, plays the role of the lothario, making comments to women that would now be considered grounds for sexual harassment.

Space: 1999 (1975–77) was also created by Gerry and Sylvia Anderson and intended as a kind of loose sequel to *UFO*. For the series, Grade insisted on recruiting two American actors: Martin Landau and his then-wife, Barbara Bain. This, and other creative choices, resulted in a hybridised product that was even more aggressively designed to appeal to the American market, and therefore lost something of its more regional 'British' flavour. The series takes as its premise a scientifically impossible situation: a nuclear blast has detached the moon from its orbit, resulting in the crew of Moonbase Alpha floating unmoored around the galaxy. The title sequence here too is action-heavy. In fact the title sequence attempts to accomplish three goals at once: in sombre, almost reverent, music and imagery it introduces its main actors. It then transitions to a faster, more upbeat selection of clips from the forthcoming episode, with the screen card 'this episode' flashing. It then transitions (through some slower credits) to exposition, telling the story in images of the initial event – the nuclear blast that detached the moon. The sequence is designed to whet the viewer's appetite for the episode to come – something American series often did by way of episode previews at the beginning.

The commander of the base, John Koenig, presides over the crew with all the expected qualities associated with a consensus-era hero: courage, selflessness, strength and rationality. Straker and Koenig are different types of leaders: where Straker is somewhat morally conflicted, Koenig is more traditionally heroic ('Koenig' is of course German for 'king', which implies the kind of unquestioned, regal authority to be found in his character, and a connection to the British preoccupation with royalty, which we will see in the *Survivors* section). Koenig exhibits qualities of selflessness, courage, modesty and little in the way of character flaws to weigh him down. But Koenig and Straker are both united in their fidelity to duty. Their definitions of morality and authority are similarly constructed and based on both spoken and unspoken rules, set around the authority of the man in charge who represents a military authority. The rules appear self-evident to all involved.

According to some of its writers, *Space: 1999* was largely designed to avoid politics. Johnny Byrne, one of the series' most prominent contributors, comments that his vision for the series was as a show 'about belief, not issues or politics. People are so tired of politics, and they want to believe, to have their imagination stimulated' (qtd in Muir, 2012: para 1). Of course, to be apolitical is not possible. As Shaun Ley reminds us in a documentary about *Doctor Who*: 'to a greater or lesser extent all fiction is political ... consciously or unconsciously, politics permeates everything we do and everything we see' (*When Worlds Collide: Doctor Who and Politics*). Indeed, there is a political structure throughout *Space: 1999*, rendered invisible because of its alignment with the status quo: a militaristic, hierarchical structure with a middle-class white man at the helm. However, the series has far less to say about contemporary political situations, perhaps partly because it is divorced from contemporary Earth affairs. If there is any subtext that connects with 1970s fears of immigration or xenophobia, it is in the premise. As a reversal of *UFO*'s alien invaders (possibly as metaphors for immigrants), in *Space: 1999* the protagonists of the series are themselves 'refugees', floating around space without a home.

Space: 1999 has a more complicated relationship with technology, but just as much 'forward thinking'. Although it is just as enamoured of organisational efficiency and the technology of the base, and of rockets and weapons, it replaces some of that faith in technology with a more ethereal outlook. Just as Cook (2006) connects *UFO* with the 1960s 'flower power' generation, *Space 1999* capitalises on the 1970s generation's eschewing of traditional faith and embracing the revival of interest in the occult. Channelling the fascination with the occultist Aleister Crowley as well as the rise of Wicca, explored by 1970s bands Led Zeppelin, Deep Purple and others, *Space: 1999* explores esoteric themes. Throughout the series (at least Season 1), it seems there is some form of supernatural force guiding the crew. The frequent appearance of metaphysical situations, such as near-deities, ghosts and mysterious forces, offsets the scientific rationalism expressed by the characters of Professor Bergman (the science advisor) and Dr Helena Russell (the medical officer). In the episode 'Collision Course', a mysterious entity appears to Koenig informing him that, while it appears the moonbase is about to collide with a huge planet, he must do nothing and allow it to run its course. Most of the crew are strongly opposed to this course of action and desperately eager to bomb the planet with nuclear weapons. Ironically, only Professor Bergman is on Koenig's side: he expresses a belief that sometimes faith is more important than rationality – an unusual position for a scientist to take, and one that suggests the biases of the writers. Finally, faith wins: the crew do nothing and the planet disappears. If indeed this scenario is mystical, then the mystical structure is benign: a positive force guiding them to a kind of enlightenment, still resonant with the theme of faith in progress, whether technological or otherwise.

The second season of *Space: 1999* was completely different from the first. Producers were unhappy with its lacklustre reception, and hired the American producer Fred Freiberger, who had overseen the last season of the original *Star Trek* (1966–69). This resulted in a series far more focused on action-adventure than the more introspective elements of the first season. The device of the supernatural force was jettisoned, as were several members of the cast, while a Spock-like shapeshifting alien, Maya, was introduced. A romance blossomed between Koenig and Helena. This moved the series much closer to an unambiguously American product, but even this didn't manage to save the series.

Space: 1999 is marginally less sexually exploitative than its predecessor. Koenig's eventual lover, Doctor Helena Russell, is a scientist with sometimes more rationality than her partner. Ogland writes:

> While it is not uncommon to have the male represent the rational and the females the emotional aspects of being human, *Space: 1999* sometimes manages to turn the tables quite nicely, giving John Koenig absurd lines and directives while Helena Russell is calm, rational and controlled. (2014: 240)

However, these minor variations are not enough to unshackle either of the series from their basic generic conventions: action-adventure science fiction series with a tendency to mythologise a conservative social and political structure with the strong, stoic white man at the helm.

BBC: liberal neutrality

The BBC, by contrast to Grade's ITC productions, treated science fiction in an ambivalent manner from its earliest transmissions: for a long time, the corporation refused to even use the term, preferring labels like 'scientific romance', or 'Wellsian fantasies', for fear of associating itself with American popular culture (see Johnston, 2009: 110). To some extent this is the result of perceptions around the quality of the product: the genre has been seen in the past as culturally inferior to other genres, and this is in part because the term is an American invention and carries with it all of the discussed 'vulgar' connotations. This again is indicative of the Establishment's dislike of American cultural values. Yet this Establishment dislike fuelled the cultural currency of the genre among those who felt disaffected by the elite.

Science fiction, at least in its early years, appealed partly to the class concerns of people who did not feel culturally connected to the ruling class. The BBC clearly felt uneasy with the genre for these reasons and, as Johnston comments, 'to the cultural arbiters of taste, for the BBC to produce genre science fiction, and to label it as such, would be an admission that the television service was, at least in part, middlebrow' (2009: 115). 'Middlebrow', of course, was merely the opinion of these 'cultural arbiters', and reflected a supercilious attitude towards this American cultural product. British science fiction television pushed in two different directions in the period from the 1950s to the 1970s: the more commercially driven, Americanised model that the previous section outlines, most commonly associated with ITV, and the 'Anglicised' product pioneered by Nigel Kneale and from which others borrowed. The latter was usually showcased on the BBC.

As mentioned in the introduction, the BBC was often accused by conservative authorities of being too 'left wing'. Lord Chalfont referred to the corporation as 'a nest of Communists, militants and left-wing agitators of all persuasions' (qtd in Cockerell, 1988: 348), while Denis Thatcher, husband to Margaret, later memorably accused the entire corporation of being 'Trotskyists' (qtd in Seaton, 2015: 6). The BBC's official policy was (and is) one of political neutrality, but there were certainly writers of a left-wing persuasion working for the corporation, and they became prominent in the 1960s, the so-called 'golden age' of television drama, which was mostly a BBC phenomenon. Indeed, this political stance among young writers and thinkers was so prevalent that Caughie, in his discussion on television in the 1950s and 1960s, notes, 'politics was part of being an intellectual [and] being an intellectual meant being left wing' (2000: 61). Some of these writers went on to write for the series of the 1970s and 1980s, including, as we will soon see, Malcolm Hulke, a prolific contributor to *Doctor Who*. This leant the series a certain socially progressive style, but not necessarily a wholly subversive attitude.

The BBC series of this era operate according to different, but in some ways similar, sets of values and assumptions to the ITV series mentioned above (some of the writers, such as Terrance Dicks, Johnny Byrne and Terry Nation, wrote for both channels). The series are also enthusiastic about the implications of technology. More liberal in their political outlook, these series are nonetheless mostly reflective of the same social structures, thereby tacitly endorsing them, and sometimes even their liberalism is ambiguous, as will be discussed. Where there is minor difference, by and large these series are less interested in the American market. As such they explore a more arguably 'British' sense of story – a focus on dialogue and characterisation over action/adventure – even if both channels present militaristic hierarchies and a collectivist mentality.

The more important differences are in their social engagement, despite the presence of conservative attitudes. The various iterations of *Quatermass* (1953–79, 2005 – though the 2005 remake is not discussed), *Doctor Who* (1963–89 – the continuation series that began in 2005 is not discussed), are more concerned with political causes, and this is one clear point of departure from the ITV series. Environmentalism, colonialism, animal rights, nationalism and multiculturalism are tackled in *Doctor Who* of the 1970s, and in each case the Doctor displays a more progressive attitude than those around him. There is more of a dialogue about the growing threat of nuclear war, and the series are still clearly affected by the lingering memory of the Second World War. There are also references to racism and xenophobia which, with some exceptions, are treated with a more direct approach than the ITV series. With these differences in mind, there are also strong similarities in the area of collectivism (with militaristic structures), authority, morality and the attitude to duty – and in the case of *Survivors* (1975–77), landing on a conservative attitude of monarchy and a return to a conservative fantasy of Britain, mitigated by dissenting attitudes.

These series all display a similar attitude to authority as the ITV series: a deference to the white, middle-class man in charge. But these series delve a little deeper in presenting a generally unquestioning acceptance of British democracy. The characters display moral dilemmas, but, like their ITV counterparts, their morality is always tethered to duty. Even when characters appear to be anti-authority, like the Doctor in *Doctor Who*, or his forerunner Professor Quatermass, there is still an ideological assumption happening: the unquestioned authority always rests with the middle-aged, middle-class white male: the mythical hero figure. Ultimately, the character himself is the authority. Foster's contention that the scientist was mythologised in this era is borne out, but I would argue that the middle-aged white man is himself mythologised, whether a scientist or not (though he usually is), and is at the centre of all social hierarchical structures. He is always trusted and deferred to, and his opinion is almost always correct.

The series

Nigel Kneale is often credited with reimagining science fiction as a genre with specifically British appeal. He achieved this partly by rejecting the American version of what the genre had become. The early *Quatermass* serials: *The Quatermass Experiment* (BBC: 1953), *Quatermass II* (BBC: 1955), *Quatermass and the Pit* (BBC: 1958–59), were the first British science fiction series to be written directly for television (the final, *Quatermass*, appeared on ITV in 1979). They are also the first to be called 'science fiction' on British television, for the first time reflecting a British sensibility in original science fiction television. Indeed, it seems that Kneale wrote them to directly challenge American science fiction:

> *The Quatermass Experiment* was supposed to be something of a critique of science fiction of the time, those terrible American films that were full of flag-waving and dreadful, crude dialogue and exhibited a singular lack of imagination and a total lack of interest in the characters. (qtd in Petley, 1989: 91)

The *Quatermass* serials are rooted in the collective. Hutchings notes, 'The *Quatermass* stories have a tendency to view individuals as existing primarily within and in relation to groups, institutions and collectives' (2009: 341). The serials always present people in various positions of authority – military, scientific, medical – working together to achieve the end result, with no individual particularly highlighted. The exception, of course, is Quatermass himself, but Quatermass has no personal relationships (as Hutchings notes, the much later *Quatermass* in 1979 reveals that he has a granddaughter, but this is the one exception). He is a distant and remote figure. Like Sherlock Holmes, from whom some of the inspiration is no doubt drawn, he is a purely rational character, without interest in personal connections: he is only really defined by his role within the group, as a rocket scientist working with other scientists and technicians.

The *Quatermass* serials engage with concerns about the environment, and questions of race, xenophobia and nuclear anxiety. They plug into cold war paranoia, with the first serial, *The Quatermass Experiment*, about a manned rocket sent out into space containing three astronauts. The rocket lingers in space too long before finally returning, but with only one crew member. Over the course of the serial, this crew member mutates into an alien monster, which possesses the crew while in space. Kneale comments:

> At that time, I think everyone was worried to bits about what might happen. They knew that very shortly before, the Russians had acquired the H-bomb ... at the same time, both the Russians and Americans were working on outer space ... [they had] stolen a lot of old German V2s and kitted them out as space rockets, and so the knowledge that this stuff exists and could drop on you was behind everything. (*Time Shift*)

The 1970 *Doctor Who* serial 'The Ambassadors of Death' borrows from this story, with some of the same concerns carried over.

Despite these apocalyptic concerns, the *Quatermass* serials still exist in a world vastly different from the world of Thatcherism. The serials are anchored in a post-war context, with memories of the still-recent Second World War at the forefront (see Hutchings, 2011). Bould comments about a Second World War that is 'already deeply mythologised', which casts a shadow over the serial: 'Enlisted men and non-commissioned officers symbolise some fundamental British decency that prompted the nation to stand firm against Hitler, while the blitz is invoked as a symbol of indomitable national unity' (2008: 212). This sentiment is starkly different to Thatcher's more individualistic and fragmented society, despite Thatcher's own insistence on rejuvenating imperial and military mythology for her 'new Britain'.

The *Quatermass* serials, even the much later final instalment, *Quatermass* (1979), are anchored in consensus-era Britain, and various assumptions about Britain and its place in the world are active in the subtext. One way this manifested was in concerns over xenophobia and ethnic cleansing. In this era, groups like Oswald Mosley's Union Movement circulated messages about racial purity. Bould comments that at the time Kneale was writing *Quatermass and the Pit*, 'immigration into Britain from the Indian subcontinent and the Caribbean increased, and as Kneale was preparing his script, mobs of white Britons attacked black communities in Nottingham and London' (2008: 212). Although all the *Quatermass* serials are about some form of alien invasion, which could be taken as a metaphor for xenophobia, Kneale mitigates against this reading and deploys Quatermass, in *Quatermass and the Pit*, to call for tolerance. In the serial, a mysterious object is found in London, which resembles a spaceship. Quatermass investigates, and discovers the remnants of Martians: insect-like creatures who came to Earth aeons ago and took humankind's ancestors to Mars where they performed genetic experiments on them and (in another science fiction echo of the Prometheus myth and a nod to *Childhood's End*) raised their intelligence and set them on the evolutionary path that led to homo sapiens. The Martians had all but died out because of a racial purge. Towards the end of the serial, Quatermass delivers an impassioned speech, which connects with the fear of racial hostilities in Britain becoming cataclysmic:

> Every war crisis, witch hunt, race riot, purge, is a reminder and a warning – we are the Martians. If we cannot control the inheritance within us, this will be their second dead planet. (*Quatermass and the Pit*)

This is Kneale's clear anti-racist comment, highlighting our tendency to destroy ourselves through arbitrary exercise of prejudice and hostility (see Bould, 2008: 212). This played against the backdrop of the then-recent Windrush generation and other immigrations from Africa, Asia and the Caribbean, but in reality the governmental attitude to race in the UK did not soften, but rather intensified, in the Thatcher era. This will be discussed in later chapters.

In the *Quatermass* serials, several themes are raised that are broadened and amplified in later science fiction series of the 1960s and 1970s. But the serials also display the primacy and authority of the patriarchal hero figure at the centre, a recurring theme throughout generic science fiction series and serials in the consensus era. Quatermass is a professor, a rocket scientist, and a subscriber to the principles of logic and reason. He uses technology wherever he can, even if it sometimes causes him problems. The series subscribes to the Enlightenment myth of rationality and reason as the path to truth. There is always a cognitive explanation for phenomena, even that which appears to be 'supernatural', as can be seen in *Quatermass and the Pit*, where images of the Devil are explained as images implanted into pre-evolved humans by an alien race (a storyline later recycled for the *Doctor Who* serial 'The Daemons', discussed below). There is always a technological element that is used to explain the more apparently irrational claims.

Doctor Who (1963–89) was (and is, in its latest form) an ever-evolving series with many different writers and producers, and indeed different actors playing the Doctor. In many ways the series is innovative, from its title sequence design – the once cutting-edge 'howlaround' sequences – to the many politically progressive messages. The Doctor is a member of the Time Lords: an alien race from the planet Gallifrey that has the ability to 'regenerate'. As a means of cheating death, a Time Lord can shed a dying body and morph into a new one. This device has allowed several different actors to play the part and allowed the series to remain fresh. In factual writing about the series, the versions of the Doctor are traditionally named for the order of actors who played the part. So William Hartnell, the first actor to play the Doctor, is usually called the First Doctor, Patrick Troughton the Second Doctor, and so on. The internal mythology of the revived series – revealing there were many Doctors before the Hartnell version – renders this numbering problematic, but it will be retained for this book. Because the series is so well documented, with countless academic and popular articles and books written about it, the following does not attempt to fully discuss its cultural impact in a thorough and meaningful way. The 1980s incarnation of the series will of course be subject to intensive treatment in Chapter 4, which assesses the changes it underwent in the Thatcher era, but in this chapter I want to briefly sketch out some elements of *Doctor Who* in the 1970s, carrying its own consensus-era political undertones, to discuss points where the series feeds into numerous debates in the 1970s around socially progressive issues, as well discourses of scientific superiority, technology, and the authority of the middle-aged, middle-class white man. The series of the 1970s presents an admirable political liberalism, but most of the time a brief overview will confirm that the Doctor is another consensus-era hero with consistent credentials, and indeed sometimes even his 'liberalism' is called into question. Because the series has hosted various writers and producers, the political messages of the series pull in different directions, but the primacy of Britain's 'superior democratic values' is usually apparent and seldom challenged, despite tensions between the military, the Doctor and the (usually unseen) government, present in terms of ideological positions expressed in the series. Moreover, the authority of the Doctor always takes centre stage. Vohlidka writes of *Doctor Who* in the 1970s that:

> the series reflected much of the tumultuousness of the time, with the Doctor serving as a beacon of calm, proper behaviour. He was first and foremost a British hero, the type many British people were waiting for to restore faith in the government and deal with the myriad of problems facing the country. (2013: 119)

The Doctor is the mythologised 'authority figure': he is a scientist, positioning him as a generic descendent to Professor Quatermass. His role requires him to deflect anxieties of the time, and as such his status and opinions must be superior to anyone else's and cannot be significantly challenged by his colleagues or friends unless there is an opportunity to re-establish his superiority. Indeed, the makers of *Doctor Who* decided that the Doctor's first companion of the 1970s, Liz Shaw, herself a scientist, was too closely aligned to the Doctor's own talents and therefore a threat to his authority. She was duly replaced with Jo Grant, a young, naive and impressionable woman who always defers to the Doctor. The companions for the rest of the 1970s followed along similar lines. Exceptions were Harry Sullivan, a doctor with UNIT (discussed shortly), who accompanies the Fourth Doctor for a short time. Harry is intelligent but naive, and somewhat more conventional than the Doctor. The other exception is Romana, another Time Lord, who is said within the series to be intellectually superior to the Doctor in an academic sense, but not as resourceful or capable of spontaneous thought.

The series in this era never directly challenges governmental authority. As Ley comments, 'The idea that *Doctor Who* has ever breached the BBC's strict impartiality rules and preached to the viewer along party political lines is the study of fantasy. What isn't fantasy is that *Doctor Who* is fundamentally political' (*When Worlds Collide: Doctor Who and Politics*). In the 1970s version of *Doctor Who*, the Doctor (played by Third Doctor Jon Pertwee from 1970–74, and Fourth Doctor Tom Baker from 1974–81) is usually on the side of passive resistance and humanism against bureaucracy. This is expressed in the face of the military and boorish government officials, but does not indicate a disquiet about the institution of government itself. In 'Inferno' (1970), the outcome of the Second World War is reimagined when the Doctor is accidentally thrust into an alternative universe version of Britain – darker and clearly fascistic, designed to contrast starkly with 'our' Britain. As Bould comments of that story, 'it is implied that, whatever its faults, British democracy is still the best available system of government' (2008: 216). This sentiment is gently restated in many Third Doctor stories, as the Doctor is often pitted against bureaucrats and officials, but as Bould points out, 'the basic tenets of democracy or the ruling power were never questioned. The series never really strays from the BBC's agenda of liberal neutrality' (2008: 215). Indeed, Wright claims that this makes the Doctor 'an extension of the programming policy' (2011: 129). *Doctor Who* in the 1970s, then, presents a mythologisation of British consensus-era democracy, with stock standard characters – the bureaucrat, the military leader, the damsel in distress, the scientist (and the 'mad scientist' in the form of the Doctor's nemesis The Master) – as essential types around whom moral stories can play out.

Like his generic ancestor Professor Quatermass, the Doctor abhors militarism and the use of weaponry, but he nonetheless works in a collegial manner with the military. From the 1968 serial 'The Web of Fear' onwards, he forms an uneasy allegiance, and later friendship, with Alistair Lethbridge-Stewart, the Brigadier of an organisation called UNIT (United Nations Intelligence Taskforce). Lethbridge-Stewart is every bit the military man – his constant order, a variation of 'Five rounds, rapid!', became a catchphrase for the character (and the title of Brigadier actor Nicholas Courtney's autobiography) – but the always-delicate friendship between Lethbridge-Stewart and various incarnations of the Doctor, which reaches (albeit stoic English) affection in later years, serves to reinforce the differences between them. Although they respect, even admire each other, their philosophies are diametrically opposed. Military tactics cut against the Doctor's pacifist tendencies, and the Doctor's solution always proves better, or at least more progressive. However, if there is an opportunity for the series to fly in the face of authority in the form of the military, it is softened by the friendship and collaboration between the Doctor and the Brigadier. *Doctor Who* can therefore operate on both sides of this ideological fence: a position of pacifism and a collaboration with the military, neither of which denies the Doctor his unchallenged moral authority. As 'scientific advisor' with UNIT, the Third Doctor becomes absorbed in the collective, though sometimes the Doctor must be reminded of this. In 'Terror of the Autons' (1971) the Brigadier says to the Doctor, 'I'm aware of your preference for acting as a one-man band, but this does happen to be a UNIT operation.' The Pertwee-era stories (and some of Baker's stories too) usually portray the Doctor and UNIT working together, succeeding where an individual working alone could not.

The Third Doctor also makes rational thinking a central weapon in his arsenal, and an antidote to magic or superstition. 'The Daemons' (1971), a serial that owes most of its storyline to *Quatermass and the Pit* (which in turn draws from *Childhood's End*) and some of its tone to Hammer horror films, finds the apparent Daemon Azal 'resurrected' in a small English village, stirring superstitious beliefs about witchcraft. The Doctor soon discovers that the Daemons are an alien race that came to Earth long ago and influenced early humans' conceptions of supernatural devils. As with most Pertwee and Baker serials, the cognitive approach to solving problems is privileged, aligning the Doctor with other scientifically inclined heroes of the consensus era.

The Pertwee-era serials of *Doctor Who* present a progressive attitude to issues around controversial topics of the era: multiculturalism, environmentalism, nationalism, animal rights and colonialism. In two serials from the 1970s: the oddly titled 'Doctor Who and the Silurians' (1970) and 'The Sea Devils' (1971) (both written by Malcolm Hulke, an outspoken member of the Communist Party of Great Britain), a long-hibernated reptilian-humanoid species is awoken, which once ruled the earth. The creatures had gone into hibernation deep in the bowels of the earth ('Doctor Who and the

Silurians') or in the ocean ('The Sea Devils'). The action of both stories occurs when the creatures (or a small cell of them) are awoken. In both cases, the Doctor attempts to negotiate a way in which the two species can coexist, but ultimately fails because the military effectively beat him to a conclusion and use weapons to destroy the species. The Doctor is horrified by this genocide, and the viewer is impelled to feel the same way. When learning of the genocide against the Silurians, the Doctor turns to his companion, Liz:

> DOCTOR: The Brigadier. He's blown up the Silurian base!
> LIZ: He must have had orders from the Ministry.
> DOCTOR: And you knew?
> LIZ: No! The government were frightened. They just couldn't take the risk.
> DOCTOR: But that's murder! They were intelligent alien beings. A whole race of them. And he's just wiped them out!

The message from the military and government is that the planet cannot be subjected to mixing with immigrant populations; the conservative order must be maintained, despite the wishes of the Doctor. The message of the series (conveyed by the Doctor) is the more progressive one, that in spite of its challenges, multiculturalism is an ideal to work towards. Working for UNIT, yet detached from its ideologies of military force and conservative values, the Doctor stands firm in his 'rebel' status, while at the same time he himself is mythologised as a patriarchal authority figure.

Other themes receive a progressive, even left-wing treatment. To take a few examples, in 'Colony in Space' (1971), another serial scripted by Hulke, the Doctor lands on a planet colonised by humans, who have oppressed the native species of sentient humanoids. The serial critiques the effects of colonialism and exploitation of resources through the mining company there and its destruction of the environment. 'The Green Death' (1973) concerns a corrupt corporation pumping toxic waste into the local environment. In 'Carnival of Monsters' (1973) the Doctor and Jo land inside a Miniscope – a device which shrinks everything, including humans, to tiny proportions and holds them inside it for the entertainment of an audience. The Doctor condemns this action and links it to zoos and other forms of animal mistreatment, telling Vorg, the owner, 'The collection of the simplest animal life forms is a dubious enough pursuit in itself, sir, but the collection of civilised intelligent beings is a positive crime!' Finally in 'Invasion of the Dinosaurs' (1974), yet another Hulke-scripted contribution, an environmental group tries to reverse time to the point where humans never existed so that the planet can be free of the harmful practices of its dominant species (apart from the environmentalists themselves, who are planning to escape the event). When the Doctor uncovers their plan he says, 'Look, I understand your ideals. In many ways I sympathise with them. But this is not the way to go about it.' The Doctor, at least in principle, is generally on the side of 'progressive' causes.

James Chapman considers the above serial a 'satire of bureaucracy and petty officialdom' (qtd in O'Day, 2010) because of the rigid nature of the authorities. There is indeed much in Pertwee-era *Doctor Who* to criticise bureaucracy. 'The Claws of Axos' (1971) also presents one of the many run-ins between the Doctor and a representative of bureaucracy. In that serial the Doctor expresses frustration at the civil servant Chinn, the 'Head of the Committee of Enquiry'. Chinn accosts the Brigadier because the Doctor is not a British citizen.

CHINN: (*to Brigadier*) ... who is he and where does he come from?
DOCTOR: (*to Chinn*) ... your petty obsessions! England for the English! Good heavens, man!
CHINN: I have a duty to my country!
DOCTOR: Not to the world?

This frustration with bureaucracy standing in the way of action is a constant refrain in *Doctor Who* of the 1970s, and echoes a wider frustration in British society. Indeed, one of the reasons Thatcher was elected in 1979 was because of her own dislike of bureaucrats and her promise to take stronger and more decisive action. Thatcher claimed that civil servants were 'complacent, inert, pedantic and incapable of appreciating the need to devise or implement radical solutions to Britain's dire problems' (qtd in Wright, 2006: 207). We will see in Chapter 3 that Sapphire and Steel play off against bureaucratic figures. Yet it also becomes apparent that neoliberalism has not delivered us from pointless bureaucracy, but rather reframed its boundaries and in many cases intensified it – a point expanded on in Chapter 4.

The Doctor's liberal humanism is often commented upon. Wright for instance, claims:

> As a liberal, the BBC Doctor occupied neutral political ground from where he criticised socially, morally, and aesthetically, the mores of his contemporary audience. His neutrality and critical role reflected the BBC's self-professed political and social agenda, which made him an extension of the programming policy. (2011: 129)

The Doctor's positions are not always politically neutral, however, especially with scripts by left-wing writers. That aside, despite his liberalism, which is in evidence in his progressive attitude, the 1970s Doctor is nonetheless a paternalistic figure with generally patriarchal values and behaviours. He is something of a chauvinist, and is most certainly a patriarchal authority hero figure throughout with an imperial attitude. Britton and Barker comment, 'Jon Pertwee played the Doctor as an implacable ultra-English hero in the Bulldog Drummond mould' (2003: 147). Pertwee had himself served in the Second World War, and was rumoured to have been involved in intelligence missions, and he brought the attitude of masculine swagger and stoicism to the role.

The Doctor has a slightly more complicated relationship to technology than other 'heroes' in 1970s television. Much like his consensus-era peers, the Doctor is generally in favour of technology – especially the Third Doctor, who is obsessed with his cars and other gadgets – but he is nonetheless wary of any technology that places itself above human endeavour. This has been the show's position since the advent of the Cybermen in 1966. The cold, ruthless Cybermen operate purely on logic, without emotion. The consistent message of the series is that the 'human factor' – the irrationality, creativity and emotional depth of humans – is vastly preferable to the cold logic of machines. The 1970s were an area of great technological development, and inherent in that development is anxiety. The anxiety of computers growing to dominate humanity also played out in *UFO*, as discussed. In 'The Green Death' the Doctor confronts BOSS, a supercomputer intent on world domination. The Doctor is insistent that this 'mere machine' does not have the capacity to do real harm, and claims, 'The whole is greater than the sum of its parts. We are more than machines', pitting the consensus-era trope of collaboration and collectivism of human minds against the machine. BOSS reveals it has linked itself to a human mind and found that 'the secret of human creativity is inefficiency. The human brain is a very poor computer indeed. It makes illogical guesses which turn out to be more logical than logic itself.' This (back-handed) endorsement of human irrationality reappears often in *Doctor Who* – in the 1988 serial 'Remembrance of the Daleks', a Dalek 'battle computer' attempts to connect itself to the mind of a human child. The Seventh Doctor explains, 'The Daleks' major drawback is their dependency on rationality and logic. The solution? Get a human, preferably young, imaginative; plug the child into the system, and their ingenuity and creativity are enslaved to the battle computer.' He calls this process 'obscene', which, of course, it is; but it seems that the general treatment of 'AI' technology in *Doctor Who* is cautious and even conservative, and the 'human factor' is always favoured over the 'artificial' mind.

There is a disturbing undercurrent of imperialism in the Fourth Doctor's era. The serial 'Genesis of the Daleks' (1975) sees the Time Lords enlist the Doctor as a kind of undercover operative to go back in time and destroy the Daleks at the moment they are created. Bould discusses how this serial, evocative of the Second World War, draws on the myth of British imperialism, with the Daleks and their fictional creator Davros as Nazis and the Doctor and the Thals as the opposing army, the victorious forces of the British Empire. This comes at the cost of disavowing 'Britain's ongoing history of colonial violence, oppression and expropriation' (Bould, 2008: 216–18). 'The Talons of Weng-Chiang' (1977) portrays a white actor playing a racially stereotyped Chinese character. The Doctor of this era refers to his companion Leela as a 'savage' because she comes from a 'primitive' tribe. More problematically, the series has a certain ethnocentric bias built into its structure. The Doctor himself (in the classic series) is always a white man, and nearly always exhibits various traits of Victorian and Edwardian English society. Loza comments that, 'although the Doctor is ostensibly an alien, he behaves like a quintessentially British dandy; he adores tea, the

European aristocracy, and fashion' (2017: 17). Charles comments that the Doctor's costumes 'visually recall the period of the height of British imperial power' (2007: 17). Even his much-touted liberal-humanism can be seen as part of the problem. As Clark comments, the Doctor epitomises 'triumphant Western humanism, with all its arrogance, self-proclaimed superiority and blindness' (2013: para 19). That is not to deny the series its progressive attitudes by 1970s standards, but simply to provide some perspective, and to point out that the character of the Doctor is sometimes able to behave in contradictory ways: both as a progressive 'liberal' and as an Establishment figure.

There is no sense of challenging traditional authority in *Moonbase 3* (1973). This dated series, which was cancelled after only one season, was created by Terrance Dicks and Barry Letts, two of the brains behind *Doctor Who* of the 1970s. It depicts a future where various superpowers have set up bases on the moon, promoting, at least in principle, a message of cooperation between nations. The United States has Moonbase 1, the Russians have 2, China has 4, Brazil has 5, with Moonbase 3 for the British. This series presents a world of government departments and budgetary cutbacks. The sets are familiar, forming a similar aesthetic to many *Doctor Who* episodes of the era – white or silver surfaces, functional equipment and metallic walls, sometimes with TARDIS-like imprints on them, but also in many ways resembling an Antarctic base. There is not, however, enough in the general tone to rescue the moonbase from its similarities to a departmental office of the 1970s, with bureaucrats here replaced by engineers and scientists who often behave like civil servants. Though it may be intended to depict the future, its aesthetic recognisably anchors it in the 1970s, but it's a drab, austere 1970s when compared to the hallucinatory moonbase of *UFO*. Instead of psychedelic colours and revealing costumes, everyone here is clad in variations on beige. Most people wear simple, austere clothing, and it is not until Episode 5 that we meet the Russians, whose outfits (perhaps ironically) display more colour.

The crew of Moonbase 3 are bound together by something approaching loyalty and respect. There are interpersonal conflicts, but they are generally resolved by appeals to decency. However, this is not enough to elevate the generally austere atmosphere of the series. Wright claims:

> *Moonbase 3*'s appeal to realism resulted in a disquieting sense of claustrophobia and isolation that undermined the optimism of its premise and captured the general mood of insularity felt (and often desired) in Britain during the early 1970s. (2005: 297)

The series once again valorises the (white male) scientist, investing him with authority and absolute trust. The antithesis (or nemesis) of the scientist is not a corrupt or incompetent government, but, as in other 1970s programmes, the bureaucrat. Bureaucracy and its frustrations became a favourite subject of Dicks and Letts, as it was for Nigel Kneale. In the first episode, the Director of Moonbase 3 says to his subordinate, 'You know why I've been sent for, don't you? Just another session with the bureaucrats of the space commission about the housekeeping.' He discusses the double bind: 'I can't produce the results because they won't give me the money, and they won't give me the money because I can't produce the results.' On the way to Earth, his pilot succumbs to a form of psychological strain associated with space, and deliberately sabotages the ship, resulting in its destruction.

There is now a need for a new Director. The Director-General of the European space programme offers David Caulder:

> A very unusual man: scientist, academic, administrator all in one. David Caulder was Lecturer in Theoretical Physics at Oxford when the troubles broke out ... a combination of student militancy and reactionary administrators brought the place to a standstill.

This recalls the 1968 student riots which would've been recent at the time. Those riots, left wing in nature and generally anti-capitalist, broke out on university campuses in France (known as the May 68 protests) and spread to other parts of Europe. The protests were calling for, among other things, a greater autonomy for the individual and less state interference. As Chapter 6 will discuss more fully, these wishes would soon be 'granted' by the Thatcher government, but in a way that completely reformulated the terminology. Caulder would have been seen as an ideal 'British chap' for the moment, because, as the Director explains, he is 'what you might call a "militant liberal", passionately committed to the middle of the road'. A 'militant liberal' or passionate centrist is almost an emblem of the BBC's 'liberal neutrality' stance: one whose good sense and general morality and fairness can calm any situation. There are times, however, when Caulder is called on to exercise more than mere diplomacy, as in Episode 5 when one of the team, Tom Hill, ends up in an accident inside a shuttle. Caulder enlists the help of the Russians against advice from the Director-General and his second-in-command, Michel. In an argument with Michel, he asks, 'What are you really worried about, Michel? Tom's life or balancing the books?' This moral determination looks set to deprive Caulder of his job – he is ordered to step down and allow Michel to take over. Caulder is not troubled by this, as he places loyalty before career.

Terry Nation (creator of the Daleks) wanted to explore the politics of a group stripped of all governmental authority. His series, *Survivors* (1975–77), is about a deadly viral outbreak that decimates the planet's population and leaves it devoid of governing structures. The series explores what happens when authority is taken away, and the vacuum is filled by individuals with authoritarian tendencies. It is therefore beginning to explore the neoliberal mindset, restructured with authoritarian tendencies in the Conservative Party. However, for *Survivors* the answer (by and large) lies in reinstituting traditional structures of authority, even if this becomes ambiguous by the end. In this series the familiar trope of the collapse of civilisation is explored, raising questions about the formation and maintenance of authority. How do the survivors build a just society? How do people discover ways to organise themselves without a central governmental structure? Who has the right to operate as an authority? Is an authority, perhaps even a brutal authority, necessary to keep the peace, and preferable to the alternative of anarchy or authoritarianism? These questions were revisited in *The Tripods* (1984–85) and, to a greater extent, *Knights of God* (1987), both covered in the last two chapters.

Survivors is particularly notable in its sense of complacency towards the established authority that existed before the event – in Britain of the time, this was the Callaghan Labour government. There is no suggestion in the series that it is the same government, but it most likely operates according to the same principles.

The government that has been destroyed in the series is never questioned or criticised, and there seems genuine fear for what will come in the wake of its loss. Sawyer sees *Survivors* as a very middle-class survival story, being 'apolitical as only the English middle-class can be' (2006: 139). This also accords with its closest influence, John Wyndham's *The Day of the Triffids* (1951), which occupies a similarly middle-class milieu (the 1981 television adaptation will be discussed in Chapter 5). Built into both stories are similar 'mythical' assumptions – that middle-class, generally middle-aged, white men, are the natural carriers of command, and that the post-war British system of governance is by and large the best system available. As the series continues, it becomes apparent that the stability and basic good sense of the English system is considered sacrosanct (as we will discover, the system for the whole of Britain is a different question). If the system is gone, as in *Survivors*, the stability of the idea remains, or must be forced to remain. The logic of the system posits that authority is required in order for peace (and often a liberal attitude) to flourish. 'Benign' hierarchies are necessary.

The series begins with the protagonist Anna, whose husband has died in the outbreak. She is searching for her son, who was at school at the time. Early on in the series she meets Arthur Wormley, who introduces himself as the 'National Union President'. Anna recognises him as such from the media. Sawyer sees this character as reflective of

> a sense of apocalyptic unease throughout the political spectrum caused by events such as the IRA mainland bombing campaign, as well as the 1973 'oil crisis' and the 1974 miners' strike, which lead to a three-day working week, power cuts and rumours of military coups and private armies. There may well be echoes of the general Middle England distrust of union activists, especially Northern ones, in the character of Arthur Wormley ... the sinister trade union president ... (2006: 135)

However, if Wormley is meant to represent a certain distrust, it seems nonetheless that the question of authority as it stood before the event is never seriously challenged. Anna asks Wormley if there is any authority now, and Wormley replies 'Not as such. Not yet. But there will be.' Wormley then outlines his 'vision' for a central governmental control with himself as its authoritative centre (echoing the sinister Torrence in *The Day of the Triffids*). It would start small, and ultimately grow. Anna asks:

> ANNA: That's how the old feudal barons operated, isn't it?
> WORMLEY: Perhaps, but it's the way that ultimately led to the finest democratic system in the world.

This position is not challenged, which suggests that Anna implicitly agrees with Wormley's assertion. Sawyer maintains that, 'Both [Anna and Wormley] represent power, but the power of the pre-plague world, which has little relevance to the new environment' (2006: 141). However, this new environment will be built in accordance with the original, and Anna and Wormley at no point deny the efficacy or 'properness' of the power that has been destroyed. There is never any indication that they want to radically alter the power structures. There is never a hint of wanting to reshape the world, but rather return it to what it was: 'the finest democratic system in the world'. Wormley wants to instil power ruthlessly and assumes 'the "right" of the last vestiges of nationalism' (Sawyer, 2006: 141). His method is contentious, but his sentiment is apparently beyond reproach.

Later, Wormley has a man shot for defending his land, and we learn that Wormley's associates are more or less thugs or vigilantes who have taken it upon themselves to install 'martial law' by some form of authority that existed before the event. When Anna has found some other survivors and they have formed a group, they go to an abandoned convenience store for supplies. Wormley's associates are there, and accuse Anna and her friends of looting, which leads to a stand-off, with Anna and her friends managing to take the supplies they need. Afterwards, as Anna and her friends are driving away from the incident, a discussion ensues:

> JENNY: Do you think they really do have any authority?
> ANNA: Yes, that's what's been bothering me. Perhaps we were in the wrong?
> GREG: Oh, come on, they're no better than a criminal gang! They just grabbed the chance to take over everything.
> ANNA: They do have some sort of organisation. I mean, we may not like what they're doing or what they are, but at least they've got some sort of order, and God knows we need it.

JENNY: Are you saying we should join up with them?
ANNA: No ... oh, I don't know.

Anna's indecision implies that any authority and 'order' is better than none. Wormley is clearly a villain, but the group largely agrees with his sentiments about British democracy. Later the group forms a kind of commune that is much more democratic than Wormley's assortment of thugs.

Survivors also extols the virtues of technology. At the school where her son boarded, Anna has a discussion with Bronson, one of her son's teachers, who tells her:

> What is important is learning again – things we've never even needed to consider before ... a book will tell you how electricity is generated, but could you do it? Right from the very beginning: find the metal in the earth, dig it up, and turn it into wire? Could you make and cast glass for a light bulb? You'll need to know every part of every process.

As already stated (and echoed by Sawyer and others) the series borrows liberally from *The Day of the Triffids*, and these ruminations are very similar to Coker in the novel:

> This is a pause – just a heaven-sent pause – while we get over the first shock and start to collect ourselves, but it's no more than a pause. Later we'll have to plough; still later we'll have to learn how to make plough-shares; later than that we'll have to learn how to smelt the iron to make the shares. What we are on now is a road that will take us back and back and back until we can – if we can – make good all that we wear out. Not until then shall we be able to stop ourselves on the trail that's leading down to savagery. But once we can do that, then maybe we'll begin to crawl slowly up again. (Wyndham, 2016: 203)

Nation himself seems to have been grappling with these questions. In an interview he said, 'I didn't know how to preserve food. I didn't know how to make anything and I suddenly realised that I and my whole generation were virtual victims of a tremendous industry' (qtd in Sawyer, 2006: 136). Much of the rest of the series depicts a return to an agrarian system. The characters realise that technology, paired with authority, constitutes a large part of the reason why people are civilised. *Survivors* takes the sudden lack of technology as a central anxiety that propels the series forward.

Greg, a character Anna meets early on, eventually becomes the leader of the group and dictates most of their decisions, though they usually take a vote on important matters. At this point, the roles of all the members are reasonably clear, and the morality of the series grounds itself firmly in a traditional framework. The characters in *Survivors* conform to a traditional group dynamic comprised of essential types, with the powerful alpha male hero at the head, and many types contained therein: the scoundrel or trickster, the grandmother, the simpleton, the damsel and others. Abby is a resourceful woman with a British reserve and resolve. Greg, closest to the hero figure, is self-sacrificing, strong, resilient and decisive (he was an engineer, which is a suitably science-based pursuit). Tom is the 'trickster' of the group: cowardly, self-serving and villainous. This arrangement and group dynamic is, ironically, not completely at odds with Thatcher's stated views. Florence Sutcliffe-Braithwaite writes, 'Thatcherites ... conceived of human nature as self-interested, but not entirely individualistic, for people were embedded in families and communities' (2012: 512). These families and communities would help each other out, and once they had looked after their community, they could look more broadly to the needs of society. It feeds into Thatcher's firm belief in Victorian values, which she called into being many times. There was of course a contradiction at the heart of Thatcher's 'social order': the neoliberal economic system which pulled in the other direction and encouraged selfish and Machiavellian behaviour, but the characters in this series have not yet experienced that system.

However, this 'natural order' as presented in *Survivors* is itself estranging, offering us an England that is both familiar and unfamiliar – in its aesthetic it resembles many rural British series of the era, with agrarian scenes. It depicts people conforming to some of the expectations of ordinary civilised behaviour, but without a central government. The interplay of the two allows for a certain 'cognitive estrangement', leading to a reflection on the part of the viewer. It compels us to contemplate the role of governmental democracy and authority, by depicting its absence. The series could be said to be pessimistic, to the extent that it portrays a world where civilisation is a weak and pallid edifice: precarious and fragile. If the series is suggesting that democracy is a thin membrane, vulnerable to the influence of despotic figures like Wormley and others, it also extols the virtues of the inherent authority and structure of this democracy through the paternalistic figure of Greg, and the democratic manner in which the commune operates.

Some of the themes that later occupy a central role in the Thatcher-era series are explored within *Survivors*, suggesting a move into darker territory. In 'Law and Order' Greg must take the agonising role of executioner, killing a member of the commune who sexually assaulted one of the others. When it is later shown that it was a case of mistaken identity, Greg and others in the know vow to keep the secret for fear of the commune descending into chaos. Greg is not averse to killing, and later (in 'Something of Value') shoots another man who threatened the commune. This aligns him, to an extent, with Straker in *UFO*, in the latter's decision about his son's survival, and points to a more morally conflicted universe; but these decisions are utilitarian – taken for what Greg considers to be the moral good of the community, mitigating against the fear of chaos or some form of anarchy, which conservative authority cannot tolerate – and Greg is a largely conservative character. In the Season 2 episode 'By Bread Alone' he is uneasy even about the introduction of religious instruction in the commune, lest it weaken his own authority. Channelling the Grand Inquisitor from Dostoevsky's *The Brothers Karamazov*, he says, 'A lot of people want authority. They're not interested in working it out for themselves, they want to be told, freed from responsibility.' Like the other characters discussed in this chapter who face moral dilemmas, Greg's primary concern is what he sees as his duty. Wright (2009), when writing of *Sapphire & Steel*, suggests that this sacrificial attitude is a conservative one, and considers *Sapphire & Steel* to be exemplary. *Survivors* is exploring these themes in nascent form, but they are taken much further in the Thatcher-era series. Similar moral decisions made by Steel in *Sapphire & Steel* are taken dispassionately, without any scruples, and at no personal cost. The Sixth and Seventh Doctors in *Doctor Who* demonstrate a much more cutthroat and

Machiavellian attitude to similar situations, and Avon in *Blake's 7* cares little for the moral consequences of his actions.

Greg's final episode emphasises the connection between sacrifice and love, and places us in the territory of the Western, overlaid with the familiar 'Churchillian stoicism' of consensus-era characters. In the episode 'The Last Laugh', third from the finale, Greg is stabbed by a group of bandits working for a duplicitous character. They dump his body in a stream, but he is still alive. He makes it to another small settlement where he finds a man dying of what he believes to be smallpox. Greg succumbs to the infection. He returns to his commune, where the same bandits are holding his group hostage, and expresses the desire to join them, even going so far as to shoot one of his own people. To convince them all that he has betrayed them he must harm his people and badmouth his wife and children. It's all a ruse, of course, and his real intention is to infect the bandits and thus kill them all. This act of self-sacrifice is particularly wrenching emotionally because there is no chance of reconciliation between Greg and his family. Brown considers narratives that involve the collision of love, vengeance and sacrifice to be derivative of the Western genre. She writes, 'The narrative code of the Old West allows vengeance ... only if it is motivated by love' (Brown, 2017: 91). The cowboy is then beyond redemption and must sacrifice himself for the sake of those he loves. Brown explains:

> the strong, virile tragic protagonist accepts full responsibility for his acts, acknowledges who he has become in full consciousness of his evil, accepts his doom stoically, and sacrifices himself in order to restore peace to society (2017: 98)

Greg's final moments are acts of vengeance, but it is vengeance that is driven by his desire to protect his family and community.

The idea of the old cowboy's death making way for the new civilisation is a theme embedded in many Westerns (Brown, 2017: 80), and plays out to some extent in *Survivors*. Greg is not a cowboy in the sense of being outside civilisation – rather, he is the primary shaper of the new civilisation; he is on 'the inside' socially. But he also embodies the heroic, mythic figure of the saviour. To that end, the series also draws influence from the eschatological texts of the Norse Ragnarök and the Christian Book of Revelation.

The eschatology in *Survivors* is grounded in sacrifice, and a 'transfiguration' to come, aligning Greg's sacrifice in a nebulous way to that of a Christ-like figure (see Brown, 2017: 91). The eschatological texts are revisited in the Thatcher-era series, but when the protagonists of *Blake's 7* (which itself shares commonalities with the Western) and *Sapphire & Steel* are sacrificed, it is against their will. When those characters make their own sacrifices, they are based on cold, Realpolitik decisions, with no consideration of love. Indeed, there is little or no love or personal connection between characters in the major Thatcher-era series. This illustrates to some extent how far British science fiction television has travelled since the 1970s consensus era.

Despite the connotations of the American Western, *Survivors* plays out, in the end, as a largely conservative celebration of British (or English) authority. Despite (or perhaps because of) Greg's death, the remains of his group see him as a figurehead. Agnes, whom Greg met earlier when she landed from Norway in a hot-air balloon, has decided that he is to be named King, and has raised a Union Jack with his initials on it. The idea that a king is needed is lightly disputed by others, but not substantially. In the penultimate episode ('Long Live the King') Agnes repeats what Greg told her, that 'You can't have freedom without authority' (Thatcher would later say in a speech to the European Foundation, 'You cannot have freedom without the rule of law'). She also holds that a currency is necessary and needs Greg (and quantities of petrol) to back it up because, 'That's all a currency needs: to be honoured by someone who symbolises the nation itself. ... [we need to] show people a central authority exists.' *Survivors* perhaps shows most clearly the value of symbolism. Symbols – like the Union Jack, money, the idea of a monarch – can unify people, naturalise (and therefore mythologise) social relations, and disguise the arbitrary nature of the concept of authority. Later, Charles says, 'Nobody need be king', but as Sawyer discusses, this point is not sufficiently unpacked (see Sawyer, 2006: 147–50 for a fuller discussion). This idea of a return to a more traditional Britain, with the hallmarks of the Establishment – the monarchy, the military (Agnes is dressed in military uniform) and presumably the Church and aristocracy as our only saviour, becomes a nostalgic dream, and an obviously conservative English one, strangely championed by the Norwegian Agnes. There is logic to this: one of the ways in which authoritarianism can take hold is through the lack of a centralised, regulated authority – something that will be explored in later chapters. But the form of authority that this series champions is not revolutionary or progressive, but largely traditional. *Survivors*, like the later (and far more conservative) *Knights of God* (discussed in Chapter 6), posits that the answer to combatting authoritarianism is not to be found in radical reform or even a re-examination of social relations, but an appeal to, even a loving reinstatement of, the benign authority of the past and all its attendant symbolism. Though Nation was reportedly unhappy with the direction *Survivors* finally took (Sawyer, 2006: 138), the seeds for its denouement were already present in the beginning, with Wormley's uncontested speech (written by Nation) about authority and leadership.

Although Greg's authority is not contested in England, things change when the characters travel, in the final episode ('Power'), to Scotland. When they arrive in Scotland, Charles and Jenny meet with McAlister, apparently the local laird. Their first encounter with him is tense. When asked about how things are in England, Charles answers:

> CHARLES: Well it's not so bad now – we've even got a sort of government established.
> McALISTER: That's an extraordinary thing to be wanting again isn't it?

It seems, as the episode continues, that people in Scotland are managing quite happily without a centralised authority and seem unconcerned to implement one. It seems the authority McAlister carries as a laird is something like communitarian, and is enough to dissuade anyone from looting or being otherwise antisocial.

The plotline casts a strange, even comedic light on the series up to this point. It seems that the preoccupation with governmental (and other forms of symbolic) authority is an exclusively English concern. The Scottish have never required it, and don't welcome its return (in part, it is implied, because English authority may oppress Scotland). This suggests that all the antisocial behaviour and attempts to remedy it have simply been an English problem, despite Scotland apparently having a much larger surviving population. Towards the end of the episode McAlister says, 'You may have a government in England, but here in Scotland we protect our own!' Charles tells him, 'Good God, man, there are few enough of us surviving without bringing nationalism into it!' This is uttered without any sense of irony, despite the fact that nationalism has been something of an obsession in England for much of the series, at least in terms of the implementation of recognisably English symbols of soft power.

This final episode is ambiguous in itself, but tends to side with localised authority over governmental. The laird is the white man in a position of power, who is largely trusted in his area, but even if that were not the case the episode can't on its own provide enough of a counterpoint to the prevailing message from British science fiction of the era, which largely reveals a conservative bias, at least in terms of the privileging of authority and order, usually in the form of a white, middle-aged man with an attitude of contentment with the government of the day. These series present a collective mentality, and a deference to political authority (or a qualified acceptance of it). Quatermass often finds himself coming up against bureaucracy, as does the Doctor in *Doctor Who*, but their indignation at the incompetence of those in governmental positions does not indicate a disquiet with the government itself, nor does it compare with the later series where there is outright hatred and dread for the powers that be. Equally, the characters in *Survivors* are sometimes pitted against those who wish to install authority, but it is never authority itself, or an overarching power, that they dread; rather, it is those who take power on for themselves, without any sense of a democratic process. This contrasts with the Thatcher-era series that privilege the individual, largely oppose political authority, and present morally compromised characters.

Where the themes of these series sail close to those of the Thatcher era, such as the morally compromised situations in *UFO* and *Survivors*, it is always an anomaly: an exceptionally difficult situation, which is resolved at great expense to the protagonist, and always in the service of a perceived moral duty towards the group. Overall these series are not as concerned with any of the prevalent issues in the series from the Thatcher era: Machiavellian behaviour in protagonists, the questioning (even hatred) of authority leading to authoritarianism, the breakdown of civilisation, which leads to dystopia, or pessimistic renderings of human behaviour. These themes begin to emerge in some series of the 1970s, but they are mitigated against by an imposition of conservative order, even to the point of installing a new king.

Paternalism does not completely disappear in the Thatcher era of course, but in the major science fiction television of Thatcher's era there is an anxiety and ambiguity at the heart of the paternal figure. The male 'leader' is never again fully trusted, and never displays the same sense of duty, except to his own version of what is worth fighting for, and that is often highly ambiguous. He seldom, if ever, displays a straightforward duty to an organisation, government or place. Where there is sacrifice, it's more often of others than himself. Motivations become murky, as the male protagonists in these series of the Thatcher era keep secrets, and even use their friends and companions as pawns. By contrast to this chapter, the major Thatcher-era science fiction series studied in this book represent the death of the traditional, mythical male hero, and give rise to a far less sure-footed male 'hero', who has suddenly recognised the oppressive nature of the authority that faces him, and has no self-evident means to contend with it. The male 'hero' in the Thatcher era has become aware of a pernicious ideology: authoritarianism. Ideology no longer contains self-evident 'truths', but a series of unpalatable ideas.

This change could be framed in what Hall called Thatcher's 'authoritarian populism' (1988: 28), weaving together social conservatism with popular anxieties. Thatcherism is at once an expression of the leader proclaiming from on high, and a populist: a politician of 'the people'. She would often achieve this double act by appealing to common-sense values of the people to push through authoritarian policies. Procter comments that

> when Thatcherism took a tough, authoritarian stance on homosexuality following the AIDS epidemic of the late 1980s, it did so through a populist appeal to traditional family values. (2004: 101)

In each instance she couched her authoritarian goals in 'populist' rhetoric. Similarly, when she wanted to strengthen the authority of the police she did so by appealing to the people's sense of safety. Even her emphatic championing of neoliberalism was framed in terms of 'freedom'.

Thatcher's mobilisation of the police and military in events was for many the final unmasking of oppressive authority: the 'false consciousness' of a naturalised authority was stripped away, and authority was laid bare as the draconian force that it had become. This is demonstrable in events like the miners' strikes in the 1980s and the poll tax riots in 1990, some of which find creative analogues in the series. Despite superficial objections to particular political actors, the man in charge in these pre-Thatcher series believes in democracy as an ideal, expressed through duty and paternalistic values. If there is discontent expressed in the science fiction television consensus era, at least in the 1970s, it may be against petty bureaucracy, and very occasionally governmental authority, but almost never against the authority of the man in charge.

Added to this, and eventually rising to the level of domination, is neoliberalism. Not all the series that follow grapple with it directly, but all contend with its new logic. The governing logic of late capitalism is that of a paradigm shift in society that affected all sectors. The individual is prized – his struggles are more important than those of the group. Democracy takes a back seat to the machinations of the individual or the power of large corporations. Contrarily the individual can behave in duplicitous ways, as he realises that authority is either corrupt, arbitrary or virtually nonexistent, and he has seen a 'gap in the market' to exploit the system and behave in any manner he decides is acceptable, often settling on a Machiavellian method.

The next chapter, a substantive analysis of *Blake's 7* and its relationship to Thatcherism and neoliberalism, will reveal the drastic change of the content of science fiction television series under Thatcherism. *Blake's 7* began in 1978, a year before Thatcher was elected. The first season is more redolent of the consensus-era themes, but even so, a new mentality is breaking through, one that favours individualism and even selfishness. After that I will devote a chapter each to *Sapphire & Steel* and *Doctor Who* of the Thatcher era, and then the last two chapters will discuss the shorter and less successful series of the era. In each case a tonal shift has occurred: authority has broken down to some extent, to be replaced with a cynical, amoral attitude. These series question what is left of the freedoms that Thatcher elevated to the mythic level and ask, how much of this newfound 'freedom' is an illusion? The series will also examine the many ways authority, and its more deleterious cousin authoritarianism, manifest in this era.

2

'Wealth is the only reality': *Blake's 7* and Thatcherism

T. S. Eliot writes in The Hollow Men: 'This is the way the world ends / Not with a bang but a whimper'. The characters of *Blake's 7* (1978–81) see their world end with such an unequivocal bang that it moved M. Keith Booker to describe the programme as 'one of the darkest science fiction series ever to appear on television' (2004: 83). The series itself has been dismissed by scholars for its failings with little assessment made of its worth. Duckworth notes, '*Blake's 7* was never in a position to compete with big-budget US genre shows in terms of production values' (2010: 52). Bould makes his distaste for the series clear, claiming:

> even as the series' fascination with the strong, sexually confident Servalan [Supreme Commander of the Terran Federation] hints at the mood of a nation prepared to elect Margaret Thatcher, its dismal tone and perpetual sense of defeat can be understood as an ironic admission of the BBC's inability to compete with US-produced science fiction spectacles. (2008: 221)

The series is dismissed by Bould as merely 'an attempt by the BBC to produce a space opera that could hold its own in a post-*Star Wars* era', which finds itself 'limping to a finale in which they are all killed' (2008: 221). The fact of the protagonists' murders in the finale separates *Blake's 7* from almost all other generic science fiction television series, ending as it does on a note of almost complete despair and futility, at least on the surface. This fact, alongside its many other departures from consensus-era series tropes, announces *Blake's 7* as the product of a new era: the era that marks the beginning of the Thatcher administration.

Blake's 7 is a British dystopian science fiction television series that follows the exploits of an often-changing line-up of rebels in a future society. This society is almost entirely ruled by a corrupt political power known as the Terran Federation. The early seasons follow these rebels as they navigate space in a ship called the Liberator (and later the Scorpio), and try to derail the Federation. On Earth and several other planets, the Federation controls every movement of its citizens, through brainwashing techniques, as well as constant monitoring, police brutality and general corruption. Parallels to Orwell's *Nineteen Eighty-Four* abound, with intimations of Huxley's 'soma'-dependent society in *Brave New World*, and the series shows its influences, drawing from this dystopian tradition of English science fiction literature (see McCormack, 2006: 176).

The series begins from a far more radical position than the other two major series that will be studied in this and the next two chapters, and indeed the shorter series studied in Chapters 5 and 6, but finds itself, by the end, adopting a much more 'libertarian' stance. While all of these series (to some extent) take a politically Machiavellian turn in this era, *Blake's 7* is the darkest and most cynical. In the characters of the crew, in particular Avon, we are able to observe many aspects of Thatcherism in emergence. More so than the other two major examples, the series is torn between the 'old world' of collectivism and consensus, and the 'new world' of Thatcherism and neoliberalism. *Blake's 7* thus exists in a kind of liminal space, wedged between two political and economic systems. Sitting on the cusp of the shift, from consensus-era Britain, to Thatcher's 'authoritarian populism', *Blake's 7* reverberates uneasily between the two poles. The series borrows from various aspects of Thatcherite logic, as well as drawing from the values of the consensus era, at least in the first two seasons, before completely abandoning them and adopting a Thatcherite attitude for most of the remainder of the series. We will recall from the introduction that Suvin accuses too much science fiction writing of recent decades of accepting the Thatcherite world view of neoliberal economics as if it is inevitable, and therefore its only concern is 'how one might survive within it' (Wegner, 2010: xxii). *Blake's 7* is an examination within generic television science fiction appearing early in the

Thatcherite landscape of this emerging system, and the possibilities of surviving within it.

In the most telling departure from the consensus-era series studied in the previous chapter, *Blake's 7* (and the other two major series) presents an intermingling of the concepts of Realpolitik and Machiavellianism. We will see that in *Blake's 7*, the mercenary and prisoner Kerr Avon stole money from the corrupt Federation. On the prison ship he explains the reason for his crime: 'Wealth is the only reality, and the only way to attain wealth is to take it away from somebody else.' This direct, bald and honest appraisal of greed and the selfish behaviour that is the corollary of Thatcherite individualism, is perhaps the reverse image of what Thatcher implied, but can be seen as the more reliable outcome of economic liberalism.

McCormack considers *Blake's 7* an anti-Utopian series, writing, 'the ultimate fallibility of technology is a recurring theme of anti-Utopian responses to Wells [*A Modern Utopia*]' (2006: 176), and falls in stark contrast to the consensus-era series studied in Chapter 2. Yet the series is also, in Moylan's sense, a 'critical dystopia' (2000: 189) – a series that exists within a dystopia, but holds open the possibilities of a better future. This better future manifests in the theme of a new beginning, which plays out in *Blake's 7* and possibly leaves the ending open to a more hopeful reading. The idea of a new beginning is also used as an ideological tool in Thatcherism. The Conservative Party's 1979 manifesto claims, 'The years of make-believe and false optimism are over. It is time for a new beginning' (sec. 7, para 4). *Blake's 7* is to some extent a call for an alternative 'new beginning' – one that is more equitable for all.

Blake's 7 appeared at a time when Britain was perceived to be on the decline by way of the collapse of the Labour Party, economic crises, and the events leading to the 1978/79 Winter of Discontent. Appropriately, the series trades in inertia and decline (see McCormack, 2006: 178–9). Every society the rebels visit is in a technological downturn, and many are reverting to a kind of savagery. If the series was conceived to be about freedom fighters engaged in a struggle against authoritarian power, it evolves into an individualistic race for Darwinian survival in which the most ruthless wins. But no one ultimately wins in *Blake's 7*. As a critique of any system that purports to be utopian, and a story of failure in the cause of revolution, *Blake's 7* carries a message of apparent futility. But ultimately, I argue that the series is a critique of the emerging system of individualism and economic liberalism that found its fullest expression in the Thatcher era. *Blake's 7* in its later seasons articulates this theme of individualism, with its Machiavellian traits seen as a consequence of greed, selfishness and the quest for profit.

There are many ways in which the series subverts the generic expectations of a science fiction television series of the era, suggesting a new Thatcherite sensibility, though it grows out of a climate of British science fiction series already discussed in this book: ATC's *UFO* (1970) and *Space: 1999* (1975–77) drawing from American utopianism, as well as Terry Nation's earlier *Survivors* (1975–77) and Nigel Kneale's *Quatermass* serials (1953–79). Their influence on the series is apparent, from critiques of authority to ruminations on the morality of duty and the use of violence. But *Blake's 7*, broadcast during the beginnings of the Thatcher era, eventually moves beyond the archetypal structures of these antecedents, exploring the brutal, Machiavellian behaviour of its protagonists – behaviour that springs from a strong sense of individualism. Also analysed in this chapter is the ambiguous messaging the series applies to the question of terrorism. Finally, the ending, in which the rebels are all murdered by the Federation, presents a message of apparent futility in political struggle, but also raises some questions about the dangers of this individualism.

McCormack considers the series as positioned between the two great post-war utopian experiments: the USA and the USSR, and their opposing ideologies (2006: 178), *Blake's 7* begins closer to a left-wing revolutionary idealism personified by Blake, but there is enough criticism within the series of Blake's position to distance it from this simple reading and move it closer to a general critique of authoritarian power. As has been discussed, a drift to the right could already be perceived in Britain from at least 1975 (Hall, 1988: 166), three years before *Blake's 7* began. In reality, discussions around economic liberalism had been taking place long before that, and Thatcher herself was advocating for it many years before she took up residence in Number 10. If the series begins as 'Robin Hood in space', a kind of consensus-era tale of rebels aligned broadly with the left, its direction from Season 3 onwards is far less buccaneering, and far more Realpolitik, seemingly aligned to Thatcher's changes in Britain of the era. Therefore, in many ways, the series anticipates and mimics the sweeping economic and social change in Britain at the time.

The series, too, throughout its run, retains some elements of consensus-era logic, while at the same time effectively 'trying on the Thatcherite suit', before finally dispensing with it and returning to the task of renewal. The new Thatcherite myths of individualism and self-interest are tried and ultimately cast aside, and the series returns to the ethic of organised collective action, even if the characters have realised too late the need for this action. The protagonists in *Blake's 7* have little idea what will replace the system; they are only possessed of the certainty that the system needs to be destroyed. In the end the system destroys them, but symbolically I believe this is not a futile act, but an act of final defiance, and an opportunity for a different kind of renewal.

Blake's 7 and Thatcherism

Blake's 7 is far more overtly political than any other series in this book in its conception of a totalitarian society as well as in its modes of resistance. It is more brutal and Machiavellian in the machinations of its characters; and finally, it's darker and more apparently futile than any other in its ending (though *Sapphire & Steel* comes close). *Blake's 7* is unique among any examples of generic science fiction television at the time for its themes and treatment of characters, but its antecedents are still discernible. In what were clearly less complicated times, Terry Nation, the series' creator, 'went to the BBC and said, "I have what I think is a terrific idea: it's *The Dirty Dozen* in space."' ('An Interview with Terry Nation', 1987), which implies a great deal of artistic freedom, especially compared with the 'checks and balances' of today's convoluted systems, and those that emerged immediately after this era, the 1980s, which will be discussed in the later chapters. Nation was informed by the BBC that he would be commissioned to write the series as long as he wrote all thirteen episodes of the first season himself. To assist his process, Nation claimed a reciprocal relationship between himself and the actors, wherein he provided the 'bare bones' of the characters' personalities, and the actors would furnish Nation with a greater depth, which he could then mould into a fuller character.

Nation's running theme had always been the corruption of power. This hints at his wartime upbringing, especially in his acknowledged (if sometimes subconscious) invocation of the Nazis as models for the Daleks. Nation comments of his most famous creations:

> The Daleks are all of 'Them' and they represent for so many people so many different things, but they all see them as government, as officialdom, as that unhearing, unthinking, blanked-out face of authority that will destroy you because it wants to destroy you. I believe in that now – I've directed them more that way over the years. ('An Interview with Terry Nation', 1987)

The dread of authority has erupted into full-blown hatred in *Blake's 7*: the series is a darker addition to Nation's oeuvre, exploring more morally and politically charged territory, with that same central concern about authoritarian power.

The dark nature of the series became ever more apparent as Nation's influence diminished by Season 2 onwards. As the series progressed, the primary creative force behind it became the script editor Chris Boucher, whose 'increased influence upon the show in its second season marked the programme's distinct turn towards the politically ambiguous' (McCormack, 2006: 175). Boucher comments:

> Terry had a much clearer notion of right and wrong than I did, and saw the series as basically Robin Hood in space. Whereas I sort of warped it a bit and tried to make it more ambiguous, so that in the end it became more like Che Guevara and *The Dirty Dozen*. (qtd in Stevens and Brown, 1992)

Boucher may not have been aware of Nation's own intention to take the series in the direction of *The Dirty Dozen*, or the recollection of history may be revisionist in one or both of their minds. In any case, Boucher did steer the series down a more politically ambiguous path. Some of this was due to the specifics of the situation: Gareth Thomas, who played Blake, left the series at the end of

Season 2, and Nation himself left soon after. This left the path clear for Boucher to change the political emphasis.

In the first episode, 'The Way Back', Earth has become a dystopia. The society that the Federation has produced is one that has naturalised certain social structures. The citizens of the citadel live a reasonably comfortable life if they don't enquire too much about the state of their existence, or venture beyond the 'forbidden areas'. The general level of affluence of the characters in the citadel – the way they dress coupled with their clipped RP (received pronunciation) accents and middle-class behaviour – suggests that the Federation is constructing a certain bourgeois approximation of reality, which it encourages its citizens to operate within. Everyone has an identity card, and like the characters in Huxley's *Brave New World*, the citizens are anaesthetised with a regime of drugs. They are presented with a naturalised society which erases history, both personal and political; much like Yevgeny Zamyatin's *We*, it even erases parts of the city that are forbidden, and presents this bourgeois existence as ahistorical and natural, recalling Barthes's notion of 'myths', as a set of constructed ideological positions which, through the erasure of history, are made to appear natural. There is absolute authority in the Terran Federation, and anyone who defies it is hunted down by Federation troopers, killed, or framed by the state for crimes they did not commit. This episode presents us with a picture of wealth and privilege for the few, as long as they are prepared to accept an unreal 'mythical' environment. Broadcast roughly one year before Thatcher was elected, it critiques the wealth divide and economic decline that was already present, but was to dramatically escalate in Thatcher's first term, when unemployment rose to over three million. This extrapolation of the reality of then-present British society, hyperbolising it to the point of near absurdity, affords us an insight into what ultimate authority might look like. This future is certainly not 'wiser than the world it speaks to' (Suvin, 1979: 36), but rather serves as a cautionary tale.

Roj Blake is introduced as a 'regular' citizen, but soon discovers that he has a rebel past. Memories of this past, and his involvement in it, have been cleared from his mind by the Federation through the use of drugs and torture. At first, he doesn't believe those who try to convince him, but they eventually persuade him to go outside the citadel, which is a crime. In the tunnels below the citadel they meet and discuss rebel plans. It is here that Blake learns his life is a myth that has been constructed by the authorities. He was told, for instance, that his brother and sister lived on another planet, but the rebels explain that they are dead, and the communications he receives are fakes created by the authorities. When Blake recovers from his anaesthetised state and sees 'behind the veil' to the reality of these authorities, he is motivated to become a revolutionary once again.

Some of the episode was filmed at Eastlays, an underground bunker originally built as a quarry for Bath stone, and acquired in 1980 by private contractors and refitted to withstand a nuclear attack: the first of its kind in the world (see Beckett, 2015: 94–8). The filming location lends it a certain feeling of cold dread. The conformity within the citadel is such that every corridor looks the same – flat, angular metallic walls and columns, and people moving largely in unison wearing very similar dress. Blake and the rebels move around the corridors, walking down metal step ladders and opening a thick metal door that resembles a bank vault. From the outside the citadel resembles a giant metal dome, reminiscent of 1970s movies like *Logan's Run*. The rebel base Blake is taken to is visually closer to an old parking lot with oppressive concrete and metal. The series was filmed similarly to most other television in the 1970s – video was used for the interior scenes and 16 mm film for the external or other location shooting. This gives the interior of the citadel a smooth but antiseptic feel, while the rebel base appears bleaker but somehow more authentic. Just as Thatcher was to grant far greater powers to the police, so the Federation mobilises black-clad stormtroopers to monitor every situation. In 'The Way Back' the rebels' gathering is broken up by stormtroopers, who kill everyone in the meeting while Blake helplessly watches on from his hiding place (a strange foreshadowing of the ending of the series). When the Federation troopers move in, they are filmed casting enormous shadows on the concrete walls, creating a strong sense of dread and emphasising the sense that the rebels are captured specimens, like rats in a cage. The Federation troopers are clad entirely in black, with masks that evoke images of gas masks from both world wars. They also call to mind François Truffaut's 1966 film version of Ray Bradbury's *Fahrenheit 451* with their black suits and helmets, and fire emerging from their weapons.

For his 'crime' of once again colluding with rebels, Blake is incarcerated, while a false allegation of paedophilia is brought against him, and he is convicted. The lawyer who tries to defend him is murdered, with a fabricated excuse offered about the cause of his death, indicating the absolute power of the Federation to control the narrative of its citizens. Blake is sent aboard a prison ship bound for the prison planet Cygnus Alpha, and there he meets the group of assorted criminals who will eventually become his crew. Between them they manage to escape the prison ship and hijack another ship christened by them as the Liberator.

In the beginning, some characters fall into archetypal roles: Blake is the hero, Vila the cowardly thief, Gan the simple-minded strongman, Jenna the smuggler and loyal disciple of Blake, Cally the telepath, providing a moral compass for the group. Even Avon could be classified as archetypal, as the trickster – self-serving: never entirely loyal or trustworthy, a sort of prototype for modern tricksters like Walter White in *Breaking Bad*, or indeed the Marvel cinematic version of Loki. The seventh 'member' of the group is the computer Zen, which controls the ship. Some of these archetypes are also to be found in Nation's earlier *Survivors* (1975–77), discussed in Chapter 1. But in *Survivors* there is no overbearing authoritarian power, only pockets of vigilantes. The protagonists in *Survivors* are far more concerned with establishing a fair and just system, which involves what they view as a benign authority. Conversely, there are never any deliberations on the possible merits of governmental authority in *Blake's 7*, only an immediate desire to destroy the system, which aligns it with political revolutionary activity. To borrow Hall's phrase, the 'hard road to renewal' (1988) for these characters is pure revolution, aligned to some extent with a Marxist enterprise in its defiance of 'bourgeois' authoritarianism. Though the characters in *Blake's 7* are never politically aligned, at least Blake considers the utopian promise of a new world, however vague, to be his starting point.

Much of the tension of the series arises from the conflict between idealism and cynical pragmatism. In the first two seasons there is something of a collectivist spirit among the crew, despite the fact that it is compromised by conflicting agendas. The rebels, led by Blake, eventually come close to destroying the Federation. But by Season 3 the ship's crew are dispersed and Blake is lost. A new crew is assembled with Blake's second-in-command, Avon, in charge. After this point the crew consistently fail in their missions. Avon more often steers them towards personal profit than revolution, and they lose sight of their goal, though sometimes there are mixed agendas. The series then changes from a Robin Hood-inspired tale of revolutionaries, to a story of mercenaries attempting to live an existence of libertarian freedom (finding fuller expression in Joss Whedon's 2002 *Firefly* series, which many consider to be directly influenced by *Blake's 7*). A sense of left-leaning idealism is tempered by the emergent Thatcherite ideology, and the series oscillates in the centre of these tensions, and remains there until near the very end. Through their new-found, self-centred and individualistic lifestyle, which roughly finds its analogue in Thatcherite values, the protagonists find themselves too disorganised and fractured to function effectively any longer as a revolutionary force. At the end, the series attempts to return to the notion of revolution, but accepts ruefully that this project is now diminished, even exhausted. Blake himself becomes a symbol of this diminishment, as we will later discover.

Even the costumes and props reflect this change. In the early seasons the characters are dressed in more colourful, Robin-Hood-in-space-inspired costumes – green and brown coats with leather trimmings. Their weapons are unusual 'guns-with-sticks', held in a way that resembles the wielding of a sword. In the second season this is amplified. Britton and Barker write:

> The aesthetic [of *Blake's 7*], especially for costumes, was transformed at the beginning of the second season, with both regulars and incidental characters for the first time dressed in a flamboyant style, calculatedly unlike the drab anoraks that dominated the first season. (2003: 138)

Though even those drab anoraks in Season 1 have a hint of Friar Tuck about them. In any case, in the harsher and more Thatcherite seasons that follow Season 2, the Robin Hood aesthetic is gone, and Avon begins to favour mostly black leather outfits. The weapons are replaced with cold metal guns. Even the new ship, Scorpio, is of a sleeker design.

As the series develops, we witness a symbiotic relationship developing between the crew and Servalan, the eventual president of the Federation. This apparently permissive relationship offers an insight into a much more insidious form of authoritarian power. In the episode 'Sand' (1981), Servalan and Tarrant, one of Avon's crew members, are trapped on a planet with aggressive, sentient sand, which confines them in a building. While holed up in this womb-like environment, it is strongly implied that they share a sexual encounter. In the episode 'Death-Watch' (1980), Servalan and Avon share a kiss. Symbolically this points to a more complex and ambiguous relationship between 'hero' and 'villain', and explores Servalan's ability to allow for the illusion of autonomy among the crew. They are allowed to believe that she has some degree of respect for them, and allows them a certain leeway. The Thatcher regime strongly encouraged independence, but at the same time it attempted to interfere with the political messaging of media outlets, including the language around the Troubles in Northern Ireland, and the Falklands. A similar relationship works for the crew in *Blake's 7* and Servalan: she allows them to operate with the illusion of independence until it is no longer expedient for her to do so. She does this because they are a useful tool for her, and also because a degree of respect develops, particularly between her and Avon. This 'illusion of independence' is even more central in *Sapphire & Steel*, which the next chapter will discuss.

Though the group are never especially cohesive in the first instance, they at least share a common goal. In the new formulation starting from Season 3, the crew appears to be far more self-serving and atomised without Blake's idealism to anchor them in their mission. Avon had always been a Machiavellian manipulator, but when he takes over as the new protagonist he proves himself ever more ruthless, operating to a large extent on selfish individual motivation, though his ultimate goals are never clear. Avon's character owes a lot to the work of Bertolt Brecht (1898–1956). The great German Marxist playwright had a powerful effect on British theatre, leading into British television. Brecht advanced the concept of *Verfremdungseffekt* – the 'estrangement effect' in theatre – to some degree following Marx's concept of alienation, breaking with the more Aristotlean notion of empathy. Among the many to be influenced by Brecht was Suvin, who used the playwright's ideas for his own concept of cognitive estrangement.

Avon, like Steel and the Sixth and Seventh Doctors in the following chapters, is an estranging character. His interests in rebellion, revolution and liberation appear to be slight, while his instinct for self-preservation is strong, and on many occasions (as this chapter will later discuss) he is prepared to risk the lives of his crew for the attainment of his own personal goals. If he does demonstrate a more humane or empathetic attitude, it is for ambiguous reasons, often treating the rescue of others as purely an intellectual challenge, or mercy as an expression of mere expedience. In 'Aftermath' (1980) he prevents Dayna from killing his assailant, simply commenting that 'he's no danger to us now'. In 'City at the Edge of the World' (1980) he defends Vila against criticism. Cally asks, 'Why are you suddenly so protective towards Vila?' Avon answers, 'He's irritating, but he's useful. We can easily replace a pilot, but a talented thief is rare', once again displaying his tendency to demonstrate either affection or steely pragmatism, depending on the interpretation. In Avon, I argue, we witness a nascent Thatcherite ideology in emergence: the individualist, shown in the rejection of 'society', the Machiavellian behaviour, and the pursuit of personal wealth (if not the actual attainment). Thatcher's regime of course never exhibited an explicit preference for Machiavellian behaviour; rather, it was an almost inevitable outgrowth of its individualist policies. *Blake's 7* plays on that outgrowth and presents Avon as a caricature of the 'ideal' Thatcherite citizen.

Avon's pursuit of wealth is often inflicted upon other crew members, even in the early seasons. In the episode 'Gambit' (1979), the Liberator crew arrives at Freedom City. Blake's quest is to find a man who can assist them with finding the Federation's mainframe computer. But Avon and crew member Vila decide to use Orac, the advanced AI unit aboard the ship, to cheat at the casino in the city, which fails. In 'Gold' (1981), the crew is recruited to steal gold from a transport ship. As always, the plan goes wrong. Anytime the crew, or individuals within it, abandons its quest for revolution for the sake of personal gain, the results are disastrous.

Servalan is also a strong individualist. Like Avon, she is Machiavellian and ruthless; she holds her ultimate plans close to her person, only releasing parts of information when necessary. Vint notes that Thatcherism led to a 'crisis in masculinity in a British society encouraged to value aggressive and uncompromising individualism, just as traditional patriarchal authority and work were disappearing' (2013: 157). Servalan uses her svelte, feline sexuality to exploit the masculine system. In one sense Servalan is the clearest comparison with Thatcher, being that both are women at a time when women in power were even less common than the present, and while little has been written about Thatcherism and *Blake's 7*, this aspect has not been overlooked. Cornea notes:

> The figure of Servalan as Federation leader legitimated female ambition, but only in the sense that she embodied a new economic agenda fuelled by amoral, aggressive competition and personal greed. Representative of Thatcher, the femme fatale characterisation of Servalan played out the 'dangerous attractions' of this new economic agenda for the left-leaning male. (2011: para 27)

Servalan marries sexuality with power, suggesting these 'dangerous attractions.' She is brutal, individualistic, and a 'threat to the masculine order'. But she also breaks out of the traditional binary structure. Servalan 'refuses to fit within the traditional binary categorisation of women in relation to men', Bignell and O'Day write, 'and blurs the boundaries between those inherited binaries, mixing the category of femininity with masculinity and power' (2004: 173). Just as Avon presents a challenge to the notion of a 'heroic' archetype, Servalan complicates these traditional gender binaries because she is in power.

The episode 'Terminal' (1980) examines the connections between these two most individualistic characters, and the porous boundaries between 'hero' and 'villain'. Avon sets out on a mission that he will not explain to the others. It turns out to be a quest to find Blake, but the 'Blake' he encounters is a drug-induced hallucination, engineered by Servalan to lure him off the ship so that she can seize it. The episode is notable for its ambiguities. Avon's quest to find Blake may be one of need for a figurehead to lead the rebellion, or it may be a drive for personal profit. The ruse involves Blake informing Avon that there is a 'discovery' that will bring them wealth and power. When Avon encounters 'Blake' (or the apparition), they have an exchange:

> BLAKE: It must've been so dull, having no one to argue with.
> AVON: Well, there were times when your simple-minded certainties might've been refreshing.
> BLAKE: Careful Avon – your sentiment is showing.
> AVON: That's your imagination. Now, are you going to tell me about this discovery that is going to make us rich and invincible?

Avon has risked everything, including his own life, for this 'discovery', yet it's unclear why he has bothered. Because of their obvious animosity, Avon's desire to find Blake after Season 2 is always unusual. There is a sense that Blake and Avon, on some level, view each other as a balm for the other's shortcomings – as the dialogue above suggests, Avon sees Blake's idealism as an antidote for his cynicism, and Blake sees Avon's ruthless pragmatism as a necessary challenge to his impetuousness. Boucher goes further, claiming that Avon had 'come to believe in Blake's love for him, and Blake was the last possible thing he could believe in' (qtd in Stevens and Brown, 1992: para 103). Indeed, this is the only real instance of 'genuine' personal connection in the whole series (there is a back story involving Avon's girlfriend, but even she betrays him when she arrives in the series). This is a constant refrain in the major Thatcher-era series: the lack of any personal, familial or romantic connection, allowing the characters a ruthlessness, but also an even greater sense of alienation, from themselves and others. In any case, Avon's motivations are always ambiguous and it is unclear whether he genuinely cares for Blake or not. Boucher himself acknowledges this, claiming:

> I was always careful to make sure that Avon could have an idealistic reason for doing something, and also a totally selfish and cynical one ... I don't think to my mind the character was really sure of his own motives anyway. (qtd in Stevens and Brown, 1992: para 103)

In the characters of Blake and Avon we may detect a contest between two ideologies: that of the 'old guard' – the leftist who believes in social justice, a product of the consensus era; and the 'new wave' – the self-interested, right-wing character emblematic of the new world of Thatcherism. Avon was originally convicted by the Federation for attempting to embezzle an enormous amount of money by hacking a computer. Already the associations become apparent. With traders in the City of London, or Wall Street in New York, the 1980s ushered in the era of the 'yuppie', some of the traits of which can be seen in Avon. Avon is doubly estranging: as a Brechtian character already, and an expression of Thatcherism at a time when this new system was still in its nascent stages.

Moral duty and the question of terrorism

Duckworth comments that *Blake's 7* 'was shot through with moral ambiguities and uncertainties' (2010: 52). Unlike the consensus-era heroes, the characters in *Blake's 7* do not display a traditional sense of duty. Blake's sense of duty is to the cause of revolution, not to an authority. Blake is comfortable with the notion that the ends justify the means. With his collectivist associations, Blake is a warning against the emerging neoliberal society. But he is also a character trapped between two moral stances: that of his perceived duty to humanity, liberating them from the clutches of the Federation, and a revolutionary position that moves closer to zealotry. By the end of Season 2, the crew has achieved its objective. They have reached Star One, the Federation's mainframe computer. To destroy it is to significantly destabilise the Federation, perhaps even end its reign. For the first time Blake's single-minded pursuit of this goal is challenged and critiqued within the series:

> CALLY: Are we fanatics?
> BLAKE: Does it matter?
> CALLY: Many, many people will die without Star One.
> BLAKE: I know.
> CALLY: Are you sure that what we're going to do is justified?
> BLAKE: It has to be. Don't you see, Cally? If we stop now then all we have done is senseless killing and destruction. Without purpose, without reason. We have to win. It's the only way I can be sure that I was right. (qtd in McCormack, 2006: 183–4)

Blake's reply is another example of Bentham's fundamental axion writ large, aligning him with other consensus heroes such as *UFO*'s Straker and *Survivors'* Greg, but pushing him several orders of magnitude further than they were forced to go, at least in terms of scale (though not personal cost, especially in the case of Straker). By the end of that episode the crew decide the cost is too great when it is revealed that an Andromedan invasion force, working with Travis, is trying to destroy all of humanity. Blake's crew alerts the Federation of the force. Blake's idealism is nearly always on the side of revolution, but at this stage at least, he retains some of his humanity. Boucher comments:

> I saw Blake as an idealist who goes down the road that idealism, and fanaticism to an extent, takes people. Although he believed that he was working for a just cause and that his motives were purely altruistic, I can't see how Blake could possibly have avoided being brutalised to some extent by the kind of guerrilla war that he was undertaking against the Federation … To infer that the end justifies the means is, to my mind, assuredly wrong, because I don't think there is an end, there are only means, and means are corrupting. (qtd in Stevens and Brown, 1992: para 96)

Boucher is clear where he sees Blake's revolutionary tendencies leading, and as the series develops towards its fatalistic conclusion, Blake's humanity is eroded, and morphs into a battle-weary cynicism. By his last appearance, which is the last episode of the series, 'Blake', he is shown to be physically and mentally deranged by his years of guerrilla warfare. Even though he is still at the business of revolution, his idealism has all but disappeared.

In the example of 'Star One', the series poses the question of whether the crew is comprised of freedom fighters or terrorists. Duckworth writes, 'Blake and his followers seek to overturn the status quo, but they do so by acts of terrorism and piracy in which civilian deaths are seen as little more than "collateral damage"' (2010: 55). Versions of the question of terrorism were arising in Britain in this era more urgently than before. Thatcher's confidante, the Conservative minister Airey Neave, was assassinated in a car bomb in 1979, and the INLA (Irish National Liberation Army) took responsibility. In the same year Lord Mountbatten (Prince Philip's uncle) was killed by a bomb for which the INLA also claimed responsibility, but other sources attributed it to the IRA. These events deeply affected Thatcher's attitude towards terrorism: she abhorred it, and was quick to label it unambiguously. Even as late as 1987 Thatcher is quoted as saying that the ANC (African National Congress), Nelson Mandela's party in South Africa, was an organisation of terrorists (1987c: para 76). Even before Thatcher was elected, the Troubles in Northern Ireland and the terrorist activities of the IRA in Ireland and Britain were commonplace. As Seaton notes, Thatcher was most displeased with the way the BBC had covered the Troubles, and when she became Prime Minister, her government decided:

> to change the constitutional arrangements around the Corporation, and then to ensure that the next chairman was perhaps closer to its view, and that the governors were more sympathetic to it politically over Northern Ireland. (2015: 70)

Indeed, this stance on terrorism brought Thatcher into conflict with the BBC, and was one of the many examples of unease between the government and the broadcaster, which intensified through the 1980s. Seaton notes that as she moved through her time as a Tory minister, then as Prime Minister, 'she increasingly made her views of the BBC public, in Parliament, in speeches, in interviews and in occasional off-the-cuff responses to questions' (2015: 9). In 1977, during the Troubles, she:

> spoke at length and with 'great feeling' about the way the BBC enhanced [Irish] Republican reputations and suggested that the prime minister, Mr Mason [Secretary of State for Northern Ireland] and Mr Rees [Home Secretary], together with the Conservative opposition, 'should make a joint approach to the BBC governors to make it absolutely clear that no increase in the licence fees would be granted while these sort of programmes were tolerated by the governors'. (Seaton, 2015: 66)

In 1974, Thatcher criticised the corporation for its apparently left-wing stance. Seaton notes, 'Usually the BBC saw itself as a "responsible" and "impartial" broadcaster, but these roles were set on a collision course' (2015: 51). Thatcher brought that collision course ever closer to its crisis point during her time in office.

It is against this backdrop that *Blake's 7* deliberately calls into question the actions of the crew in operating outside the law. McCormack writes that '*Blake's 7* scrutinises the response of government to terrorism and considers in what kind of society armed resistance becomes a logical activity' (2006: 179). In the earlier cited exchange in the episode 'Star One', Blake is challenged about whether they are 'fanatics'. That, and Boucher's comment about the untenable premise that the end justifies the means, suggests that the series is critical of what it calls 'fanatical' behaviour. This fanatical behaviour by the time of 'Star One' amounts to terrorism. Yet at the same time, Blake in particular is portrayed as a heroic figure, even if his particular 'heroic' qualities are becoming obsolete in the world of the narrative – giving way to more cynical qualities that are exemplified by Avon. The series is, in the end, ambivalent about whether or not Blake and his crew are terrorists, and whether that moral position can ever be defended. Ultimately Boucher tends to think not, yet the series certainly portrays the struggle against the system, including those we would consider as terrorists, as noble.

Avon has little sense of moral duty. In the third episode of the series, 'Cygnus Alpha', we witness the first hint of Avon's Machiavellian character when he and crewmate Jenna discover valuable jewels aboard the ship while Blake is on the surface of a prison planet. The two debate whether or not to leave Blake on the prison planet or teleport him back up to the ship:

> JENNA: What about Blake?
> AVON: What about him?
> JENNA: No.
> AVON: We could own our own planet.
> JENNA: We're not leaving him there.
> AVON: We have to. He's a crusader. He'll look upon this as just one more weapon to use against the Federation. And he can't win. You know he can't win.

In most series of the era, the heroic struggle would be rewarded with success, but not in this case. The most telling departure from most generic science fiction television series, whether British or American, is that Avon is proven to be correct. In the long run, Blake cannot, and does not, win. This conversation, coming as it does so early on in the series, sets the tone. This crew is not a collection of 'merry men': there is dissent from the beginning, which never dissipates. The audience is tempted to see Avon as the 'villain' who might derail the crew, yet his Realpolitik arguments are reasonable: the idea that Blake cannot win, and the suggestion is to simply exploit the situation by accumulating wealth. In an echo of Suvin's comments about the emerging neoliberal mindset, this exchange is both a 'concession' to that mindset, and a stark warning against it.

Avon's cutthroat attitude appears constantly. As early as the second episode, 'Space Fall' (the first appearance of Avon), we are provided examples of where the character sits:

> VILA: (*referring to Avon*) He came close to stealing five million credits out of the Federation banking system.
> BLAKE: What went wrong?
> AVON: I relied on other people.

Soon after, Avon explains his attitude:

> AVON: Wealth is the only reality, and the only way to attain wealth is to take it away from somebody else.

For Thatcherites, wealth is also the only reality that can lead to freedom, just as it is with Avon. Avon's version represents a more cynical aspect of wealth accumulation, or perhaps a more honest one – it cuts through the Thatcherite rhetoric of greater economic prosperity for all through trickle-down wealth, deregulated markets and economic growth, and presents it instead as a zero-sum game.

When Avon takes over charge of the ship and its crew, it is clear that his motives are far darker and more ambiguous than Blake's ever were. Although he appears to be part of the crew, it becomes apparent at certain junctures that Avon has his own agenda, his own interest in self-preservation, and will do anything, even kill other crew members, to achieve it. In 'Terminal' (1981) he explains:

> AVON: I don't need any of you ... I don't want you with me, I don't want you following me. Understand this: anyone who does follow me, I'll kill them.

In the episode 'Orbit' (1981), Avon and Vila find themselves trapped in a ship that can't quite break the atmosphere. In order to do so and escape, they need to jettison 73 kg. Orac (the computer) informs Avon that this happens to be the exact weight of his crewmate Vila. Avon pulls out his gun and shrieks, 'Vila?' Vila has by now taken the initiative to hide, and narrowly escapes death when Avon discovers something else he can sacrifice.

Final episodes

After more quests for wealth, the last two episodes leading up to the final, 'Blake' (1981), see a change of heart for the crew. Avon rediscovers his revolutionary streak and attempts to assemble a new rebellion in 'Warlord' (1981), and is only thwarted because of internal politics. Then, in the final episode, Avon, presumably driven by the quest for rebellion once again, discovers where Blake may be. This time it heralds success in the sense that they locate Blake, but ultimately it leads to the crew's demise. The crew has learned, too late, that the only way to fight the power of the Federation is with organised, collective action. They attempted to operate within the values of individualism and self-centred behaviour, reflecting Thatcherite values in Britain, and it led them down a blind alley. The series finally warns against the temptations of this new system and lends itself to a redemptive reading.

The crew go to the planet Gauda Prime, where Blake is living as a bounty hunter. In reality he's working to assemble a new team of resistance fighters. He is shown beaten and battered by his struggle for survival. One of his eyes is damaged and permanently closed, calling to mind Odin, the Norse God, who gives one of his eyes for knowledge of Ragnarök, the impending apocalypse that sees all the gods killed. This may be intended to foreshadow a similar apocalypse – the deaths of all the crew at the hands of the Federation. The symbolism of the all-seeing eye links us to the notions of wisdom and foresight, though in this instance Blake is completely ignorant of the catastrophe ahead.

As cover Blake pretends to be working for the Federation, and 'captures' Tarrant, intending to brief him on the new rebellion once he is sure Tarrant is not a Federation spy. At the same time, Avon and the others find their way to Blake's new base, where Tarrant, escaping from his phony confinement, warns Avon that Blake has 'sold us ... all of us ... even you'. Avon is unable to process this information, asking, 'Have you betrayed us, Blake? Have you betrayed *me*?' Before Blake can properly answer, Avon shoots him, apparently out of his feelings of betrayal. Blake dies, falling at Avon's feet. The Federation troops storm in soon after and kill all the crew members (while sustaining many deaths of their own), with only Avon left alive. Troopers surround him, echoing the disturbing images of the riots in England during that same year. Avon slowly lifts his weapon, looks at the camera, and ambiguously smiles. The screen cuts to black, accompanied by the sound of gunshots.

One way to read the final episode of *Blake's 7* is to cede to the notion of complete failure and futility. Boucher considers this reading of the ending, which connects to Thatcherism. When asked about whether the crew could have ever won, Boucher replies:

> No, I don't think it was possible. Although on occasion it was suggested that there were other freedom fighters about the place, they were never of any real threat to the Federation. So really when you came down to it, there was only Blake and his four companions, fighting alone and against overwhelming odds. (qtd in Stevens and Brown, 1992: para 154)

This kind of admission points, on one level, to a futility that is applicable in Thatcher's Britain: it applies to the fractured and defeated political left. But on the other hand, Boucher sees the failure of the rebels as the failure of the individual. If the rebels had managed to assemble a larger rebellion with a clear set of objectives, they may have had a chance. This suggests that only a sufficiently large and organised collective can succeed against corrupt power. The rebels in *Blake's 7* fail in the main because they are a disparate collection of individuals, combined in neither philosophy nor motivation, and therefore the series is a dark caricature of the kind of individualism Thatcherism championed.

The characters in *Blake's 7* are never united in their 'hopeful resistance': they are all fighting for their own personal reasons. Only Blake is truly interested in overthrowing the system, and his position is morally questionable. There is never any mention of the 'more humane and democratic' alternative to the system: indeed, echoing Thatcher herself, there is never *any* alternative. Avon never embodies any of these attributes of hopefulness or humanity, and is mainly in pursuit of his own selfish and cynical goals, even if they are ambiguous and tempered somewhat by the occasional revolutionary streak. There is some temptation to read the ending as a cry for freedom against corrupt authority, even if one's life is taken in the process. It would therefore align with a more straightforward left-wing revolutionary agenda: to die for one's cause if necessary. However, that is not how the ending plays out. Instead, Avon is clearly characterised in a manner that is too cynical for that kind of idealism. Blake, the idealist, is killed not by the Federation but by Avon himself. This would suggest that individualism has killed idealism. But individualism is not a viable alternative: it leads to the destruction of all parties. The ending most clearly presents a critique of the atomised individualistic spirit that emerged as part of the right-wing, Thatcherite discourse: there is no chance for the 'ordinary' individual, with their own personal motivations, to beat the system, or even, in many cases, to live in an equitable way within it. Only a unified front can achieve true revolution. The ending of *Blake's 7* is ultimately about the failure of the individual, at least when he or she operates in a self-interested way without thought for others, and it therefore criticises Thatcherism and its inherent individualistic policies and ideologies.

Another way to interpret the ending is in a redemptive reading, which also aligns with the Thatcherite world view. As in late *Doctor Who* and *Sapphire & Steel*, the eschatological undercurrent lends sense to the series overall, because it frames it as a struggle for renewal, which culminates in the ending and assists in understanding it. In this last episode, Blake is a symbol for the struggle of the left itself: he is weakened, eroded, until there is little remaining. He goes about the same actions that have ceased to be effective in a radically altered world. Thatcherism, as I have discussed, saw itself as a 'new beginning' – an ideological reset. It swept through the chaos and failure of the consensus era and positioned itself as the saviour of Britain and its dormant identity. Throughout Thatcher's reign the left struggled to articulate an effective oppositional voice to Thatcherism, but Hall (1988) expressed the search in terms of a need for 'renewal'. Hall was well aware that Thatcher's power was in her use of imagery, writing, 'Mrs Thatcher has totally dominated that idiom, while the left forlornly tries to drag the conversation round to "our policies"' (1988: 167). Hall knew that the left required its own use of imagery, its own 'common sense'. Like the 'forlorn' left wing in Britain, Blake continues the futile process of trying to assemble yet another rebellion, where all others have failed.

Blake's 7 finds its own 'rebirth' to be another kind of ending, as the characters have failed in their revolutionary goals, failed even to accommodate to the new libertarian ways. The only victory left is to find their own new beginning. They need to die and shed the individualism and selfishness that derailed their mission: analogous to the philosophies that guided Thatcherism in practice. In this formulation, the suggestion is that the rebels die for the sake of 'the greater good', and become martyrs. Bignell and O'Day pose this kind of reading:

> the efforts of Blake and his crew to overthrow the system in favour of a more humane and democratic one can seem like futile and insignificant blows against it. Nevertheless, the values of the British (or more accurately English) middle class that these resistant and hopeful characters possess are attributed with potential to become the lynchpins of progress towards a more enlightened future. (2004: 177)

Perhaps there are other rebel groups who will follow in the aftermath, leading to that 'more enlightened future'. In the first episode, when Blake first encounters the rebel leader, he says to Blake, 'They could've killed you, but that would've given the cause a martyr.' If this philosophy still applies to the ending, it implies that the crew's deaths will resonate and give the cause the martyrs they needed. This leads us, to some extent, back to the Christ-story and the theme of sacrifice. It also aligns to some extent with the myths of the Western: as discussed by Brown, the old hero must die if there is to be hope of a new civilisation: he has committed too many 'sins' in the name of love, so he must sacrifice himself. However, there is no love, personal or collective, that obviously motivates the characters in *Blake's 7*; in fact, it is something closer to hatred.

The characters in *Blake's 7* display an outright hatred of authority, matched with a strong sense of individualism and a morally complicated position. Blake and Avon appear at different times as the protagonists, and their moral positions are almost diametrically opposed. Blake is an idealist, while Avon is a cynical pragmatist. But their attitudes do converge occasionally, and they display an ambiguous need for each other. Blake champions a kind of reckless idealism, leading to fanaticism, and he is prepared to take his crew down that path. Avon's motivations are much more ambiguous. At times he is more in pursuit of personal gains, and will happily leave (and endanger) his crew in danger for the sake of this goal. At other times he will fight for his companions. His search for Blake in the latter two seasons appears to be both for personal gain and for the cause of revolution at the same time. Indeed, Boucher himself thought there was no clear line of motivation for Avon. Yet Avon's connection to the culture that built up around Thatcherism is clearer: a ruthless, Machiavellian pursuit of profit and personal gain. Blake and Avon's opposing positions are in some ways reflections of Britain's changing political climate, from social-democratic principles and the consensus-era social democracy to Thatcherite neoliberalism, with its 'conviction' politics and emphasis on individualism.

3

Sapphire & Steel: the illusion of independence

Sapphire & Steel (1979–82) is the most mysterious and ambiguous of the three major series studied in this book, and there is very little serious critical, or even fan-based, writing devoted to it. What is written about the series usually comments on its impenetrability, surrealism and mystery, and makes passing comparisons to *The Prisoner* (1967–68) for its equally baffling structure. Wright notes that, with the exception of *The Prisoner*, '*Sapphire & Steel* remains the most perplexing British television science fiction series to date' (2006: 192). *The Sci-Fi Freak Site* claims:

> When the final, definitive work on science-fiction television is written, the only series that will stand any chance of matching *The Prisoner* for sheer bloody-minded impenetrability will be *Sapphire & Steel*. (para 1)

The 'impenetrability' is not surprising considering that television writer Peter J. Hammond, the series' creator, has been very sparing with his commentary, claiming that he himself does not understand the characters' backgrounds or the 'mythos' of the series (Haley, 2007). Nonetheless, some of the oblique statements Hammond has made provide useful insight, and will be discussed in this chapter.

Sapphire & Steel was conceived by Hammond with little connection to the tradition of Lew Grade-produced science fiction television on ITV. Grade was involved with the ATV company that produced the series, but its style was vastly different from the Americanised series of Grade's ITC ventures. Rather, *Sapphire & Steel* derives from a chain of science fiction television series designed to compete with *Doctor Who*. The website *Doux Reviews* comments: '*Sapphire & Steel* was ITV's last real attempt at trying to create their own *Doctor Who* ... and certainly its best, as well as its most confusing' (Grieg, 2015: para 4). Hammond explains of the series' beginnings that '[TV producer] Pamela Lonsdale ... asked me to put together a ... self-contained first episode ... that could possibly spin to a series ...' (*Counting Out Time*). Hammond goes on to explain that a first episode was made, which was rejected by various companies, until a producer at ATV saw it and 'it frightened the life out of him, and he said, "I don't want to see any breakdowns," he said, "I want to do it as it is"' (*Counting Out Time*).

Despite showing little connection with Grade's output, *Sapphire & Steel* bears some of the same hallmarks of its antecedents in Grade-produced science fiction-related drama. Like *The Avengers* (1961–69), the two protagonists in *Sapphire & Steel* are a man and a woman, stylishly dressed, who solve crimes (in a sense). Joanna Lumley, who plays Sapphire, was also a main actor in *The New Avengers* (1976–77), and David McCallum, who plays Steel, was a main actor in *The Man from U.N.C.L.E.* (1964–68), an American series, so there was a certain cultural capital that these two actors brought to their roles. Indeed, many *Avengers* and *New Avengers* episodes, as well as episodes of *The Man from U.N.C.L.E.*, revolve around science fiction plots. Tonally, however, *Sapphire & Steel* is very different to either. In *Sapphire & Steel* the 'crimes' that the titular characters solve are always science fiction-related, but all of the Americanised elements previously discussed in this book – in action, pace and dialogue – are absent.

Sapphire & Steel was predated by two related series: *Timeslip* (1970–71) and *The Tomorrow People* (1973–79). *Timeslip* was created by children's producer Renee Godard for ATV and written by Bruce Stewart, specifically designed as a programme that could challenge *Doctor Who* (Stewart, 2002: para 1). Stewart devised a series about children who 'slip' through time. In the first episode the children fall through one of these 'timeslips' into Britain during the Second World War. Stewart comments, 'I was impressed by his notion ... that adolescents may be open to "energy" still surging around from the past. This would provide among other things an explanation for ghosts' (2002: para 5). This provides some of the clues as to the inception of *Sapphire & Steel*, which borrows the concept of 'ghosts' as expressions of time distortion from *Timeslip*, but takes it in a very different direction. Reversing the standard concept of the protagonists travelling in time, Sapphire and Steel are sent to investigate situations where the past or future has broken into the present by way of time corridors, which will soon be explained. Similarly, *Sapphire & Steel* invokes the war as an inescapable trauma, which it shares with *Timeslip* and, to an extent, consensus-era series like the various iterations of Quatermass (save for the final entry in 1979, which was a departure in many ways).

Sapphire & Steel concerns two 'operators': the eponymous Sapphire and Steel. The title narration describes them as 'medium atomic weights', and the title sequence illustrates a shining blue stone for Sapphire, and a ball of barbed wire for Steel, suggesting that they are, in their 'purest' form, the actual element (or compound) of their name. They are presumably aliens, or from another dimension, and they come to Earth to investigate rifts in time. In all stories they simply appear where they are required, though it's later explained that there is a structure. First the 'investigators' appear to assess the problem, then the 'operators' are sent in (these include Sapphire and Steel), and finally the 'technicians' are sent if there is a specialised job the operators cannot carry out, which sometimes occurs in the series, and in these instances Silver or Lead are dispatched. None of the stories are named. Rather, there are six stories (sometimes called Adventures or Assignments, as in the Carlton DVD release) and they are divided into four, six or eight parts – half-hour episodes (in practice usually 22–24 minutes in duration), in the same format as *Doctor Who* of the era. There are six stories in all. For the purposes of this chapter, they will be referred to as A1, A2, A3, A4, A5 and A6, with the A standing for either 'Adventure' or 'Assignment'.

There are very minor clues seeded throughout as to the true nature of Sapphire and Steel and the other operators. The title sequence explains that there are several of these 'transuranic elements', and sometimes, as mentioned earlier, others appear, including Silver, Lead and Copper. In A1, Sapphire and Steel reveal that they were present for the Marie Celeste, which implies that they are either able to travel in time, or they have lived several human lifetimes (A1). They have certain types of powers that code them as non-human: Sapphire is psychic and can manipulate time. Steel is able to manipulate metal, and has the ability to freeze his body temperature to absolute zero. However, despite the suggestion in the title sequence that they are minerals, their human form is apparently their authentic one. In A4, Sapphire comments, while talking to 'Shape', the faceless antagonist, 'Our true faces: these are ours. The only ones we possess, I'm afraid.' In A5, Steel is asked if he is alien, and answers 'in an extra-terrestrial sense, yes'. But aside from these minor insights, we are offered very little background information on the characters, where they come from, and under what authority they operate.

The series draws from several different generic traditions, some of which Hammond had written for earlier in his career. These include gothic horror, detective fiction, fantasy, and, of course, science fiction. Hammond draws upon all of these generic traditions to tell his stories, with the idea of 'interstellar detectives' and 'ghost stories' a common theme. But the final combination of elements is something else entirely. *Sapphire & Steel* appears as a kind of symbolic theatrical drama within a science fiction premise. Fisher, in *Ghosts of my Life*, compares the series to Pinter's *No Man's Land*, a spare, symbolic and oblique piece that is nearly impenetrable. I would agree with Fisher and add that *Sapphire & Steel* is similarly close to Beckett, especially *Endgame*, and to Pinter's early output – *The Birthday Party* (1957), *The Caretaker* (1960) and *The Homecoming* (1965). In this cryptic exchange in *The Caretaker*, the homeless Davies is questioned by Aston, a man who takes him in for the night:

> ASTON: What did you say your name was?
> DAVIES: Bernard Jenkins is my assumed one.
> ASTON: No, your other one?
> DAVIES: Davies. Mick Davies.
> ASTON: Welsh are you?
> DAVIES: Eh?
> *Pause*
> ASTON: You Welsh?
> DAVIES: Well I been around, you know ... what I mean ... I been about.
> ASTON: Where were you born then?
> DAVIES: (*darkly*) What do you mean?

Here, Pinter plays with a sense of evasion over the most apparently simple questions that becomes both comical and threatening. The characters in his plays typically have no past, providing only basic clues as to their background. Steel in *Sapphire & Steel*, when asked about his childhood, implies that he has a past, if not a childhood in the conventional sense: 'I have very positive origins. Inexpressible, maybe, but positive.' That same oblique language found in Beckett and Pinter, and the same sense of unknowability about exposition, is used in *Sapphire & Steel*.

There is a similar sense of sparsity and foreboding in *Sapphire & Steel* as there is in these Absurdist plays, as well as their common heritage in Brechtian estrangement – Sapphire and Steel are estranging characters. Each story is populated by a very small cast, and the stories never quite explain themselves. A1 takes place in a Victorian house. The opening shot is the oppressive ticking of clocks, all at their own pace – clocks on the wall, and a grandfather clock. There is a deliberate nod to traditional British ghost stories here, including *The Innocents*, the 1961 adaptation of Henry James's *The Turn of the Screw* (1898). Then, suddenly, all the clocks stop. The boy becomes scared and calls for his father. Sapphire and Steel appear as if from nowhere. They determine that the parents have disappeared through a fissure in time, which Sapphire explains as being like a corridor:

> It surrounds all things, and it passes through all things. But sometimes time can try to enter into the present: break in, burst through and take things, take people. The corridor is very strong, it has to be. But sometimes in some places it becomes weakened, like fabric, worn fabric.

In order to understand the time rift, the children are instructed to recreate the scene of their last interaction with their parents, in which they were reading. Sapphire reads 'Ring a Ring o' Roses' as if it were an alien text, completely unfamiliar to her. This causes clocks to stop and a door to open. An apparition of a Victorian maid walks into the scene and screams, and then the room distorts and turns into an elongated corridor, echoing scenes in Roman Polanski's *Repulsion* (1965) as well as the distorting effects of German expressionist cinema. Nursery rhymes here function like incantations, dispelling evil spirits, as Sapphire reads the rhyme backwards to somehow reverse the corrosive effect of time. This all has the effect of estrangement – of making apparently familiar items – clocks, nursery rhymes – appear alien.

Sapphire & Steel is presented in far more austere and conservative tones than *Blake's 7* or *Doctor Who*. Wright's thesis is that it appears to be more supportive of a Thatcherite world view than many of its contemporaries. Sapphire and Steel are, in many ways, Thatcherite figures, from their conservative dress (Steel usually wears a suit, while Sapphire wears traditional dresses) to their austere manner. This chapter will draw extensively from Wright, the only commentator to have written comprehensively about the relationship between *Sapphire & Steel* and Thatcherism. I will engage in dialogue with Wright's analysis, but also extend it in some parts, especially in terms of the last adventure. In this last story, Sapphire and Steel discover they have been betrayed by their superiors. This is where the series comes the closest to an anti-Thatcher, anti-neoliberal commentary. The protagonists in *Sapphire & Steel* reveal they had been granted a certain independence, which allowed them to operate to some extent free of the hierarchy. They surmise that other operatives envied this position, and (presumably sanctioned by the authority) turned against Sapphire and Steel, confining them to endless suffering in a free-floating prison in space. Their fate becomes more ambiguous than that of the characters in *Blake's 7*, but no less severe, and becomes a statement about the futility of attempting to evade authority, specifically in a Thatcherite context. I contend that, despite its outward appearances as a pro-Thatcher text, the series is ultimately a critique of Thatcher's illusory promise of independence. Sapphire and Steel are Thatcherite heroes for their conservative nature, but they fail to understand the true power dynamic of an authoritarian system. They fail to understand that, under the 'authoritarian populism' of the Thatcher government, independence is an illusion.

Sapphire & Steel and Thatcherism

Wright maintains that this series, broadcast at the very beginning of the Thatcher era, betrays a conservative attitude throughout its run.

Because of its broadcast date, beginning in 1979 and following the Winter of Discontent, Wright argues that it was a welcome series for the British public:

> P. J. Hammond's sombre and symbolic *Sapphire & Steel* (1979–82) presents Margaret Thatcher's election as the triumph of conservative order over social chaos. The eponymous Thatcherite protagonists defend the temporal order against metaphorical versions of the perceived contemporary social malaise: ineffective politicians, immigrants, faceless bureaucracy. After the Winter of Discontent, it was not surprising that Sapphire and Steel were greeted as heroic figures, despite their misanthropy. (2009: 98–9)

Certainly, Sapphire and Steel behave much more like Thatcherite characters than those who preceded them in generic science fiction television, and the world from which they emerge seems to be more authoritarian than earlier examples, at least from the information available. What we know of the social structure of their world implies a strongly hierarchical order – the chain of investigator-operative-technician; the pragmatic and ruthless attitude of the two (particularly, if not exclusively, Steel) and indeed the regressive, patriarchal gender politics. Steel is, as his name suggests, cold, logical and ruthless, while Sapphire carries many of the traits of a traditional feminine character: she is empathetic (at least more so than Steel), she is able to 'sense' and 'feel' the situation, which is why she is an asset to Steel, whose cold attitude precludes any intuitive responses. She is often interested in 'making herself pretty' by using her power to summon elaborate clothes – ball gowns, evening dresses – for no obvious reason. Even her 'name' is a precious stone often used in jewellery. Finally, and in keeping with Thatcher's anti-feminist stance, she defers to Steel whenever a 'serious' decision must be made (not to suggest that Thatcher herself ever deferred to anyone).

Wright believes the first story, A1, sets the tone for the series in the sense that it is about preserving family as the 'mainstay of the social order' (2006: 199). Indeed, Wright's assessment of the 'ghosts' that emerge in the series is that they are a metaphor for the unions, which were so prevalent in the preceding Labour government, and which were shown little mercy by the Thatcher administration, as insurgents marching into the frame, which need to be neutralised (2006: 199–200). In these motifs: the preservation of family and property, the discharge of duty, and the repelling of insurgent forces (in this case, unions), Wright sees a strong authoritarian drive. Family, duty and responsibility are at the forefront of Thatcher's Britain, all connected to her Victorian ideal. The dramas that are played out in the series mythologise these notions.

I would agree with Wright that Sapphire and Steel are conservative characters, but I contend that there is a disturbing theme at the core of the series which renders the two protagonists more ambiguous than they first appear. Unlike *Blake's 7*, I am not suggesting that the protagonists are outright subversives or saboteurs, except to the extent that they are perhaps defiant of the authority merely by working independently. They are careful not to change anything in the social order, but they are 'independent of the state' and fiercely proud of that independence. Thatcher was highly enthusiastic about independence, discussing it on many occasions and linking it to her concept of economic freedom. In a speech in Finchley in 1979 she said, 'We stand for the independence of the individual, for the fundamental freedom of the individual' (para 4), and would repeat the sentiment on many occasions. But *Sapphire & Steel* suggests that, in practice, independence amounts to something quite different. In practice it seems that there is no escape from conformity, and those who operate with the illusion of independence are eventually disabused of that notion.

Thatcher's first term did not represent a full implementation of her neoliberal policies. Instead it was a transitional term in which her policies forced people out of work, with no apparent benefit. In the term 1979–83, unemployment was at a record high due in part to Thatcher's decision to increase the interest rate. Unemployment rose to 12 per cent of the working public, about three million people, in 1981. This, and other factors, such as race, immigration and general deprivation, would eventually lead to the 1981 riots in Brixton and other cities around England. This mood of tension and loss of economic security is reflected in a particular way in the series: lack of any clear place or time, what Fisher, quoting Franco Berardi, calls 'the slow cancellation of the future' (2014: para 16), despite Thatcher's election promise to reverse the decline of the previous Labour government. Her popularity did not start to manifest until the Falklands War in 1982. In her first term people were left with little security as Britain appeared to deteriorate without any clear direction. *Sapphire & Steel* represents a world where there is no change, no strong sense of the present, and no march towards the future.

The series' main writer, P. J. Hammond, was strongly influenced by ghost stories, and the atmosphere of many of the *Sapphire & Steel* assignments displays that influence. A1 takes its aesthetic lead from Victorian ghost stories, and A2 is about a ghost hunter who is looking for spirits in a deserted railway station. This lends an eerie atmosphere to the series, but also produces the effect of stasis and loss. *Sapphire & Steel* is nearly always set in unkempt, almost deserted places: dilapidated apartments, empty railway stations, deserted petrol stations. All these spaces are what Fisher calls 'non-places ... generic zones of transit' (2014: para 8). They all combine to create a picture of inertia, meaninglessness and loss. In that sense, *Sapphire & Steel* paints a bleak picture of Britain of the time, as a desolate wasteland, emptied of specificity. Whether this is an indictment of the Labour Party's collapse, or of Thatcher's early years is unclear, though it shows no signs of progression in the Thatcher era, or Thatcherism's promised 'new beginning'.

McCormack sees this stasis as part of anti-utopian texts of the twentieth century's 'preoccupation with the false promise of progress' (2006: 178), a promise which was abundantly visible in the earlier 1970s series, but in decline within this series. The only exception is the lavish mansion of A5, the outlier because it is tonally very different, due to its status as the only story not written by P. J. Hammond (this point, also covered by Wright, will soon be discussed). Added to this is a sense of political failure. Wright, discussing A6, which is set in a petrol station trapped in some kind of time loop, reminds us that the former Conservative government, led by Ted Heath, had lost a crisis election in February 1974. The Arab–Israeli Yom Kippur War in October 1973 dealt a fatal blow to Heath's government, when oil prices were quadrupled. Wright explains that the crisis was repeated to an extent in 1980 when the Shah of Iran was deposed, leading to another explosion of oil prices (Wright, 2009: 211). Wright goes on to state, 'For modern

Conservatives, [a petrol station] signifies a place of danger and political downfall' (2009: 212). The Conservatives promised to tidy up this state of affairs: their manifesto of 1979 reads, 'there has been a feeling of helplessness, that we are a once great nation that has somehow fallen behind' (para 11). For this 'falling behind' Thatcher blamed Labour's 'actively discouraging the creation of wealth' and its crippling of 'enterprise and effort' (Conservative Party, 1979: sec. 2, para 5). However, this series is firmly set in Thatcher's Britain and shows no improvement.

Many of the stories communicate a sense of homogeneity. The main theme of A4 is the idea of being 'frozen in time'. Liz, the main character besides the protagonists, talks about people in photos 'going nowhere' (A4). Wright comments, 'the idea of going nowhere is the key to assignment four. It defines the pawnshop, connotes a moribund bureaucracy and a weak economy, and summarises Liz's plight' (2006: 208). Indeed, these 'generic zones of transit' are often associated with movement – a train station, a petrol station – and yet the stories depict the opposite. Not only is there nowhere to go, but there is often 'no-when'. All time zones begin to resemble each other. In A5, Sapphire and Steel arrive at a mansion in 1980 in which the guests are having a party. They are all in 1930s dress. The actual year of 1930 is also invading the house, so that the past and present are indistinguishable from each other. In A6, Sapphire and Steel arrive at a diner, which exists in three separate timelines. A 'commoner' called Johnny Jack materialises in 1981, but he is from 1957. When informed of this, he comments nonchalantly, 'All places look the same to me.' This constant sense of inertia – no time and no place – pervades the tone of the series and adds to the sense that Thatcher's Britain is a place of no forward progression.

The tone of *Sapphire & Steel* sits poised between the old and the new Britain, rummaging in the wreckage of the old, perhaps anticipating the new, but certainly not holding out any hope. Like *Blake's 7*, the only 'hope' that can be generated is in clearing out the old altogether: the removal of Sapphire and Steel themselves, which occurs at the end of the series. *Sapphire & Steel*'s constant strategy is to draw parallels between the time arrived in, and the time that has 'intruded' through the corridor, and more often than not the conclusion to draw is that little has changed, few promises have been delivered upon. This is particularly obvious in A6, but also apparent in some of the others: A3 makes no distinction between 'now' and the 'future' in the clothing or behaviour of the two interlopers, visitors from the future, except to cite their names, Rothwyn and Eldred, which they anachronistically drew from Britain's deep past in a misguided attempt to assimilate. The ruptures in time – the more obvious changes between 'then' and 'now' – are not about the surface but about a kind of trauma: they are most often emotional ruptures rather than physical ones. The trauma that results is usually a trauma that pits the progressive hopes of humanity – the hope for instance that the war will end and usher in a better age, or that lives lost will be atoned for – against the stasis of the present.

Within this context – this formless limbo – Sapphire and Steel, and particularly Steel, behave with some of the emergent traits of Thatcherism. The kind of morality seen in earlier examples of generic science fiction television is replaced here by a ruthless, Realpolitik attitude based on pragmatism without regard for individual human lives. They exhibit Machiavellian traits throughout the series. Thatcher talked at length about compassion, often linking it to the rights of the individual and the defence against the 'cruelties' of socialism. In a speech to Finchley conservatives she said:

> In the desperate situation of Britain today, our party needs the support of all who value the traditional ideals of Toryism: compassion and concern for the individual and his freedom: opposition to excessive State power: the right of the enterprising, the hardworking and the thrifty to succeed and to reap the rewards of success and pass some of them on to their children: encouragement of that infinite diversity of choice that is an essential of freedom; the defence of widely distributed private property against the Socialist State; the right of a man to work without oppression by either employer, or trade union boss. (Thatcher, 1975: sec. 3, para 10)

But in reality she was often comfortable with Realpolitik solutions to problems, such as government deregulation, selling state assets, hiking up interest rates, and abruptly cutting off incomes by closing down the mines and other allegedly unprofitable industries. This, of course, meant a surge in unemployment, but it was all in service of the neoliberal economic reforms that Thatcher believed would create wealth in the longer term.

If Wright is correct that Sapphire and Steel are heroes, then they are heroes set in a new mould, markedly different from what the 1970s science fiction audience would consider heroic. They have no emotions that are available to be read in a conventional manner. They have no discernible past and no relationships. They do not invite empathy or compassion in any way. Much like the 'new heroism' of Avon in *Blake's 7* and the Sixth and Seventh Doctors in *Doctor Who*, they behave in a way that estranges. Like Avon in *Blake's 7*, Steel is a Thatcherite character in many respects, from his manner of dress and speech, to his conservative attitudes about immigration. He and Sapphire both work independently, as is later discovered. They are, in a sense, a Thatcherite ideal: conservatives who work independently of the state, yet answer to authority. They also possess a moral world view that is vastly different from science fiction characters who came before them. For this reason, they are not naturalised in any way that a traditional conservative would recognise as heroic. If indeed they are meant to be understood as heroes, and their tactics as heroic, then they are both a forewarning and an advertisement for the kinds of behavioural traits a neoliberal economy would produce. Thatcher was, right from the start, insistent on the 'freedom of the individual'. Even the party's first election manifesto claimed, 'No one who has lived in this country during the last five years can fail to be aware of how the balance of our society has been increasingly tilted in favour of the State at the expense of individual freedom' (1979: para 8). As discussed in the previous chapter, this 'individual freedom' under a neoliberal economy would lead to the kind of behaviour often associated with Machiavellianism. As the 1980s progressed, this behaviour became naturalised and mythologised: individualism and its selfish connotations (often enacted) became part of the fabric of a neoliberal society. *Sapphire & Steel*, along with *Blake's 7*, is one of the earliest television representations of this kind of behaviour in a consistent fashion. If Sapphire and Steel are heroes, they are heroes for the neoliberal era, and presumably their heroism appeals to a socially conservative, economically liberal audience.

Steel often exhibits a cut-throat, Realpolitik attitude. In A2, the characters arrive at a railway station where they encounter Tully, a middle-aged man who operates as a 'ghost hunter'. Tully is a mild-mannered, even feckless character. During the course of the story Sapphire, Steel and Tully discover that a malign entity known as the Darkness is trying to feed off the negative emotions of people who died unfairly. This trauma is carried into the present: a First World War soldier, a fighter pilot, and a group of people dying in a submarine, all from different time zones, enter into the space of the train station, through the 'rifts in time' that have been described, and appear as ghosts. Sapphire and Steel must then interpret their trauma to understand the situation. Steel's eventual solution to the problem is to sacrifice Tully to the Darkness, so that the entity will feast on a living soul and close the rift. Steel shows no compunction about doing this. In A3, Steel is so angered by the presence of Rothwyn and Eldred in contemporary England that he suggests they commit suicide in order to repair the timeline. His behaviour can be compared in superficial ways to Straker in *UFO*, and Greg in *Survivors* (as discussed in Chapter 1), but for both of those men their sacrifice was an aberration from their usual duties, and an agonising decision to make, which came at great personal cost. By contrast, Steel's behaviour is more or less standard procedure and costs him nothing personally. This shows, to some extent, the distance that this more cut-throat Realpolitik attitude has travelled since the election of Thatcher.

Wright considers Steel's actions to be indicative of a Thatcherite reasoning, which finds 'no irony in, or critique of, Steel's character; no sense that he is a satirical figure. Rather, the series suggests that strong leadership and social stability will require suitable sacrifices' (2006: 204). This pattern is repeated several times, and it becomes clear that Steel regards humanity to be beneath his contempt. If Wright is correct, it means that this Thatcherite view of Realpolitik action has been mythologised by the series: it is now viewed – within the TV series and perhaps as an emergent trait within Thatcherism – as self-evidently 'correct' to take Realpolitik decisions over more compassionate ones. However, Brecht's *Verfremdungseffekt* was designed to bring about (left-wing) social change through presenting alienating or estranging scenarios in theatre. There is no suggestion that *Sapphire & Steel* has such lofty goals, but nonetheless the series does present estranging characters often behaving in ways that are amoral. This can lead the viewer to abhor their actions, and in doing so begin to formulate a more compassionate solution. The series is so open to interpretation, and viewers are left with the option of applauding or criticising Steel's actions depending on their ideological position. Just as with Avon in *Blake's 7*, the critique of Steel's behaviour and attitude is dependent on the ideological position of the viewer.

Sapphire and Steel are authority figures, and they in turn seem to answer to a higher authority while retaining some form of independence. They seem to champion a form of individualism and independence. As we have seen, Steel in particular tends to behave in a purely pragmatic way, measuring the variables of the case in a Realpolitik manner. There is more clear evidence that the series favours authority throughout its run, and little to suggest a critique of Thatcher's insistence on authority until the end, where the whole of the series lends itself to a retrospective anti-Thatcher reading. This last assignment will be discussed in the next section, but here I will only highlight the instances of authority deployed in a Thatcherite manner.

A4 presents the character of Shape, an evil figure with no name (except in the credits) and no face. The central problem in A4, that Shape is able to trap people in photographs, shows a certain political bias. Shape is a parody of a bureaucrat: suited, with a hat, and with no face. In his demeanour he projects several different impressions at once: the concept of 'faceless bureaucracy', but also a kind of authority figure who is threatening in his lack of discernible expression, which draws to mind Terry Nation's comment about the Daleks, seeing them as 'government, as officialdom, as that unhearing, unthinking, blanked-out face of authority that will destroy you because it wants to destroy you'. In his blankness there is something of what Suvin calls 'the constant intermingling of imaginary and empirical possibilities' (1979: viii). Without a stable set of features his face becomes a blank canvas, available for several possible interpretations. These possibilities turn out to be both pro- and anti-Thatcher in their connotations.

Wright certainly believes that Shape is the antithesis of a Thatcherite character. He sees in the character a retrograde figure: an embodiment of old, 'dry' Tory values, something that Thatcher, in her radicalisation of the party, was eager to dismiss. Added to what Thatcher said about civil servants – that they were 'complacent, inert, pedantic and incapable of appreciating the need to devise or implement radical solutions to Britain's dire problems' (qtd in Wright, 2006: 207), Wright goes on to claim that Shape trapping people in photographs is analogous to the civil service trapping society in 'traditional bureaucratic administration like a fly in amber' (2006: 208). But, as Wright himself comments, 'For conservatives, there can be no freedom without authority' (2006: 195), and therefore Shape is a conservative symbol to both the traditional 'wet' and radical 'dry' Tories – a bureaucratic symbol, but also a symbol of impersonal authority. That is not to say that these two factions of the Conservative Party are essentially the same, but that they both have reverence for authority, power and tradition, and Shape, in his ambiguity, comes to represent both.

One of the attractions of the neoliberal system was its promise of eradicating bureaucracy. Jon Pertwee's Third Doctor in *Doctor Who* saves his most pointed criticisms for the bureaucrats who use endless official objections to halt progress. Thatcher too professed to a hatred of bureaucrats. Yet, as Fisher points out, bureaucracy under neoliberalism has grown rather than diminished:

> Initially, it might appear to be a mystery that bureaucratic measures should have intensified under neoliberal governments that have presented themselves as anti-bureaucratic and anti-Stalinist. Yet new kinds of bureaucracy – 'aims and objectives', 'outcomes', 'mission statements' – have proliferated, even as neoliberal rhetoric about the end of top-down, centralised control has gained pre-eminence. It might seem that bureaucracy is a kind of return of the repressed, ironically re-emerging at the heart of a system which has professed to destroy it. (2009: 43)

Part of the logic of the 'mission statements' is to sketch out a 'better future' for the company. But this better future is endlessly deferred, never actually attained. What in fact happens in the neoliberal workplace is, more commonly, maintenance – endless meetings to achieve the same results. This new form of bureaucracy is, in fact, embodied not only by Shape, but Steel himself. Steel may not be interested in 'mission statements' and such, but in the way that he carries himself and discharges his duties, which are largely about maintenance of the timeline and are in no way innovative except in his occasional extreme solutions, he differs little from Shape. Even his solutions are merely temporary. He never fully vanquishes an enemy, but simply neutralises them for a time. Steel and Shape are both, in a sense, bureaucrats in the new neoliberal tradition – functionaries (literally faceless in the case of Shape) who are ultimately responsible for nothing, as few individuals under late capitalism ultimately are (this point will be discussed further in Chapter 6).

The question remains as to whether Sapphire and Steel are part of the solution, or part of the problem: a radical balm to old-fashioned bureaucracy, or another manifestation of that same system. My contention is that they see themselves as progressive figures, and in the context of the series this means conservative in a Thatcherite sense – neoliberal figures who believe in the efficacy of the individual while retaining many traits of a traditional conservative. In the series, time itself is characterised as a malevolent force, penetrating people's lives and causing havoc, and requiring an authoritative figure to tame it. Sapphire and Steel can be seen as the 'good-sense' protagonists entering the scene in order to clean up the error, often taking authoritarian measures. This would align them with a Thatcherite mentality. But they also do nothing to change the conditions under which people live, and they very rarely solve any of the problems they encounter in the long term.

Many times, the protagonists make a distinction between the 'old and the new', and their job is, in general, to clear out the debris of the past to make way for the (always deferred) progressive future, which in itself draws us back to the 1979 Conservative Party manifesto and its promise of a 'new beginning'. In A3, Sapphire and Steel have a small exchange:

STEEL: Left hand?
SAPPHIRE: The past.
STEEL: Right hand?
SAPPHIRE: The future.

If this can be interpreted as a working model of left- and right-wing politics, it illustrates where the two characters, and the series, sit, with the progressive way of the future clearly to be found on the right. Yet it also reveals that this future is not yet here, and it is achieved by way of summoning the past. By the very style of the programme, history is constantly being integrated into the present, and therefore understood in present terms, in a way that often conflates and obfuscates. In A3, the past is called into the present in the form of the Victorian era, so much admired by Thatcher. Victorian children are summoned into the present by Shape. In A1, the house that Sapphire and Steel enter is Victorian. In each case it is a nostalgic version of the past. So, in *Sapphire & Steel* we experience history filtered through a particular right-wing ideological perspective, and in so doing we notice the conservative influence on the series. This lends the series a Thatcherite mythology: the present is understood as one that summons touchstones of the Victorian era and the Second World War, with its socially conservative values intact – courage, patriotism, community, family and social cohesion. Yet, by the end it would appear that all this apparent summoning of Tory values (at least on the surface) is mere subterfuge, designed to lead the protagonists (and the audience) astray. By the end, when the protagonists are betrayed by their own side, it appears that the values Sapphire and Steel buy into – independence, authority, order – are deceptions.

One aspect by which *Sapphire & Steel* differs markedly from the science fiction series that preceded it is that it is so claustrophobic and parochial. While most series were about humanity going 'out there', to discover what is in space or on other planets – *UFO* depicted a base on the moon, which *Space: 1999* carried on; the Quatermass serials were about human exploration of the moon and other planets, as well as alien invasion; *Sapphire & Steel* is about history coming 'in here' – penetrating the inside, interior world of Britain, and perhaps spilling into its hermetically sealed society: something intolerable to conservatism. Every *Sapphire & Steel* story is set predominantly in an interior space, with time itself breaking inside. The parallels to xenophobia have not escaped Wright, who discusses A3 in these terms:

> In suggesting that illegal immigrants like Rothwyn and Eldred [the characters from the future] should be returned, *Sapphire & Steel*

seems to subscribe to the contemporary Tory attitude towards immigrants and, possibly, to the late-70s zeitgeist. (2006: 206)

Thatcher herself warned that 'people are really rather afraid that this country might be rather swamped by people with a different culture' (1978: sec. 1, para 4), and it is in this vein that A3 can be read as a warning against immigration, naturalising the fear of the 'other', or outsider.

However, mitigating against this reading of the fear of outsiders, though still allowing for a Thatcherite reading, is the fact that many of the forces breaking into the present are 'ghosts from the past'. In A2 they are soldiers and military characters; in A4 they are Victorian children. *Sapphire & Steel* often mixes nostalgia with trauma, and suggests that the 'ghosts' are reminders of better times, when Britain was an empire and there was a stronger sense of identity, despite the life that was expended. These are notions about which Thatcher would be strongly enthusiastic, and so the 'intruders' are sometimes Thatcherite figures too. Thatcher would eventually summon these 'ghosts' when she began to mythologise Britain and herself, constantly comparing her Britain to the Victorian era when the country 'became great', and evoking the ghost of Churchill when she wanted to suggest a principled battle and a proud, imperial (or post-imperial) past.

As well as a vaguely patriotic summoning of the past and its collectives (soldiers, families) the series trades in the new myth of individual achievement. Instead of the group mentality favoured by characters in earlier series such as *Space: 1999* or the *Quatermass* serials, *Sapphire & Steel* presents two individualistic characters, who never work in teams but only together, with an occasional third member who is most certainly not part of the crew – they do not work as a cohesive 'team' but as three individuals with separate jobs to do. Steel often makes decisions without even consulting Sapphire, and in doing so exerts an authoritarian tendency consistent with the new neoliberal structure. Neoliberalism, as several writers have discussed, was designed to 'unshackle' the individual from authoritarian state practices, yet in many cases it achieved the opposite. In the wake of governmental authority, authoritarian individuals emerged; in the wake of responsible parties, Machiavellian characters took charge. Von Dirke writes that the neoliberal model of 'flat hierarchies left the underlying power structure intact while deliberately removing the mediating practices of legitimate authority' (2017: 331). Without this structure, authoritarian tendencies are given space to emerge. Clint Eastwood's Dirty Harry kills criminals without any thought to 'officially sanctioned' authority, taking control into his own hands, as do Stallone and Schwarzenegger's characters throughout the 1980s. Similarly, Steel has become his own authority and seemingly has free rein to exercise his authoritarian powers as he sees fit. There is a lack of accountability to any authority (at least until the end). This mimics several of the structures of the new neoliberal world view. There are clues throughout the series that the individualistic mindset is becoming more favourable in Thatcher's Britain, especially A5 as we will see, yet at the end the protagonists are trapped and confined to a hellish fate because they choose to work alone.

A5 concerns a rift in time, where two separate timelines exist alongside each other. Arthur Mullrine has thrown a party to celebrate fifty years of Mullrine International. He built it off the success of his earlier business partner, George McDee. McDee died fifty years earlier. The partygoers from 1980 must dress in the fashion of 1930 in order to replicate the time when the company was founded. McDee then returns to the house, existing in a simultaneous timeline that is actually 1930, rather than a replication of it. It is explained that McDee wanted to cure the world of all disease, and he was betrayed by Mullrine, who exploited his work for commercial profit. A5 is a murder mystery – people begin to die throughout the house and Sapphire and Steel must solve the case. In its utilisation of the murder mystery genre, it uses and exploits generic conventions in a far more telling way than usual *Sapphire & Steel* episodes, to the level of pastiche. It demonstrates to an extent that the writers – Don Houghton and Anthony Read, representing the only instance in which the series was written by someone other than its creator – had departed from Hammond's much more oblique and symbolic tone. A5 is considered by Wright to be the least successful of all the serials, and in some ways its weaknesses are clear in the more obvious subtext, of Sapphire and Steel as Holmesian detectives. Wright takes the opportunity to deconstruct this story, connecting Sapphire and Steel to a long line of 'detectives', starting with Holmes, through the line to Poirot, and connects them with Thatcher, because they all 'champion the cause of bourgeois values' (2006: 198). The mythology plays out in quite predictable fashion here, with archetypes of Victorian (or Georgian) enterprise pitted against the vilified socialism. Wright notes that the serial recommends 'the benefits of capitalism to humanity' (2006: 210), once again connecting the series with an emerging neoliberalism. The characters, then, are to some extent Victorian 'types', and the drama brings us to the conclusion that 'economic salvation lies in the hands of individuals rather than collectives' (Wright, 2006: 210). This story, as stated earlier, is the outlier in the series, especially in the straightforward manner in which it borrows from other genres, and the more simplistic exploration of its themes. The message of A5 – extolling of the virtues of capitalism – perhaps makes explicit what the rest of the series keeps contained within its subtext: that the neoliberal world view is beginning to become the dominant mode of social expression. The series as a whole explores the outgrowths of neoliberalism – the favouring of the individual and the move towards authoritarian and Machiavellian traits.

Sapphire & Steel is, like the other series studied, a multilayered text with several contradictory meanings. However, by its final story it displays its tensions with Thatcherism most strongly. It critiques Thatcherism, as it were, from within, showing that the kind of independence Thatcher championed is ultimately an illusion. Hall (1988) points out that social conservatism, calling back a Victorian sense of nationalism and statism, does not chime with economic liberalism which seeks to relinquish state control and throw itself open to the whims of the marketplace. Fisher attempts to reconcile the two contradictory positions:

> Despite evincing an anti-statist rhetoric, neoliberalism is in practice not opposed to the state per se ... but rather to particular uses of state funds; meanwhile, neoconservatism's strong state was confined to military and police functions, and defined itself against a welfare state held to undermine individual moral responsibility (2009: 61)

Fisher sees neoliberalism as meeting statist concerns with marketplace realities in the form of a 'common enemy' – the 'nanny state', a particular target of Thatcher's ire. In this model, instead of jettisoning its interventionist aspects wholesale, the government simply removed some (unprofitable) aspects and enhanced others. Responsibility for the citizen's welfare was greatly reduced by the state, and seen as a matter of individual concern. But the state still retained many authoritarian aspects, which it sometimes enhanced. This contradiction – between state control and individual responsibility – renders the idea of political independence virtually meaningless, or at least deeply contested. Though *Sapphire & Steel* was produced by ITV, an example from the BBC illustrates Thatcher's contradictory goals: while she encouraged the BBC to operate independently and become more of a commercial channel, presumably to dislodge it from government or public control, at the same time she installed many of her own ministers to the Board of Directors and policed the corporation as much as she could. Of this tendency, Crisell comments: 'The government reasoned that if the board was to be a creature of anybody, it should be a creature of the government rather than of the BBC' (2002: 233). She attempted to control the language around the Troubles in Northern Ireland, and the Falklands, both on the BBC and in newspapers. She outwardly favoured independence, yet repeatedly imposed control over ideological messages. *Sapphire & Steel* in the end suggests that, despite official encouragement, intellectual and personal independence – especially in the political or ideological realm – in a socially conservative state is too contradictory to sustain.

The final story: individualism and futility

There is a particular type of futility that *Sapphire & Steel* explores. Unlike *Blake's 7*, which ultimately points to the futility of fighting the system without cohesion and collectivism, *Sapphire & Steel* is perhaps even more disturbing: it suggests that even working independently but 'within the system' is not sustainable in the Thatcher era; rather, it violates neoliberal logic. Despite Thatcher's proclamations of individual freedom, *Sapphire & Steel* posits that there is no freedom from an authoritarian state. The State will allow the illusion of freedom, but that will be revoked when the independent operator proves no longer useful – or indeed shows signs of becoming subversive. The final *Sapphire & Steel* story, A6, amounts to a critique of Thatcher's stated position on individualism and independence. Before presenting this position, I will cover all the ways in which the series explores its themes of futility, culminating in the series' final critique of Thatcher's ideology.

More so than the other two major series, *Sapphire & Steel* shows no sense of human endeavour leading to any greatness; rather, there is a sense that humanity is incompetent and requires the operatives to correct its mistakes. *Sapphire & Steel* as a series is not concerned with progress, but rather a kind of futile, Sisyphean process of 'maintenance' of the problems that have already occurred in the timeline. Malignant forces that lurk in the timeline are never defeated as such, but merely restrained or neutralised for a time. In A2, the Darkness is arrested but not vanquished. In A4, Shape is confined to a kind of endless prison, but not destroyed (strangely foreshadowing the fate of Sapphire and Steel themselves). There is also a multiplicity of viewpoints and 'meanings' to the series. The series carries with it contradictory interpretations because its subtext is so fertile – nothing is ever developed explicitly, and the final story ends on such an ambiguous note, that several readings are possible at the same time. The remainder of this chapter will explore Wright's persuasive reading of the final story, A6, and then will present my own interpretation.

In A6, Sapphire and Steel arrive at a diner attached to a petrol station, where they discover that Silver has already been dispatched. Sapphire senses a great deal of fear, which she interprets as a fear of death. They encounter a couple at the diner who claim to be from 1948, though the present year is 1981. It soon transpires that the couple were each trying to escape their marriages and had begun an adulterous affair, arriving at a diner that would become the present petrol station in 1981. Later, Sapphire and Steel encounter a man from 1925 who appears as an apparition, though Sapphire surmises that this time she and Steel are intruding into his timeline. Finally, a travelling musical performer who calls himself Johnny Jack appears, and states that his timeline is 1957. Sapphire and Steel begin to question what is happening – Sapphire begins to suspect that the fear she initially sensed is emanating from her and

Steel, and in some way, this is a premonition of death. They begin to suspect they are being betrayed by someone – agents like themselves, but who answer to a higher power.

The deserted petrol station is laden with advertisements for various products – Castrol, 7up, and so on – and the camera pulls our focus, lingering on these advertisements, but no sentimentality is afforded to them: they are presented as meaningless signs of consumerism, providing no insight, situated to show what Jameson would call 'depthlessness'. Jameson sees, in late capitalism, 'the emergence of a new kind of flatness or depthlessness, a new kind of superficiality in the most literal sense' (1991: 6). In *Sapphire & Steel*, this depthlessness manifests as a sense of futility: that all the capitalist excess – the abundance of 'signs' in the semiotic sense, of both advertisements for products as well as the products themselves – have culminated in nothing of any meaning. Thatcherism would usher in a new era, already beginning in the mid-1970s, that would bring consumerism and excess to the general populace, and this serial in particular anticipates this new brand of social mobility, even if at this point there is only inertia. The bricolage of times in A6, from 1925, to 1948, to 1957 and finally arriving at 1981, adds to this inertia because of its suggested generic quality.

Fisher surmises that:

> the emotional austerity that had characterised the series from the start assumes a more explicitly pessimistic quality in this final assignment. The le Carré parallels are reinforced by the strong suspicion that, just as in *Tinker Tailor Soldier Spy*, the lead characters have been betrayed by their own side. (2014: 1)

Sapphire and Steel are proven right, as the others in the diner all turn out to possess powers comparable to Sapphire's, and with the aid of a small box that manipulates time, they are able to trap Sapphire and Steel in the cafe, unmoored from its surroundings and forever floating through space. This is where the series ends, on this final note of the apparently eternal imprisonment of the two main characters. This is not as 'final' as the ending of *Blake's 7* (the protagonists don't actually die, and so there is hope of rescue) but it is every bit as bleak.

Wright believes this story complies with a conservative order, but with the final act of Sapphire and Steel's banishment he sees a triumph of social democracy. Wright claims that everything about this final story, from the setting to the characters, is coded in a certain way, which complies with the central notion that Sapphire and Steel 'champion the cause of bourgeois values' (2006: 196). The station itself – an abandoned petrol station – alludes to conservative fears about oil prices. He then interprets the characters who eventually join together to trap the protagonists as representatives of, at least the principles of the Social Democratic Party who, as Wright reminds us, were for a short period a real opposition for the Conservative Party. It consisted of a 'gang of four' politicians: Roy Jenkins, David Owen, Bill Rodgers and Shirley Williams. Wright argues that A6 has its own 'gang of four' attempting to take down Sapphire and Steel. They are the couple on an adulterous excursion, the old man and Johnny Jack. Of the couple, the man is fourteen years the senior of the woman. To Wright they signify

> non-traditional freethinkers. From a conservative perspective they stand for infidelity and, in their 14-year age difference, impropriety. They are the antithesis of Thatcher's advocated Victorian morality. (2006: 213)

The old man from 1925 represents to Wright the year Conservative Prime Minister Stanley Baldwin was establishing his 'new Conservatism'. Finally, Wright connects Johnny Jack, the travelling troubadour, to a working-class mentality. Together, they represent 'the kind of interclass and cross-generation appeal the SDP were hoping to achieve' (2006: 213). If indeed Wright is correct, then the final scene (which he does not discuss in great detail) represents a triumph of social-democratic opposition to conservatism. It also allows for an easy Barthean reading: the four characters are all essential types – Johnny Jack the 'common man' and troubadour, the couple (implying somewhere a cuckold), are the illicit lovers, and the old man is a throwback to an earlier age. Sapphire and Steel are then seen as representatives of an older England – Victorian, upper-middle-class, privileged and authoritarian – while the four are seen as progressive, and the story is a clash between these two powers, with the progressive winning and indeed 'banishing' the

Tories (Sapphire and Steel themselves). This is not, then, a story where the dominant, bourgeois values are viewed as triumphant (as are all other *Sapphire & Steel* stories) but rather a surprising reversal of the notion.

Another possible reading, one that reverses his position and hints at an alignment with the apparent futility that ends *Blake's 7*, is to suggest that Sapphire and Steel are not simply representatives of the conservative order, but agents who have dared to operate independently of this order, and have ultimately failed. This reading would suggest that the four characters in A6 are not social democrats, as Wright surmises, but in fact the ultimate conservative order – higher representatives of the same side, as Fisher has suggested in his le Carré analogy, from which Sapphire and Steel have broken away. Therefore, whatever 'radical' attributes the 'gang of four' possess – the couple being sexually liberated, or Johnny Jack behaving as a wandering troubadour – are overridden by their conformity to this 'higher authority'. Thatcher's contradictory position allowed for all manner of deviation from her preferred social values, and this began a loosening of conservative social values that are still active today. It is in this way that Keith Spencer can claim:

> In our everyday reality, progressive identity politics and authoritarian politics already exist separately; that's how the left was able to win the culture war in the United States while losing the political war. (2018: para 30)

The left or the progressive side of politics has made significant gains in the last thirty years: gay marriage, abortion, drug laws and so on, because the neoliberal ordering of Western society thrives on social change, whether liberal or conservative, ultimately absorbing all 'social trends' into the marketplace. The authoritarian nature of conservative politics remains largely unchallenged. To that extent, these characters can fit into a neo-conservative world view, one that embraces the vicissitudes of the marketplace, while defying some of Thatcher's social conservatism, a trend that was beginning to emerge in the Thatcher era with issues such as homosexuality being freely alluded to and discussed despite Thatcher's strong opposition to it. In any case, Johnny Jack and the old man are Thatcherite characters in the sense that the old man represents older conservative values, and Johnny Jack represents the mobilisation and emancipation of the working class that Thatcher envisioned through her liberalisation of the market.

After Sapphire, Steel and Silver encounter the old man from the 1925 timeline, Sapphire comments, 'We were the ones that didn't belong ... he wasn't a ghost: if anything, we were the ghosts to him' (A6). This reversal of expectations or perceptions hints at a deeper reversal, that perhaps throughout the series Sapphire and Steel have effectively been 'the ghosts'. In every assignment, they have been as foreign and unknowable as the intruders they have set out to vanquish. It perhaps implies that they were themselves rebels.

Later in A6, when Sapphire realises they are being betrayed, she comments about the other characters in the diner: 'They're like us. ... [but] I think they answer to a higher authority' (A6). Usually the word 'higher' connotes several meanings, involving 'greater', and more morally upright. Indeed, being 'like us' reinforces the assumption that they are on the same side. Their dialogue continues:

> STEEL: They resent us ... they resent our achievements.
> SAPPHIRE: More than that – they resent our independence.

The mention of 'resentment' implies that this 'higher order' is in some sense petty. The mention of 'independence' matched with the claim that the others 'answer to a higher authority' tends to suggest Sapphire and Steel do not work for an authority, at least not in the straightforward sense heretofore implied. Rather, it suggests they have departed from that authority to an extent; they have their own autonomy outside and beyond this higher authority – they are 'free agents'. Thatcher's ideology was so connected to the word 'independence' that this implication is difficult to avoid.

There is also an interesting reference to an eschatological source here. Just as Sapphire and Steel are confined to the 'nothingness' of space, apparently forever, so in the Book of Revelation, the Beast (often considered analogous to Satan in the popular sense) is cast out to the 'lake of fire': 'And the devil that deceived them was cast into the lake of fire and brimstone, where the Beast and the false prophet are, and shall be tormented day and night for ever and ever' (*New American Standard Bible*, Rev. 20:10). This stands as a warning against defying the patriarchal and authoritarian message of the Christian tradition: authority must be adhered to. Milton's version of the Devil in *Paradise Lost* is also the rebel, cast out from heaven for choosing to operate independently, tolerated as long as he doesn't cause trouble or interfere with the social order. With mention of the word 'independence', and the contextual clues that indicate Sapphire and Steel (and possibly Silver) are of a lower order than the eventually named 'transient beings', seeking to trap them, the 'revelation' arises that Sapphire and Steel are akin to 'fallen angels' in the series, finally cast into their own 'lake of fire' at the end for defying authority. This reading anchors the series in the apocalyptic tradition in which *Blake's 7* (and to some extent, late *Doctor Who*) also dwell.

Sapphire and Steel may behave conservatively and show some traits of Thatcherite behaviour, but as independent operators who make decisions without reference to the higher authority, they are (like Milton's version of the Devil) threats to the conservative order. One of Thatcher's core principles was independence, and she would reiterate this point constantly, with reference to home ownership, income, and most other aspects involving her economic version of 'freedom'. But in practice she worked to ensure that pillars of British society – like the Church, the universities and the media – conformed to her messages (her clashes with Archbishop Robert Runcie are discussed in Chapter 6). Though well past *Sapphire & Steel*'s timeline, Thatcher became furious with ITV for broadcasting a documentary, *Death on the Rock*, in 1987, about IRA terrorists being killed by the SAS (Brown, 2009: para 8). Many believe this led to the abolition of the Independent Broadcasting Authority in 1990. Sapphire and Steel's fate is a warning about the pitfalls of operating independently and ignoring authority. The portrayal of the authorities as insidious and deceptive can be read as a critique of Thatcher's strong but hypocritical stance on independence.

To reconcile the two positions, of operating independently but also within general rules of authority, we might frame the representation of Sapphire and Steel's fate in the most disturbing manner of all, one that resonates with events such as Occupy Wall Street, or Extinction Rebellion, but also with the way Thatcher dealt with the media: that under a neoliberal system, especially of the authoritarian style that Thatcher and Reagan did so much to mobilise, even the 'independent' voice is integrated into the system. That, like Sapphire and Steel, their actions are made part of the machine, largely indistinguishable from those they oppose or break away from, and they are used and disposed of when no longer required. Downing defines recuperation as the way in which 'the ruling class could twist every form of protest around to salvage its own ends' (2001: 59). This description of the integration of protest and rebellion into the capitalist machine is also summarised by Hall: 'This year's radical symbol or slogan will be neutralised into next year's fashion; the year after, it will be the object of a profound cultural nostalgia. Today's rebel folksinger ends up, tomorrow, on the cover of *The Observer* colour magazine' (1998: 484). Indeed, Fisher comments, '[Kurt] Cobain knew that ... nothing runs better on MTV than a protest against MTV' (2009: 9). Capital reabsorbs dissent into the system and neutralises it. Sapphire and Steel were not actively protesting against this authority, but the realisation of their betrayal in the final story is a realisation that their position has always been untenable. Their very autonomy has been little more than a ruse, tolerated by the ruling power because it allows the power a degree of control. If interpreted this way, Sapphire and Steel in the end are victims of the capitalist strategy of recuperation: they have been allowed to operate outside – and perhaps in defiance of – the true conservative order without opposition and given the illusion of independence until it is no longer politically expedient, at which point they are lured into a trap; their fate made to look as if it was of their own devising. In the end Sapphire and Steel are neutralised in a literal way. They are not simply rendered irrelevant, but removed from space and time altogether.

Sapphire & Steel is unusual among the major series studied, in that it is by far the most impenetrable. While all reveal similar concerns, *Sapphire & Steel* is the most difficult to interrogate. This is in part due to the lack of any solid antagonist: Sapphire and Steel never face an 'enemy' that has any realistic qualities. Instead, they find themselves battling ideas, apparitions, metaphors. These metaphors usually communicate a sense of inertia, of going nowhere. It is also because the series lacks any clear mythos of its own devising: Sapphire and Steel have no known history, relationships, or even real personalities other than the purely functional. But beneath the surface, *Sapphire & Steel* reveals a network of meanings because it exists, as Barthes would say, as a 'fabric of quotations' (1989: 53), 'quoting' various generic traditions, and remaining available for several contrasting and sometimes contradictory readings. *Sapphire & Steel*'s themes and style run deeper than *Blake's 7* or *Doctor Who* because of this reason – its presentation is so often reliant on either blank surfaces onto which we must impose our own meaning, or an accumulation of surfaces that have been emptied of the meaning they once had.

If *Sapphire & Steel* is predominantly a conservative programme, as Wright suggests, then its version of conservatism – lost among the empty and desolate spaces that were once productive – is a diminished and pessimistic one. If the counter-reading presented here is correct, then *Sapphire & Steel* is more subversive than it appears: an enactment of the myth of the end times, clearing the way for a new beginning. This is the position from which it negotiates with Thatcherism, as an enactment of the illusory nature of independence in a Thatcherite context, and a yearning for something new. Despite the Conservative Party's promise of a new beginning, *Sapphire & Steel* suggests that Britain was, in Thatcher's first term, little more than a collection of the old, signalling stasis and depthlessness. *Sapphire & Steel* is a yearning for that change, without any glimpse of what form it may take.

4

Rewriting the Doctor: *Doctor Who* in the late Thatcher era

At the end of 'Logopolis' (1981), Tom Baker's last *Doctor Who* story as the titular character, the Doctor has been mortally wounded, and must regenerate in order to survive death. In this particular story the regeneration was foreseen within the plot. As his companions crowd around him, the Doctor proclaims, 'It's the end, but the moment has been prepared for.' The period 1979–83 was 'the end' for consensus Britain, and the moment certainly had been prepared for. *Doctor Who* itself took a little longer to recognise the shift in British politics, and began to contend with Thatcherism around 1983, where this chapter's analysis begins.

It may be important to note that this era was the least successful or popular with audiences. Many fans consider it to be unworthy of much critical attention. Colin Baker and Sylvester McCoy frequently rate as the least favourite Doctors among fans, though it is often pointed out that they are not wholly to blame. The internal conflict behind the scenes, particularly in Baker's era, weakened the series as a whole. In that era (1983–86) the series was 'rested' for eighteen months, so that Colin Baker's tenure amounted to only two full seasons. The second season, a fourteen-episode-long story called 'The Trial of a Time Lord' (1986) seemed for a moment to usher in a new and better phase of the series. The first shots are of the TARDIS in space, in the grip of a tractor beam as it is pulled into a spaceship, accompanied by a soundtrack that seems faintly inspired by the Vangelis soundtrack for Ridley Scott's *Blade Runner* (1982). This sequence used some of the most sophisticated and expensive visual effects of the era, far surpassing anything previously seen in the famously rickety 'special effects' for *Doctor*

Who. But the rest of the story proved a disappointment, and ultimately controller Michael Grade fired Colin Baker from the role. Three years later Grade cancelled the series.

Doctor Who was conceived in 1963 and, up until 1989 when the original series ended, it largely followed what I will call a story-based format. Each 'story' would contain somewhere between two and twelve episodes of roughly 23 minutes' duration, each one ending on a cliffhanger until the resolution in the following episode. This structure eventually settled on a loose format of an average of four to six episodes per story. Typically, a year's output would consist of four to six stories. In the Colin Baker era, the producers experimented for a short while with a (roughly) 44-minute format, but this was soon abandoned (to be reused in the modern series that began in 2005). When this chapter uses the term 'story', it refers to the collection of episodes that make up the story, whereas the word 'series' refers to *Doctor Who* as a whole.

Sydney Newman, the driving force behind the creation of *Doctor Who* in 1963, once described science fiction as 'a marvellous way – and a safe way – of saying nasty things about our own society' (2010: para 3). The Doctor has always been a rebel and an outsider, and *Doctor Who* often engaged with politically charged situations. As we have seen, many of the Pertwee-era stories carried a political and ecological subtext. Many of the writers of that era, including Malcolm Hulke, Barry Letts and Terrance Dicks, were committed to left-wing causes. Although Thatcher-era *Doctor Who* began with the very late end of the run of Tom Baker's Fourth Doctor (1974–81) and into Peter Davison's tenure as the Fifth Doctor (1981–83), the series showed little deviation from the well-trodden path already established, of the Doctor as liberal-humanist, intervening in others' affairs. While shunning the official authorities, the Doctor himself becomes a (trusted) authority figure in his own right.

In the mid to late Thatcher era, from 1983–89, containing the last years of the original *Doctor Who* series, the political subtext changed considerably. *Doctor Who* of the Colin Baker, and particularly Sylvester McCoy, years reflected on the changing world of Britain, and engaged ever more directly with Thatcherism. This contention is bolstered by the admission from several figures who were instrumental in the show's production that they had every intention of reflecting Britain under Thatcher, and they were strongly against Thatcher's authoritarian policies. McCoy himself claimed, 'Our feeling was that Margaret Thatcher was far more terrifying than any monster the Doctor had encountered' (qtd in Adams, 2010: para 5). The political leanings of the writing team are obviously the clearest point of departure from the other series studied, yet the simple claim of an of anti-Thatcher agenda could not hope to encapsulate *Doctor Who* of this era because of its complexity as a series, and its tendency to pull in many opposing directions.

This chapter will discuss examples of where the Doctor's 'rebellious' nature, inherited from his previous incarnations, is intact and even sharpened by the rise of Thatcher and the neoliberal world. From the examples mentioned in Chapter 1, it seems relatively straightforward, at least until the Colin Baker era, to concur with Bignell and others who claim the Doctor was always a liberal-humanist. But that stance is itself a political position, containing an inbuilt political bias, which will be explored further in this chapter. However, in those earlier years the Doctor never exhibited party politics, and never directly or indirectly criticised the (contemporaneous British) government. There was usually an unspoken contentment with consensus-era politics and a respect for British democracy, if only in the abstract. From 1983 onwards, where this chapter's analysis begins, the series engages much more urgently with the contemporary politics of Thatcherism (albeit cloaked in metaphor). Unlike the chapters on *Blake's 7* and *Sapphire & Steel*, which discussed the early years of Thatcher's time in office, this chapter is about late *Doctor Who* in the mid to late Thatcher era. So, where I claim that those earlier series were anticipating some of the extremes of Thatcherism, this chapter analyses the way late-era *Doctor Who* is responding to Thatcher's by then familiar regime. It will show moments where the 'liberal-humanism' of the Doctor shines through in a way that is reflective of the times, especially on issues such as race relations and immigration. But the chapter will also discuss examples of where the series becomes curiously supportive of some of the stances of Thatcherism.

In keeping with the preceding two chapters, *Doctor Who* of this era uses eschatological imagery to articulate the need – not for a new beginning, but rather several new beginnings. The societies the

Doctor encounters ostensibly operate on principles of order, justice and peace, but in fact conceal a dark reality. This tendency does not fully manifest until the McCoy era, where the bulk of this chapter's focus lies, but it was beginning in the preceding Colin Baker era. In the McCoy era nuclear anxieties, the new consumer culture of Thatcherite Britain, racism and xenophobia are all treated in various ways as apocalyptic scenarios that require change and renewal. In 'Remembrance of the Daleks' (1987), Britain's racist and xenophobic past is explored, drawing parallels to the then-present of the 1980s. 'Ghost Light' (1989) explores the mythologies of Victorian Britain, seen to be at an end and desperately in need of change and renewal. In 'The Greatest Show in the Galaxy' (1988) the Doctor enacts a certain kind of apocalypse to see 'behind the veil' to the true authoritarian rulers of the society, who happened to be named after the Norse myth of Ragnarök. In 'Battlefield' (1989) the Doctor must prevent a nuclear apocalypse. 'The Curse of Fenric' (1989) continues the Norse myth theme. In each case there is an urgent need for reformation.

This chapter will reveal two sides of *Doctor Who* that are revamped in the Thatcher era. One side is the politically progressive version. In the McCoy era (1987–89) it becomes clear where the writers, led by script editor Andrew Cartmel, intended their anger and discontent with Thatcherism to break through. This manifests in several ways, including the treatment of themes like racism, xenophobia and nuclear warfare. These issues are treated with sensitivity and from a liberal perspective, even at times with a left-wing revolutionary spirit. But there is another component lurking in the subtext, which ultimately draws the Doctor down a darker path. Traces of it begin in the preceding era of Colin Baker (1983–86) when the Doctor encounters rapacious mining organisations, brutal police states and societies that condone violence. These stories can be taken as commentaries on Thatcher's Britain, but the character of the Doctor is more complex and compromised than previous incarnations, embracing Realpolitik solutions to problems rather than the more humanistic stance his predecessors would have taken. Then in the McCoy era he assumes an even darker edge, encapsulating what became known as the 'Cartmel Masterplan', in which Cartmel and his team attempted to retrofit the Doctor's character.

The writers felt that some of the mystery had been drained out of the series, and the 'Dark Doctor', as fans came to know him, was an attempt by Cartmel and his team to reintroduce some of that mystery, by showing the Doctor to be in possession of 'forbidden' knowledge, which he conceals to the last moment. Suddenly he is not trusted by even his companions, and, to borrow Fisher's comparison in *Sapphire & Steel*, his motives are as murky as a character from a John le Carré novel. He is in possession of absolute knowledge of the origin of the universe, and he speaks in a quasi-religious language about good and evil and its beginnings. However, despite the writers' political leanings, the effect of the Dark Doctor, I will argue, is to bring the Doctor closer to a Thatcherite position: not just an authority but an authoritarian; someone who believes himself to be an absolute power, even a god (this possibility is strongly hinted at). *Doctor Who* of this era, like Thatcherism, contains contradictory positions on topics. The Doctor is seen to be both the champion of the dispossessed, and the ultimate authority figure, perhaps becoming himself an 'authoritarian populist'.

The Doctor had always shunned authority, but he had in the consensus era been himself an authority figure of a certain variety: the middle-class white man, a paternalistic figure to whom others defer. Here he transitions into a different type of authority figure. In alignment with the other two series studied, the Doctor becomes a Machiavellian figure, one who is not automatically trusted, or if he is, he erodes that trust through his own manipulation. This chapter therefore argues that the Thatcher-era *Doctor Who* series departs significantly from its earlier incarnations, and begins to delve into different subject matter that engages with, and reflects, the tropes of Thatcherism in all their contradictory measures.

The Sixth Doctor: resembling madness

The series took a decisive turn when Colin Baker was cast as the Sixth Doctor in 1983, a year after the epoch-defining moment in Thatcher's government: the winning of the Falklands War. Baker's Doctor is portrayed as unstable, irascible and aloof. His Doctor is given to violence, or the intimation of it, in a way that would've been unacceptable to the audience or the characters in previous incarnations. The Sixth Doctor is an estranging figure, sharing a quality with Wright's description of Steel in *Sapphire & Steel*, as a new kind of Thatcherite hero. However, Colin Baker's low popularity with fans would suggest that the gambit did not succeed. The blame for this cannot be placed squarely at the feet of the actor: the overall direction of the series was lagging, and it resulted in poor plotting and direction on many occasions. This led to an eighteen-month hiatus of the series in 1985–86. Finally, Baker was fired – the only time an actor playing the Doctor has ever been forced to leave the role (though of course Sylvester McCoy was effectively fired when the series was cancelled three years later). Baker's Doctor was the first sign of a strong shift in political and social consciousness in the Thatcher era, including a sharper focus on violence and a more Realpolitik attitude in conflict resolution.

The Doctor has always been an essentially Victorian or Edwardian adventurer. He is partly modelled on the character from Wells's *The Time Machine*, and partly on Sherlock Holmes. As discussed in Chapter 1, the Doctor himself has, at various times in the character's history, become a symbol of Empire through his dress, his predilections for British style, and his attitudes. Britton and Barker write:

> The ideological underpinnings of *Doctor Who*, its gender stereotypes, and the evocation of myths of Englishness that made it popular at home and abroad are essentially the values of British colonialism. The Doctor, a leisured gentleman-traveller, represents the sort of self-important moral arbiter so familiar from the era when 'the sun never set' on the British Empire. Thus, it is not surprising to discover that the Doctor's quaint sartorial image belongs essentially to the golden age of empire, the Victorian era ... (2003: 144).

The Doctor's dress sense is usually indicative of this Victorian bias. All the incarnations of the character up to this point had worn variations of a Victorian or Edwardian outfit – always a jacket or coat, often a frock coat. The First Doctor wore a simple coat and tie, the second a loose-fitting suit. The Third Doctor's array of velvet smoking jackets and Holmesian capes both nodded to the Victorian influence and borrowed from contemporaneous fashion.

The Fourth Doctor wore frock coats and waistcoats under his ludicrously long scarf. The Fifth Doctor returned to a simpler combination – the outfit of an Edwardian cricketer, again wrapping his cricket jersey in a cricket-themed frock coat. The Sixth Doctor, while still wearing the same basic combination of frock coat, shirt, waistcoat and trousers, was given a garish, clashing, deliberately unpleasant colour palette. His multicoloured coat was designed to suggest a sense of tastelessness which would in turn convey an unstable personality.

The Sixth Doctor's harsher edge was consciously executed on the part of producer John Nathan-Turner and script editor Eric Saward. Saward comments: 'because we wanted to make the Sixth Doctor different, we decided to make the regeneration so extreme that it would resemble madness' (qtd in Howe et al., 1993: 146). A decisive shift in moral behaviour throughout all of Baker's short tenure as the Doctor is evident. Very early on the series starts to explore themes of violence, suffering and torture, with Baker's Doctor himself a morally ambiguous figure: unstable, erratic and colder than his previous incarnations.

Added to the emphasis on violence, several other aspects of Thatcher's Britain are reflected in the Sixth Doctor's series, such as the surveillance society and increased militarisation. Often these are set on dystopian planets. Violence and discontent were erupting in the UK around the time of Baker's run as the Doctor, with the 1981 Brixton riots only a few years recent, with the more contemporaneous 1985 riot, beginning after the shooting of Cherry Groce, mother of Michael Groce, firmly planted in the public consciousness. Added to this, the IRA's many bombings and terrorist activities were in full swing, including their attempt to assassinate Thatcher herself in 1984. Discontent around the government's aggressive neoliberal agenda, specifically the planned closure of coal mines, led to the 1984 miners' strike, and Thatcher's response on all of these occasions was to increase the powers of the police.

The Sixth Doctor's moral stance is no longer that of the simplistic campaigner that the Doctor had hitherto been, but an advocate of the Realpolitik attitude of Thatcherism. Baker's Doctor is far more violent than his previous incarnations, and sometimes the violence is portrayed in a casual manner. In 'Attack of the Cybermen' (1984) the Doctor and his companion Peri are confronted with two policemen aiming guns at them (they are later revealed to be merely disguised as policemen, but the Doctor and Peri don't realise this at the time). Peri holds one off while the Doctor overpowers the other and apparently gives him a beating, knocking him unconscious. When the Doctor returns from the (unseen) altercation, wearing the helmet of his opponent, Peri asks, 'What happened to the other one?' The Doctor replies somewhat flippantly, 'He's er ... having a little lie-down.' Later the Doctor and Peri are both armed, and even later still the Doctor shoots and kills a Cyberman.

'The Two Doctors' (1985) manages to be implicitly racist as well as unusually violent. The Second Doctor has travelled to the space station to talk to a scientist called Dastari. While there he discovers that Dastari has been experimenting with genetic manipulation – augmenting the intellectually feeble (and physically repulsive) species known as Androgums with 'higher' characteristics. Dastari's efforts have paid off with an Androgum, Chessene, who appears blemish-free and behaves in a sophisticated manner. The Doctor strongly disapproves of Dastari's attempts at eugenics, but not for any reason other than his distaste for Androgums and his belief that they are irredeemable. He tells Dastari, 'You give a monkey control of its environment, it'll fill the world with bananas.' Chessene appears in contrast to her friend Shockeye, a 'natural' Androgum who is physically grotesque, with huge orange eyebrows and large warts exploding all over his face. His obsession is with food, and in particular with cooking and eating the Doctor's companion, Jamie. Later in the story, the Sixth Doctor kills Shockeye by covering his face with cyanide-soaked cotton wool, perhaps able to do so because of his antipathy towards Androgums, violating a (usually) unspoken rule that the Doctor does not kill.

In discussion of this often-gruesome violence, Howe, Stammers and Walker note that:

> Some commentators ... suggest that season 22 [Baker's first] marked a temporary departure from the strong moral standpoint, which has previously been one of *Doctor Who*'s most distinctive and popular features. No longer, it was said, was there any clear delineation between good and evil in the stories. (1993: 152)

Saward attests that there was always moral ambiguity in *Doctor Who*, and all that had changed was its presentation. This claim is too simplistic. It is true that there has always been violence and moral ambiguity in *Doctor Who*, but the key to this change is in the character of the Doctor himself. With very few exceptions, in past incarnations, the Doctor had been disgusted by violence, only occasionally (and reluctantly) resorting to it. By comparison, the Sixth Doctor's seasons *embrace* violence: the Doctor often instigates it, and if not he tacitly condones it, and seems unmoved by its fallout. Like Steel in *Sapphire & Steel*, he sees it in a Realpolitik manner as merely the most expedient way to resolve a situation. Compare him with the Fifth Doctor (and most of the previous incarnations) who was never able to commit murder, and was horrified even at the death of his sworn enemies, and the difference becomes strikingly apparent. In 'Resurrection of the Daleks' (1984) the Fifth Doctor has the chance to kill Davros, the creator of the Daleks, who have under his rule committed atrocities throughout the universe. He points the gun at Davros, announcing that he has come as his 'executioner', but lingers too long.

> DAVROS: You hesitate, Doctor. If I were you, I would be dead.
> DOCTOR: I lack your practice, Davros.
> DAVROS: You are soft, like all Time Lords. You prefer to stand and watch. Action requires courage, something you lack.

The Doctor cannot bring himself to shoot Davros, and loses out on the opportunity. Similarly in 'Warriors of the Deep', the Doctor encounters his old adversaries, the Silurians and Sea Devils, working in unison here to bring down humanity. When, in the end, the two species are both killed the Doctor is forlorn, proclaiming, 'There should've been another way.'

The Sixth Doctor's much more aloof response to death in 'Vengeance on Varos' (1985) demonstrates the contrast:

> *The attendant turns around, raising his hands, and knocks his companion into the acid bath. The Doctor grabs a gurney then the stretcher to use as a shield as he and the attendant struggle. The one in the acid reaches up and grabs his friend's trousers, pulling him into the acid too. The Doctor puts down the stretcher and picks up his jacket.*

DOCTOR: You'll forgive me if I don't join you. (*Doctor Who* transcripts, 2021: para 644–5)

This illustrates their very different attitudes. Colin Baker's two *Doctor Who* seasons are interlaced with moments of callousness, disregard for life, and violence similar to this, including the (faked) death of the Doctor's own companion Peri, demonstrating a much darker and more abrasive attitude on the part of the Doctor, and indeed the producers of the series. To some extent this once again illustrates the move into neoliberal territory. The new neoliberal Doctor takes matters into his own hands, sinking to the level of the aggressor in what appears to be a casual manner.

In 'Vengeance on Varos', the Doctor and Peri find themselves in a brutal, dystopian, ex-penal colony where executions are televised and voting can change the outcome. There is a mineral, Zeiton-7, which is the subject of a price war. The Galatron Mining Corporation have sent their representative, Sil, a slug-like creature, to negotiate the deal. Sil is portrayed as a physically repulsive, as well as deeply nefarious, representative of his mining corporation. In a 2012 review, Christopher Bahn writes of Sil that, 'His belligerence and leering, greedy, toad-like personality is clearly meant as a parody of corporate capitalism' (para 6). The portrayal of both government officials and private business representatives as corrupt and brutal is deeply disturbing. The parallels to Thatcherism are implicit: as well as the bleak dystopian setting redolent of a police state complete with total surveillance, the aforementioned 'parody of corporate capitalism' is apt in the fact that Sil represents a commercial mining company. This story was produced only a year after the 1984 miners' strike, in which Thatcher closed down many mines because of their alleged lack of commercial viability.

The violence in the story is also telling of the times. Thatcher claimed to abhor violence, but she was nonetheless criticised for granting the police much greater powers. She considered arming the police during the 1981 riots. In addition, Tharoor writes:

> Thatcher's government is also alleged to have funneled arms to Iraqi despot Saddam Hussein and to have provided training and technical assistance to Cambodia's murderous Khmer Rouge, who, in Western eyes, was a hedge against Soviet-backed Vietnam in Southeast Asia.

> Defenders of Thatcher's legacy argue that such policies were the necessary product of the Realpolitik of Thatcher's age. But as the image of Thatcher as a moral titan gets burnished in the press, they also cast a necessary shadow. (2013: para 6)

The Realpolitik attitude of the Thatcher era is reflected, and not thoroughly critiqued, in the Sixth Doctor's era. However, in the era of the Seventh Doctor the Thatcherite zeitgeist is given a fuller analysis.

The Seventh Doctor: the 'Dark Doctor' as both liberal and conservative

Sylvester McCoy's foreword to Andrew Cartmel's book, *Script Doctor* (2005), which discusses Cartmel's time as script editor on *Doctor Who*, recounts the following incident. At Cartmel's job interview, the producer John Nathan-Turner asked him:

> 'If you could achieve one thing with *Doctor Who*, what would it be?' Andrew, without an instant's hesitation, replied, 'Overthrow the government'. (15)

Cartmel has since suggested that it wasn't as dramatic as that. However, Cartmel's role in shaping the direction of the Seventh Doctor was considerable – in some ways akin to the influence of what would now be called a showrunner, though the producer John Nathan Turner was theoretically the greater influence (however, Nathan-Turner was a deeply controversial figure, which this section does not have space to discuss). The Seventh Doctor introduces the dilemma the writers of the series imposed on themselves by choosing to deal with Thatcherism, in a sense, head-on. Cartmel claims, 'I was very angry about the social injustice in Britain under Thatcher and I'm delighted that came into the show' (qtd in Adams, 2010: para 8). Nonetheless, the character of the Doctor, intended as a critique of Thatcherism, was often made to reflect some of the tropes of the Thatcher government and its neoliberal agenda – authoritarianism, the polarisation of good and evil, and the triumph of the individual over the collective. The first part of this section will discuss the ways in which *Doctor Who* of the

McCoy era combatted what it saw as the evils in Thatcher's Britain, including racism, xenophobia and war, and in this respect the series was progressive in its political and social agenda. The second part will delve into the character of the 'Dark Doctor' as envisioned by Cartmel and his writers, and explore how aspects of that version of the character mitigate against the more progressive messages in the series and align themselves uncomfortably with Thatcherism and sometimes Thatcher herself, despite the best intentions of the writers and script editor.

The Seventh Doctor as liberal progressive

'Paradise Towers' (1987), the second Sylvester McCoy story, operates on the principle of what O'Day considers to be satire – a mode that *Doctor Who* frequently operates within, though I would also add pastiche as a category in many of the Seventh Doctor's outings. O'Day quotes Chapman, who considers 'Paradise Towers' to be redolent of the race riots in Britain in the 1980s (2010: para 24), a theme to which I will shortly return. 'Paradise Towers' was part of Sylvester McCoy's first season as the Doctor, and the actor was still finding a satisfactory method to play the character. The next season's 'Remembrance of the Daleks' (1987) substantively engages with many of the concerns of Thatcherite Britain. The story is politically and socially engaged: a comment on Britain in the 1980s through the lens of the past – that of the 1960s. In the case of this story, the targets are racism and xenophobia, and they are echoed in the later 'Ghost Light' (1989). 'Remembrance of the Daleks' is set in 1963, the year *Doctor Who* was created, but its themes are firmly entrenched in 1980s Britain. At one stage the Doctor has lunch in a cafe, where he starts a conversation with John, an African-Caribbean man who is serving him:

DOCTOR: What if I could control people's tastebuds? What if I decided that no one would take sugar? That'd make a difference to those who sell the sugar and those that cut the cane.
JOHN: My father, he was a cane cutter.
DOCTOR: Exactly. Now, if no one had used sugar, your father wouldn't have been a cane cutter.

JOHN: If this sugar thing had never started, my great-grandfather wouldn't have been kidnapped, chained up, and sold in Kingston in the first place. I'd be a [sic] African.
DOCTOR: See? Every great decision creates ripples, like a huge boulder dropped in a lake. The ripples merge, rebound off the banks in unforeseeable ways. The heavier the decision, the larger the waves, the more uncertain the consequences.
JOHN: Life's like that. Best thing is just to get on with it.

The scene described here presents a moment of humanity for the Doctor: listening to the man's history without judgement, appearing in no way patronising and merely allowing him to speak, and in hearing him speak, the implications of social injustice are clear. The scene is not crucial to the plot and could easily have been deleted. The political position of the scene is clear within the man's telling of the story: a sympathetic, anti-xenophobic statement at a time when Britain was beset by race riots and the contested history of the Windrush generation.

A somewhat xenophobic approach to race and immigration that eventually became the position of Thatcherism began long before Thatcher, but it grew more prominent in Thatcher's tenure. Thatcher was clearly not in favour of immigration, even considering putting an end to it altogether (see Bourne, 2013: sec. 1, para 5). But it is also clear that she favoured some forms of immigration over others. Thatcher's rhetoric often strayed into areas that bolstered her opinion of who should be included in Britain, and who should be excluded. Thatcher once again couched her rhetoric in mythical language, attempting to evoke an essential 'British' character to differentiate from the 'other' of the immigrant. But she was clearly referencing a certain type of non-white immigrant, as will soon be shown. Though she claimed to 'condemn' racism, she nonetheless hosted South African apartheid head of state P. W. Botha in 1984 (see Tharoor, 2013: para 6) and condemned Nelson Mandela's ANC party. On many occasions, her language reflected a clear bias against non-white members of society.

In a similar tone to Powell's 'Rivers of Blood' speech, Thatcher's 'authoritarian populism' was monocultural, and again this was part of the package of the social structure of the Victorians. As part of her general desire to reconnect with the more monocultural flavour of Victorian Britain, Thatcher often allowed subtle racist, or at least parochial, remarks to slip into her language. She constantly referred to the Falkland Island residents, for example, not as strangers, but rather as 'our people' (Seaton, 2015: sec. 1, para 22), which contrasts with the immigrants in Britain, especially those not ethnically European, which presumably were not 'our own people'. Interlaced with the Victorian vision, then, is a vision of a culturally 'pure' Britain, a nationhood constructed around a regressive ideal of social cohesion. Samuel comments, 'In the face of multiculturalism, she resurrected the mythology of a unified national self' (1992: 18), and that 'national self' was white and European.

In 1978, Thatcher claimed that the figures estimated a rise of four million immigrants, but this was from 'the new Commonwealth or Pakistan' (sec. 1, para 4), the only actual region she mentioned by name. She went on to comment:

> Now, that is an awful lot and I think it means that people are really rather afraid that this country might be rather swamped by people with a different culture and, you know, the British character has done so much for democracy, for law and done so much throughout the world that if there is any fear that it might be swamped people are going to react and be rather hostile to those coming in. (Thatcher, 1978: sec. 1, para 4)

The clear bias against non-white people is demonstrated, as well as a vague summoning of 'the British character', without any reference to its specific characteristics (except perhaps a reference to the rule of law, carrying with it the implication that the 'outsider' will not assimilate to the expectations of British law). The use of the term 'rather swamped' demonstrates a clear framing of the idea of immigration (from the new Commonwealth and Pakistan) as something to be avoided. As Jonathan Charteris-Black comments:

> The 'swamp' metaphor arouses feelings of fear and was revived in connection with asylum seekers who some politicians claimed to be swamping the country ... clearly the association of being overwhelmed by something unpleasant, as if in a swamp, has a strong negative force. (2011: 24)

This is consistent with other evidence that Thatcher's anti-immigration bias was directed more towards non-whites whom she did not recognise as 'British'. She was, for example, against 'BAME' (Black and Minority Ethnic) immigration, and 'Her private papers show, retrospectively, how strong her objection to BAME immigration was, while feeling that white immigration would not be a problem' (Tomlinson, 2013: sec. 1, para 5). This polarising attempt to foreground the 'British' character as coherent and of measurable qualities: white and European, summons a particular, ethnically narrow, version of society.

In a Granada interview from 1978, Thatcher elaborated on her idea of Britishness:

> We are a British nation with British characteristics. Every country can take some small minorities and in many ways they add to the richness and variety of this country. The moment the minority threatens to become a big one, people get frightened. (sec. 1, para 13)

This creates a clear dichotomy between 'British' and 'not British', with the latter category including 'small minorities', again inferring those who are not white or of European descent. Based on the statement that 'the British character has done so much for democracy, for law and done so much throughout the world', we can assume she is referring again to the Victorian mindset, which was an imperial one. Masking the true history of Victorian Britain, which colonised countries like India and subjected them to British rule, she portrays Britain as the victim of immigration from the very places the Victorians conquered and subjugated.

There are also references to fascism in 'Remembrance of the Daleks'. One of the characters, Ratcliffe, is seduced by the Daleks into working for them. It becomes clear that Ratcliffe has Nazi sympathies, and has formed a group called The Association, which also secretly includes Sergeant Mike Smith, with whom Ace is becoming romantically involved. Ratcliffe says, 'This country fought for the wrong cause in the last war. When I spoke out, they had me imprisoned.' There was strong movement from the National Front in Britain at this time, and though Thatcher condemned that organisation, her comments about 'outsiders' over the years, such as her 'rather swamped' comment, were authoritarian and similarly nationalistic and 'far right' in their tone.

Another example from 'Remembrance', between Ace and Sergeant Mike Smith, who is revealed to be working for Ratcliffe, illuminates this further:

MIKE: Ace, I didn't know it was the Daleks. I was just doing Mister Ratcliffe a favour.
ACE: Do me a favour and drown yourself.
MIKE: I thought it was the right thing. Mister Ratcliffe had such great plans. Ace, I never really wanted to hurt anybody. It's just you have to protect your own, keep the outsiders out just that your own people can have a fair chance.
ACE: I said shut up! You've betrayed the Doctor, you betrayed me. I trusted you. I even liked you ...

Although Ace is primarily horrified that Mike is working with the Daleks, it is clear that she is just as disgusted by the racist and xenophobic implications in Mike's comment about 'keeping the outsiders out'. Earlier at the boarding house that is hosting her, Ace discovers a sign that reads, 'No Coloureds'. She looks appalled and takes it down. These examples of Ace's anti-racist position and the Doctor's lack of racial prejudice support a strong anti-xenophobic stance.

Race and xenophobia are also alluded to in 'Ghost Light' (1989), in which the Doctor and Ace travel to Gabriel Chase, a house that Ace burned to the ground in 1983 because she sensed an evil presence. The Doctor takes Ace to the house in 1883, a hundred years earlier, to discover what that presence might have been. This story is set in Thatcher's favourite era, the Victorian. Gabriel Chase is revealed to be an experiment in cataloguing species. Various species are abducted from Earth's history and deposited in the house, including Nimrod, a Neanderthal. Nimrod is the butler in the house. He is forever subservient, and unlike the others, his position is fixed (the others change and evolve during the course of the story). In the house he is relegated to what Larsen calls 'a subhuman class not for his species but rather his perceived socio-economic/racial position' (2017: 158). The Doctor corrects the racist/xenophobic interpretation of him from Inspector Mackenzie:

MACKENZIE: I suppose this must be the manservant. Nasty looking customer. Must be a foreigner.
DOCTOR: Neanderthal.
MACKENZIE: Ah, gypsy blood. I can see it in him. Lazy workers.

Despite the Doctor's intention, Mackenzie aligns the term 'Neanderthal' with 'gypsy', and 'gypsy' with the pejorative, as a culturally backward character, and therefore (in his assessment) a foreigner (see Larsen, 2017: 158 for a fuller discussion). Throughout the story there are examples of this comparison between Nimrod and 'undesirables', which the text ironically highlights, and counterpoints with the Doctor and Ace's more 'liberal' reactions.

In the McCoy era, there is often a cruel secret at the heart of societies (or sometimes smaller communities). Certain values have been brought to the fore – a selective type of 'happiness', or a Victorian household, or family-friendly entertainment. The secrets that lurk behind the veneers are revealed as not only dark, but an indication of 'forbidden knowledge' on the part of the Doctor. This comes in stark contrast to earlier, pre-Thatcher *Doctor Who*, wherein the most common storytelling device was to use British democracy as a given, and enact a story that reinforces and naturalises the 'myth of Great Britain', as Great Empire, as a nation victorious in the war, and as a nation with a democratic system that is the envy of the world. This simplistic (and highly selective) portrait of Britain breaks down in the Thatcher years, and a new myth arises: one that pits the Doctor against a particular enemy in a particular scenario, and then shows us 'behind the veil' to the truth, and in so doing, exposes the tools with which the 'myth' is constructed.

The Seventh Doctor's era confronts Thatcherism – apparently head-on. 'The Happiness Patrol' (1988) is set on a dystopian planet: an Earth colony called Terra Prime. The story portrays a world presided over by Helen A. The writer of the story, Graeme Curry, stated, 'I can't deny that I think Margaret Thatcher was at the back of my mind when I was writing Helen A' (*When Worlds Collide: Doctor Who and Politics*). However, he goes on to mention that many other political situations are referenced that are worse than Thatcherism, and indeed there is a strong hint of the North Korean regime within the story. The precept of this colony is that the inhabitants are forbidden to be unhappy, on penalty of death. This idea is stretched to its illogical limit, and the story functions more as pure satire than science fiction drama (see O'Day, 2010: para 24). The irony of enforced happiness is not directly related to Thatcher herself, but the portrayal of an authoritarian figure who demands a certain type of behaviour and language from her subjects resonates with Thatcher's authoritarian-populist approach.

Of course, any departure from this already nebulous idea of happiness is punishable by death, and much like Thatcher, Helen A controls the language used, which must always include a reference to happiness. This obviously creates a contradiction: one cannot be happy when one is coerced into using certain forms of language on fear of death. There are also hidden factions of this society that have been rendered invisible by Helen A. and her administration, just as Thatcherism concealed the racism and suppression of human rights in Britain. The Doctor eventually locates the disaffected workers, the 'pipe people', forbidden to enter the city, who are protesting against their conditions, and encourages them to down their tools and revolt, echoing the miners' strikes in Britain. The Doctor, in this story, appears to be the workers' champion, a proletarian revolutionary.

In 'Ghost Light', Gabriel Chase is apparently occupied by Victorian archetypes. The Doctor first discovers Redvers Fenn-Cooper, an explorer very much in the imperialist vein of the Victorian era. But the difference is that Redvers is insane. He had long ago lost his sense of reason, and is now a raving lunatic, crawling through the bowels of the house, talking gibberish. This first representation of the 'Victorian gentleman' (which is a constant refrain in the story) then, is a confused one. Redvers appears to be both aggressor and victim. He displays all the traits of an imperial mindset – he seems to believe he had been in Africa on some sort of colonial mission – but now has been reduced to a madman. The patriarch of the house is the Victorian gentleman, Josiah Samuel Smith. It is eventually discovered that Josiah is in fact an alien, and the house itself is a spacecraft (borrowing from B-movie science fiction such as *The Rocky Horror Picture Show*, itself a pastiche of science fiction B-movies), containing various aliens and creatures from Earth's past. What initially appears natural is in fact deeply artificial.

Josiah is presented as the ideal Victorian gentleman. But because he is really an alien, he is changing. Over a short period of time his skin starts to decay. On a metaphorical level, with all the discussion around the perfect Victorian gentleman, Josiah's condition symbolises the decay of this archetype itself. The corrosion of Victorian authority and the Empire it spawned pervades the entire story. There is a tacit acknowledgement throughout the story that change is inevitable, and that the inhabitants of this house are fast becoming extinct. This points to the acknowledgement that the ideals of the Victorian era are now extinct: a rumination on the idea that the time for 'Empire' is over and was an insane quest from the start, despite Thatcher's attempts to call it into being again, especially during the Falklands War. The suggestion, then, is that the Victorian 'ideal' was never anything more than a fantasy. The house is merely a veneer for something darker, exposing the truth behind the mask. As in many of the McCoy-era stories, 'Ghost Light' connects with eschatology: calling for change, for a new beginning of its own – to shed the skin of the Victorian era and allow for something new to take its place.

'The Greatest Show in the Galaxy' (1988) presents a different kind of Victorian archetype. The Doctor and Ace are invited to the 'psychic circus' on the planet Segonax. While there they discover an array of characters from a seeming variety of different times and places in Earth's history. In this story there is no collective 'society' – the area outside the circus is a wasteland, populated by nomadic travellers. In this wasteland, the Doctor and Ace meet Captain Cook, but not the historical figure. This Cook is a famous 'intergalactic explorer'. He is dressed somewhat in the manner of Gilbert and Sullivan's 'modern major general'. When the Doctor and Ace first encounter him, he is drinking tea. These obvious reference points make him instantly recognisable as a Victorian English figure, but in the context of a post-apocalyptic setting, the cognitive remove produces a dissociation. Cook is like an alternative version of the Doctor – fascinated by the Victorian sensibility, taking part in an imperialist aesthetic. But Cook is not presented as a sympathetic character, and is in a sense the darker mirror-image of the Doctor. Like the Doctor, he has a companion, a young woman. But whereas the Doctor treats his companions with respect (though he is also manipulating them, as we will soon see), Cook dehumanises his assistant, calling her a 'specimen', and caring little for her welfare. Later, Cook is shown to be entirely self-serving in his actions, and even worse for the British sensibility, boring. The Doctor calls him out, declaring, 'You're not only a scoundrel and a meddling fool, you're also a crushing bore!' This deconstruction of a Victorian archetype, and the parody of its values, is once again a criticism of Thatcher's constant extolling of the virtues of Victorian England.

'The Greatest Show in the Galaxy' is already a post-apocalyptic fable, a pastiche of postmodern punk-inflected *Mad Max* landscape of barren nowheres, reminding us of Fisher's 'generic zones of transit'. There are indications in that story of excess, consumerism and instant gratification, reflecting Jameson's 'depthlessness' (1991: 6). Just as the Thatcherite generation of 'yuppies' was constantly calling for more and more gratification, the audience members in the circus ring (who are later revealed as the mysterious 'Gods of Ragnarök') are in need of more entertainment, and if they are unhappy with the entertainment offered, they kill the performers. This metaphor stands for the excesses and indulgences of late capitalism, and the consumerist culture that Thatcher promoted.

The story once again presents a veneer, and allows us a glimpse behind the veil. This enactment of a 'revelation' is an eschatological theme in itself. This time the apparent setting is a circus: mythologised as a safe and pleasant family atmosphere. But once again this story presents an apparently harmless and even family-oriented activity as the site of something far more sinister. This time it is the motif of the circus-as-arena. In the story there is always a family in the audience, watching and applauding. However, with the threat of death, the theme of safety and entertainment is threatened by the realisation that safety is only possible with complete obedience, a theme that parodies Thatcher's ever more vitriolic defence of the police and the authoritarian state. By the end of the story, the Doctor discovers (or already knows) that the 'family' is in fact a group of malevolent beings called the 'Gods of Ragnarök', who feed on the energy of the performances. In the scene where the Doctor passes through the dimensional portal and is able to see them for who they really are, he literally passes through a threshold that lifts a veil, calling to mind the original meaning of the word 'apocalypse', as a revelation. The naturalised environment of the circus is made to look intensely unnatural, and in fact is reformed as a kind of ancient gladiatorial ring, with the stone-like Gods of Ragnarök revealed as the true force behind the construct.

Doctor Who of this era explores, in several different environments, the myth that is disseminated by the ruling power, and the reality that is concealed, and in doing so enacts a kind of apocalypse, each time calling for a new beginning. Thatcherism propagated many myths about Britain, about Empire, and about the return to Victorian values, already discussed in this book. The 'lifting of the veil' in the *Doctor Who* stories serves the purpose of exposing the corruption underneath, just as the 'reality' of Britain underneath Thatcher's rhetoric paints a very different picture of the country – unemployment, race riots, nuclear anxieties. But, moreover, it exposes the lie. The construct that the characters see, always calling itself truth, is no more than a narrative built around exploitation of what seems desirable to them, and indeed natural. In reality it is a way to control and subjugate them.

War, and in particular nuclear war, is also a target in this era. There are several instances where the series takes a strong stand against nuclear war. The ideological war between communism and capitalism that drove the cold war, and the sense of fatalism – fear of nuclear destruction – had been a constant source of anxiety since the end of the Second World War, and reached a crescendo in the 1980s. Thatcher was vocal on many occasions about her hatred of communism, and the need for the nuclear deterrent. The cold war continued until the end of her tenure, and the nuclear anxieties escalated. In *Doctor Who* of the era, traditional myth is used as another way of describing British society of the 1980s.

'The Curse of Fenric' (1989) is shot through with references to Norse myth, connecting it to notions of an Earth destroyed by toxic waste, and using eschatological structures. 'Fenric' is a name that finds its antecedent in Fenrir, the Fenriswolf in Norse mythology. In 'The Curse of Fenric', Viking ships had visited the small English town that the Doctor and Ace visit centuries later, and carried with them in a vase (like a genie trapped in a bottle) the evil known as Fenric. In this convoluted story, Fenric summons the Haemovores: deformed creatures evolved from humans. They come from Earth's distant future when their mutation was the result of the planet suffering chemical contamination for which Fenric itself is responsible. The writer of 'The Curse of Fenric', Ian Briggs, saw fit to use a Norse myth to serve as the inspiration for an endgame that destroys the whole planet. The resultant creatures resemble deformed victims of toxic contamination, thus combining

Norse myth with an apocalyptic anxiety, and exploiting the fears of the era around nuclear radiation and annihilation, which Thatcherism did nothing to suppress, and indeed amplified.

'Battlefield' (1989) delves even deeper into the theme of nuclear anxiety. It borrows the traditional mythical structure of King Arthur and his knights (something that is used again, without the sense of transformation, in *Knights of God*, covered in Chapter 6). In the story, Arthurian knights from another dimension invade England. Late in the story, the Doctor has to prevent Morgaine from firing a nuclear missile, and uses a rousing speech to do so:

> DOCTOR: All over the world, fools are poised ready to let death fly.
> MORGAINE: What do I care? This is war.
> DOCTOR: Machines of death, Morgaine, are screaming from above, of light brighter than the sun. Not a war between armies nor a war between nations, but just death, death gone mad. The child looks up in the sky, his eyes turn to cinders. No more tears, only ashes. Is this honour? Is this war? Are these the weapons you would use? Tell me!

Andrew Cartmel, who wrote the speech, comments on it that the Doctor achieves his goal 'by the unusual expedient of talking ...' (2005: 158). But language is not an unusual expedient in *Doctor Who*. The series has always been aware of the power of language. This, and the earlier example with John in the cafe, illustrates this power put to the task of combating racism and war respectively.

Thatcher's position on nuclear weapons was clear: they are the only effective form of deterrence. She claimed, 'A world without nuclear weapons may be a dream but you cannot base a sure defence on dreams' (1987d: para 21). Her government was constantly butting heads with the Campaign for Nuclear Disarmament (CND), for which there were many demonstrations in London throughout the 1980s. Cartmel notes that his speech in 'Battlefield' was 'irreverently' referred to as 'the CND speech' (2005: 158). However, for all his socially progressive stances, by the end of the series the Doctor himself becomes an authoritarian in some ways, combining his advanced knowledge of the universe with a certain kind of absolutist moral structure. The next section will outline how this Messianic and authoritarian tendency reaches a crescendo, and how the Doctor's character can therefore be read consistently since 1983 until the end of the original run as an expression of both the 'populism' and also the 'authoritarianism' of Thatcherism and neoliberalism.

The Dark Doctor

A *New Statesman* article asks 'Is *Doctor Who* a Lefty?' (Harrison, 2013: para 1) with strong reference to the direction taken in McCoy's stories. There are indeed many apparently 'left-wing' poses that the Seventh Doctor assumes throughout his run, which have been discussed. But running through the Seventh Doctor's era is a problematic undercurrent. The Doctor is slowly morphing into something darker and more elemental. The Doctor can of course be both: a liberal, progressive character and a darker, 'godlike' character, but the problem is that the latter position carries with it an uncomfortable strain of authoritarianism in the neoliberal mould. In his invocation of absolutes, the Doctor begins to sound like a Thatcherite character. Gareth Roberts (who wrote for the revived series) comments:

> The really odd thing I think about Sylvester McCoy's time as the Doctor and Andrew Cartmel's time as the script editor is that they're there to throw down the government supposedly and to ... bring these left-wing messages to people, but the Doctor himself behaves more like ... George W. Bush than anyone else. (*When Worlds Collide: Doctor Who and Politics*, 2012)

If Roberts is citing the actions of Bush as an example of the right-wing, authoritarian tendencies of Western politicians, then I would agree. In this era the Doctor starts to proclaim upon the notions of absolute good and evil. He uses these convictions to play duplicitous tricks on those around him, and to carry out Realpolitik solutions as he sees fit. He plays his companion Ace like a pawn on a chessboard. He becomes the opposite, in a sense, of what he had always been: from a liberal humanist, and a court jester to the powers that be, he becomes the ultimate authority himself.

McCoy's first season as the Seventh Doctor is unremarkable, and many of the faults that had been building throughout the series since about 1983 in terms of plotting and direction reach a crescendo. But with the beginning of Season 25, 'Remembrance of the Daleks' (1988), the tone of the series changes. Alongside all the progressive messages of the story, there are darker themes that begin to develop. The Seventh Doctor is suddenly portrayed as something other than merely a Time Lord. He becomes what Muir calls 'the tyrant of time, the controller of destinies, the master manipulator' (1999: 61). This is the beginning of what was later referred to in fan circles as the 'Cartmel Masterplan'. To the extent that there was any 'masterplan', it was the aim of Cartmel and his writers to reintroduce some of the mystery into the series and the titular character by suggesting that he is in essence a kind of cosmic manipulator, with access to powers deeper and older than time itself. This led to mixed results that both repudiated and supported a Thatcherite position.

Thatcher created a mythical Britain, and placed herself at the helm, calling into being Britain's already mythologised figures: Queen Victoria and Winston Churchill most prominent among them. These near-Messianic tendencies are reproduced in late-era *Doctor Who*. Where he had previously been subject to the universe, now the Doctor seems to be its custodian, and even in some way its progenitor. In earlier seasons of *Doctor Who*, he was an anti-Establishment figure. The Time Lords, his people, were depicted as bureaucrats, a reflection of the English class system: they were the House of Time Lords, the Tories of the universe, and the Doctor was perpetually at odds with their stultifying practices. But the shift, which reached its zenith in McCoy's era, is almost diametrical. It is now implied that the Doctor is not *merely* a Time Lord, but the *prototypical* Time Lord. In some ways he is responsible for the direction of his home planet – that he is older than time itself, that he was present in the early days of Gallifrey, shaping it, presiding over it (the 2019 series of *Doctor Who* seems to address these possibilities with its reference to the Timeless Child). The suggestion even goes as far as implying that he was present at the genesis of the universe itself. The way the character reveals this information places the Seventh Doctor in the company of Steel and Avon: scheming and Machiavellian. But unlike those two he does not possess the cynicism. He has something darker: authoritarianism.

This quasi-religious, authoritarian impulse is entirely new in *Doctor Who*, and parallels the authoritarian nature of Thatcherism: the recourse to ultimate moral authority, and the reformulation of myth in her favour. It also mimics the authoritarian tendencies of neoliberalism.

'Remembrance of the Daleks' hints at the idea that the Doctor was around long before anyone realised; that he was in fact one of the architects of Gallifrey's political beginnings. Far from being a dissident or a rebel who stole a TARDIS and left the staid society for some fun (as was the original understanding), this story implies a much longer, and darker, story. This arose out of a discussion with Cartmel, the writers, and McCoy himself, who wanted to take the Doctor in a darker and more mysterious direction. Cartmel explains: 'I set about restoring the awe, mystery and strength to the character ... I set about making the Doctor once again more than a mere chump of a Time Lord' (2005: 135). The re-established mystery involved some incarnation of the Doctor at the very beginnings of Gallifrey, co-creating a device called the Hand of Omega, with Gallifrey's founding figures, Rassilon and Omega. This is hinted at in an exchange between the Doctor and his companion Ace in 'Remembrance of the Daleks':

> DOCTOR: The Hand of Omega is a mythical name for Omega's remote stellar manipulator, a device used to customise stars with. (*Laughs*) And didn't we have trouble with the prototype?
> ACE: We?
> DOCTOR: (*tentatively*) They ...

Despite the many socially progressive commentaries in 'Remembrance of the Daleks', it is also the story where the Doctor exercises his ultimate authority by committing genocide – using the Hand of Omega to destroy Skaro, the Daleks' home planet, without giving it a second thought – a very authoritarian decision to make.

It is also suggested throughout the last two seasons that the Doctor is something more than a Time Lord, with powers that had not been guessed at earlier, though some of these exchanges were omitted from the final broadcasts, such as in 'Remembrance of the Daleks':

DAVROS: In the end you are merely another Time Lord.
DOCTOR: Oh Davros, I am far more than just another Time Lord.

Another appears at the end of 'Survival' (1989), the last broadcast story of the show's original run. It depicts an exchange between the Doctor and his nemesis, The Master:

MASTER: You're not a Time Lord!
DOCTOR: Well, strictly speaking ... that is to say ... well, not *just* a Time Lord. We all have to evolve a bit as the years go by. (*Quietly*) Evolve or become extinct.
MASTER: What are you?
DOCTOR: (*Drawing himself up and grinning wickedly*) Shall we just say I'm multi-talented? (qtd in Howe et al., 1993: 133–4)

Why these passages were omitted from broadcast is unknown, but these are the hints that the Doctor is far more powerful and authoritative than was ever previously realised.

Doctor Who in this era also begins to show strong signs of individualism winning out over the collectivist mentality of much pre-Thatcher science fiction television. Rollman considers that the Doctor's ethos is 'grounded in individual morality, rather than political ideology' (2016: para 6), which he also calls 'situational morality' (2016: para 7). I agree that the Doctor has never explicitly stood for any partisan cause as such (except for certain positions sketched out in Chapter 1, around ecology, multiculturalism and so on), but I argue that his 'individual morality' in the later years studied in this chapter becomes problematic. The Doctor plays out his own individualist and sometimes Machiavellian agenda in the later series. He has become, by these series, the embodiment of detachment. He is an alien and always has been, but in his earlier incarnations he was at least a 'humanist' alien. The Sixth and Seventh Doctors embody estrangement, as a Brechtian character would, by rejecting an empathetic understanding of themselves or their motives, often appearing aloof and detached. The Sixth Doctor achieves this by means of an antisocial personality, while the Seventh Doctor holds information close to him and only allows others the benefit of his knowledge when he believes it to be expedient to do so. Echoing Fisher's comments about *Sapphire & Steel*, that it calls to mind a le Carré world of deception, the Doctor in these later series behaves like a cold war spy: never disclosing information until it is absolutely essential. This information seems more and more like intergalactic 'state secrets', with the Doctor as an agent of some sinister force (this concept is explored further in the spinoff books called *The New Adventures*).

The latter series of *Doctor Who*, specifically Seasons 25 and 26 that were the final in the original series, both critique and glorify individualism. Though the Doctor has always been a loner in some ways, rejecting his society to wander the universe essentially alone, he has nonetheless traditionally worked with organisations, most famously UNIT – and often involves himself as an ambassador in negotiations between different sides of a conflict ('The Monster of Peladon' [1974] is an example). The Seventh Doctor's stories never feature any organisations or collectives with which the Doctor aligns himself: he largely operates alone, apart from his companion, and he seldom involves her as an intellectual equal. The Seventh Doctor goes significantly further down the path of individualism than his predecessors, except for the immediately preceding Sixth Doctor.

In 'The Curse of Fenric' (1989), alongside a collective idea, the theme of faith emerges, and the two coalesce in the climactic scene. The question of what we believe, and how strongly, is explored literally – there is a 'psychic barrier' that faith creates to ward off the invading creatures of the piece – and metaphorically – a kind of collective mentality is invoked: believing in each other. However, the psychic barrier proves, in the end, to be the very obstacle that requires defeating, much as Thatcher believed that individuality was the antidote to the collectivist mentality. In that story there is a contest enacted between a collective mentality and an individualist one. Russian soldiers have arrived at a base in England in the Second World War. The two sides decide to join forces, with one saying, 'War, a game played by politicians. We were just pawns in the game, but the pawns are fighting together now, eh, comrade?' Later, another Russian soldier declares, 'Workers of the world unite, comrade.' This inference of socialism follows from the political leanings of the writers, but this is complicated by the position of the Doctor.

In the climax there is a chess game that determines the outcome of the battle between the Doctor and the evil known as Fenric (which has now inhabited the body of one of the other characters).

This clash between the notion of the collective joining together and the individual dispelling evil comes to a head when Ace gives away the winning chess move. In an illogical but symbolic turn, she declares that the game is won if the opposing pawns join together to topple the king. She is tricked into giving the final move to Fenric, and he apparently wins. But the Doctor is on hand with the true 'checkmate' – in apparently humiliating Ace and destroying her faith in him, calling her 'an emotional cripple', in front of those assembled, he allows the leader of the heamovores, the 'Great Old One', to kill Fenric (removing the 'psychic barrier', in this case Ace's faith in the Doctor, that is necessary for blocking the haemovores). The Doctor therefore demonstrates that it is not teamwork that wins, but the duplicitous machinations of the individual with power and authority.

In 'The Curse of Fenric' the Doctor is seen as the ultimate authority – he is in control of elemental forces, and his arrogance is such that he manipulates others without even informing them of their part in the drama, because he believes, as authoritarian leaders do, that ignorance is better for them – that 'the truth' would be more than they could manage, and that, in their naivete, they could derail the whole delicate situation if in possession of knowledge. In that story, Ace voices the frustration she feels at the Doctor's authoritarian streak:

ACE: You know what's going on, don't you?
DOCTOR: (*Wearily*) Yes.
ACE: You always know; you just can't be bothered to tell anyone. It's like it's some sort of a game and only you know the rules.

The Seventh Doctor believes his version of morality is absolute. Like Blake, he believes that good and evil are objective realities, but beyond Blake's revolutionary aspirations, the Doctor believes he has access to ultimate knowledge about good and evil, and is therefore the only one equipped to decide on the best outcome. In 'The Curse of Fenric', more than ever before, the universe has been reduced to a series of absolutes which, in their description, resemble the foreign policy rhetoric of both Thatcher and Reagan. It is explained in the story that only the Doctor knows what is happening and who Fenric is, implicitly because he was there at the time of Fenric's creation. In describing Fenric's origin, the Doctor posits a creation myth, which seems to preclude all others:

> DOCTOR: Evil, evil since the dawn of time ... the beginning of all beginnings. Two forces: only good and evil, then chaos. Time is born; matter, space, the universe cries out like a newborn. The forces shatter as the universe explodes outwards. Only echoes remain, yet somehow, somehow the evil force survives: an intelligence, pure evil.

This quasi-religious description, and the exclusive knowledge the Doctor has of it, positions the Doctor as a religious figure himself. Andrew Cartmel claims that he saw this version of the Doctor as 'one of these half-glimpsed demigods' (2005: 135), and would have pursued this further had the series not been cancelled in 1989. We can certainly detect this deified status in the above speech.

Some of Thatcher's comments on the subject of 'good and evil' also lapse into the quasi-mythical, such as an interview from 1984 in which she claimed that 'evil men have been born since the beginning of recorded time' (para 50). She echoed this in 1985 in a discussion about natural disasters when she claimed that the laws of physics were 'fixed at the beginning of creation' and this led her to proclaim that 'each of us is so vitally important we have a choice: this is the choice between good and evil' (Thatcher, 1985b: para 122). Reagan, too, in his famous 1983 'Evil Empire' speech to the National Association of Evangelicals, implored his audience not to 'remove yourself from the struggle between right and wrong and good and evil' (Parry-Giles, 2015: para 48). While there is nothing new about politicians declaring themselves on the 'good' side of an ideological struggle, the polarisation of the two states, heavily dowsed in religious language, that Thatcher and Reagan used in their rhetoric seems to be at one with the Doctor's speech, which in its absolutism seems to allow him the position of ultimate moral arbiter. This too has its precedents. As early as 1965, the Doctor, then played by Patrick Troughton, claimed, 'There are some corners of the universe which have bred the most terrible things. Things which act against everything we believe in. They must be fought' ('The Moonbase'). But this is not a creation myth; it does not locate the Doctor in a position of ultimate authority or custodian of 'forbidden knowledge'. It has no quasi-religious element. Equally, the personification of good and evil has been hinted at before, with the Black and White Guardians: elders of the universe who exist to guard good and evil. But when he works for the White Guardian, the Doctor does so only as an emissary, not as an authority. The Seventh Doctor's speech in 'The Curse of Fenric' is more elemental in its quasi-religious reach, its polarisation of good and evil, and thus closely aligned to Reagan and Thatcher's rhetoric.

Thatcher's tenure brought a resurgence of Manichean ideas of 'good' and 'evil': the absolutes that dominated in the times of Empire, and dwindled under the consensus era of post-war Britain. Later in Tony Blair's time and the build-up to the Iraq War, matched with (and instigated by) his American counterpart George W. Bush in Washington, this language re-emerged. In *Doctor Who* in this particular historical moment, we witness an attempt to combat Thatcherism in broad terms, but at the same time, not only a retreat back into Manichean rhetoric of good vs. evil, but a reinforcement of it, edging closer to these polarities than ever before (see O'Shaughnessy, 1996: 297). In *Doctor Who* of the era, the Doctor is elevated from the status of the rebel and outsider, to the authority figure himself, and in dispelling Fenric and labelling it as some form of ultimate evil, the Doctor positions himself as the ultimate moral authority. If we are to read the Doctor's character and actions as consistent since 1983 until the end of the original run, the logical conclusion to reach is that when the Doctor evades authority, or indeed rises up against it, it is not because he is a 'rebel' in the traditional sense; it is because he believes himself, even if reluctantly, to be the greater authority. This is seen in the Doctor's actions, specifically the Seventh, when concealing vital information from his companions, playing them like pawns, and finally in 'The Curse of Fenric' positing his ultimate creation myth.

The era of *Doctor Who* discussed in this chapter was socially progressive, but ushered in a peculiarly bleak and Machiavellian version of the central character. The Doctor had hitherto always been a 'liberal humanist', but in Colin Baker's and (more notably) Sylvester McCoy's incarnations, he became a dark and unknowable figure, willing to expend the lives, and exploit the trust, of others for the sake of his own 'masterplan'. This afforded the production staff a remit for the character that was perhaps too broad: he could variously play the role of the 'clown', the 'hippie', the 'revolutionary' and the 'dark manipulator'. In their ambition, the writers realised a character who straddled both sides of the ideological divide. In *Blake's 7*, this argument is articulated between its two principal characters, Blake and Avon; but in *Doctor Who*, the roles of both liberal and conservative fall simultaneously on the shoulders of the Doctor. The Seventh Doctor, then, embodies a certain kind of 'authoritarian populism'. He is both an authoritarian in his dealings with his companions and others, and he is 'with the people' in examples such as 'Remembrance of the Daleks' and 'The Happiness Patrol'. Despite his 'revolutionary' stances, he embodies many of Thatcher's socially conservative principles, as well as her proclivity for individualism.

The stories around the Doctor were constructed out of the remnants of Norse mythology, British mythology, Victoriana, and various emblems of the 1980s, which seemed to articulate both the writers' dread of Thatcher and the anxiety around nuclear war. In each case the writers turned these positions into mythologies: ideological positions communicated through the selection of essential types. Often the writers were successful in communicating their anti-Thatcher agenda, both explicitly and implicitly, as well as articulating a left-wing perspective on race, immigration and hegemonic systems of power. Ultimately, however, the Doctor himself edged closer to a Thatcherite figure, with his invocation of absolutes and his reliance on individualistic motives. In his polarisation of good and evil, and in the position he occupied of ultimate moral authority, the Doctor became a much more conservative character than ever before.

5

'A precarious existence': science fiction television adaptations of the 1980s

The 1980s brought about a radical restructuring of television drama. Cooke writes of a drift away from 'quality' programming and one towards commercialism:

> The larger budgets required for the television film and for the expensive drama serial led to more co-productions, often with American companies, and the freedom from editorial control that playwrights, directors and producers had previously enjoyed, especially at the BBC, was gradually eroded in this changing economy of television production. (2015: 151)

Blake's 7, *Sapphire & Steel* and *Doctor Who* were all commissioned in the era that preceded Thatcherism, and as such the creators were afforded a degree of artistic licence that became rare to nonexistent as the decade continued. In the 1980s, television producers were subject to much tighter controls. One result of this was that science fiction output – seen as too expensive – was radically diminished, and another was that there tended to be more adaptations of novels because of the perceived 'trustworthiness' of the source. Geraghty writes of 1980s science fiction television (and television in general) that 'the original text had to be of a standard to warrant a large budgetary outlay, and be popular enough with a broad enough spectrum of people to guarantee a dedicated audience' (2011: 106). To that extent, there was much more emphasis on adapting well-known novels across the board. On ITV, the most memorable were *Brideshead Revisited* (1981) and *The Jewel in the Crown* (1984).

Adapting science fiction novels was an even more precarious undertaking, due to their complicated production values and special effects. As Bould explains:

> In the 1980s, as new effects technologies enabled increasingly spectacular science fiction cinema and as importing U.S. productions became relatively economical, British-produced series became less common. (2008: 221)

Nonetheless, there were some science fiction series commissioned in the mid to late 1980s in Britain. Most were adaptations of novels, and some of these will be studied in this chapter. The next chapter will be devoted to the series written directly for television in the era.

The two series selected here are the adaptation of John Wyndham's 1951 novel *The Day of the Triffids* (1981), famously described by Brian Aldiss as a 'cosy catastrophe'; and the 1984–85 adaptation of John Christopher's *Tripods* novels (1967–68), with the majority of focus on the latter. Both series in their own ways have updated the source material to reflect a changing Britain, commenting on the creeping sense of authoritarianism in the country during those years. Though the novels were written before the neoliberal Thatcher era, some of the aspects of the post-catastrophe science fiction landscape were already in evidence – the emerging Machiavellian behaviour of those under pressure (or those who can see a way to exploit the system), the authoritarian tendencies of the military and members of the Establishment, and the duplicitous behaviour that enters to fill the vacuum left behind by a loss of traditional authority. In the case of *The Day of the Triffids*, the differences from the novel are slight but significant, whereas for *The Tripods* they are wide-ranging.

While traditional authority is always contested and problematic, it is nonetheless a kind of anchor in the 1970s series. In the series of the 1980s the reverse is shown – in most cases a world much more closely resembling the world of neoliberalism, emerging strongly in the Thatcher era, where it is no longer clear who is in charge, and individuals, in this deregulated environment, take it upon themselves to be authorities. Because of the nature of competition, that tendency is also Machiavellian – the most cynical, manipulative and often 'ironic' personality wins. We witnessed the birth of this character in the protagonists of the major series studied in the preceding three chapters. In the novel adaptations of this chapter the Machiavellian tendencies are (by and large) not those exhibited by the protagonists. What these series do that the longer ones did not is examine the impact on a wider society that has been thrust into a situation of totalitarianism or chaos.

The protagonists in these series behave, on the whole, more like consensus-era characters. Bill and Josella in *The Day of the Triffids* are resolutely middle-class English characters, determined to make the best of their situation, while also developing some darker tendencies. Will and his friends in *The Tripods* are boys of 15, not yet brutalised by the system. These characters are basically trustworthy and do not display the level of duplicity that their longer-form television cousins do. They belong more to the ethos of the 1970s – their predecessors or forebears are the good-sense, pragmatic characters of *Survivors* or *Space: 1999*. But they are clearly operating in a different world. There is no simple, pastoral England to return to, there is no sense of nationalism (though this topic will be addressed again in the 1980s with *Knights of God*, in the next chapter). The world of the Triffids is too annihilated to ever return to any nostalgic past, and in the series there is no desire for it in any case, though the resolute characters are determined to create some kind of future. The boys in *The Tripods* never knew a world other than the parody of a bucolic Eden that they were raised within, and those with clear vision could see that it was an illusion from the beginning. Their world is radically altered, and around them they see characters who are adapting the skills to survive – cynicism, self-interest, ruthlessness. All around them are 'official' authority figures who have merely capitalised on the situation and become authoritarian. None are worthy of any trust or respect.

The focus of this chapter is *The Tripods* (1984–85). For television the story has been expanded and brought into the range of 'family' viewing. I will argue that the main aspects of *The Tripods* mimic the authoritarian tendencies of the Thatcher era, as well as the new logic of neoliberalism, in which traditional social units were replaced by the individualism, self-interest and arbitrary logic of a social order that has abandoned history – both personal and cultural. The other series receives shorter treatment. *The Day of the Triffids* (1981) was largely faithful to the source material, so its engagement with Thatcherism or neoliberalism is minimal. However, it is worth discussing because the novel (along with *Childhood's End*, *The War of the Worlds*, and, to an extent, *1984*) served as a kind of founding text for British science fiction television (I have discussed the many similarities between the novel and *Survivors*), and many of the character choices and interactions appear as templates or prototypes for the more extreme characters that emerged in 1980s television drama.

There are other television adaptations in this era. *The Nightmare Man* (1981) adapted from David Wiltshire's novel *Child of Vodyanoi* (1978), plays out as a throwback to 1970s *Doctor Who* episodes, and was scripted by long-time *Doctor Who* writer Robert Holmes. Added to this was an adaptation of H. G. Wells's *The Invisible Man* (1984). But the series I have selected for this chapter seem to me to exhibit most clearly the evolution of television science fiction in the UK and the move into neoliberal territory in its themes.

The Day of the Triffids (1981)

Concerns about nuclear warfare, big business and satellite surveillance are discussed in the 1981 television adaptation of *The Day of the Triffids* (scripted by Douglas Livingstone), though some of those concerns were already present in the novel and are merely accentuated by the serial. The serial was written in the late 1970s, and acts as a kind of transitional piece, engaging with issues that were to become prominent in the Thatcher era. Though it was broadcast around the time that *Blake's 7* and *Sapphire & Steel* were reaching their conclusions, it does not contain the same level of biting commentary of emerging neoliberal attitudes. As a reasonably faithful adaptation of the novel, there is little that can be said to be *directly* critical of Thatcherite society or neoliberalism (though writers like Geraghty see connections, which will be discussed shortly), but the series can be viewed as a precursor to the darker terrain explored by series like *Star Cops*, or even *The Tripods* (its common connection to *The Tripods* is that both were highly influenced by *The War of the Worlds*). It is useful to analyse the serial here because it (and the novel) provides many of the 'prototypes' of characterisation and social commentary that were to become more prominent in the Thatcher era.

Protagonist Bill Masen is often torn between competing facets of his conscience – his desire and sense of duty to help others – and his own selfish impulses. This is ruminated on many times in the novel, and brought out in the series on occasion. This central dilemma serves as the basis for many Thatcher-era characters – many like Avon, Steel and the Seventh Doctor tend to occupy both sides of this dilemma between serving the community and serving oneself. There is an appetite for change in *Triffids* which is absent from *Survivors* and, broadcast in the early stages of the Thatcher era, it can be seen as both a supportive gesture for the new government and a fear for the future. What emerges most clearly is a discontent with any 'authority' that robs the individual of their autonomy and tries to impose its order upon them – a concern that would be highlighted in the Thatcher era.

The Triffids are carnivorous plants with the ability to kill humans by stinging them. It is unknown how they first appeared, but it seems unlikely they were alien in origin. Bill begins the story in hospital. He narrates to us the history of Triffids, and the way their oil was exploited by capitalists (early on we're shown a scene of 'disreputable' businessmen discussing deals over Triffid oil). Before the catastrophe Bill worked for a Triffid farm, where they harvested the oil that the plants produced, and he had been stung by one and temporarily blinded. While his eyes were in bandages the world experienced a mysterious light in the sky so bright that it blinded anyone who looked at it. Because Bill was convalescing with his eyes under bandages, he was not affected. When Bill takes off his bandages he discovers that almost everyone else is blind. He walks the streets and discovers the country is transformed into chaos – people rioting and looting, and no semblance of authority. Geraghty notes:

> In *The Day of the Triffids* a critique of Thatcherism can be clearly read in the fact that little is learned or seen of the government or emergency services after the meteor shower makes the country's population blind and vulnerable to the Triffids' attacks. The blind are left to fend for themselves on the empty streets of London, small bands of looters and thugs terrorising shopkeepers and stealing what supplies they can. (2011: 106)

Certainly it is telling that Bill walks past a deserted Westminster with the Houses of Parliament ominously empty in the background, signalling the loss of authority. It is also clear that the riots in the streets mimic the actual riots that had occurred a few months earlier in London and other parts of England (this point will be discussed further in the next chapter). The seeds of this are in the novel, but the implications are drawn out, and problematised, in the series. Both novel and series depict a disarming lack of response to the disaster, and a rapid (if not entirely believable) descent into chaos. In the series people are looting shops, roaming the streets chanting football songs in a threatening manner, and stealing people's cars. An old tramp attacks a girl, Josella, whipping her and treating her like a dog on a leash, leading her around to help him find the supplies he needs. Bill saves her from the old man, and they team up as two sighted people amid the blind population.

There is a cold war paranoia building. When Bill and Josella decide to fall in with a group of people – academics and military men – they watch as the academic David Beadley gives a speech. In the book it is the following:

> I would like to point out to you that this, even now, is not the worst that could have happened. I, and quite likely many of you, have spent most of my life in expectation of something worse. And I still believe that if this had not happened to us, that worse thing would. (Wyndham, 2016: 115)

In the series he says, 'At any point during the last thirty-five years the earth could've been destroyed by a nuclear holocaust. It has not been destroyed.' Much like its contemporaries, the series trades on the nuclear war paranoia.

Bill is a character torn between duty and self-interest. He serves as a kind of prototype for much more ruthless and Machiavellian characters like Avon and Steel, though these characters were presented to the British television viewing public earlier. What he articulates – in the book and the series – is something like a developmental stage in the post-war British character, at least in terms of science fiction narratives. Bill doesn't help anyone unless it is expedient for his own purposes, and the narrative of the book contains several hand-wringing speeches concerned with the most 'moral' response. Early on Bill and Josella come across a man (later revealed to be Coker) delivering an impassioned speech through a gate to the military man on the inside, about how selfish they have become, electing not to help out the blind people. The ensuing 'argument' that Bill and Josella have, about which side they should align themselves with, is given detailed treatment in the novel, and basically repeated for the series. The following is the version presented in the series:

> JOSELLA: He's right isn't he, that man? We've got to help them.
> BILL: He's right ... and he's wrong ... Oh, we could show some of them where to find food for a few days, for a few weeks, and what happens afterwards?
> JOSELLA: So we should just walk out and leave them to rot?
> BILL: I think it comes to a very simple choice. Either we say, 'There's been a catastrophe, let's start again, let's save what really can be saved,' or say, 'No: those people will die, we must keep them alive as long as possible.' On the face of it that's the most humane choice. For us it's probably suicide. We die, they die, we'd all die. Would that be making the best use of ourselves?
> JOSELLA: You've made up your mind.
> BILL: Look, I don't like it anymore than you do, but, well, in the end do we make the moral gesture – and that's all that can be: a gesture – or do we join those people in there and start to rebuild some kind of life for ourselves?

Here we witness the emergence of a mentality that is beginning to belong to the right wing, the Thatcherite world of self-interest; the 'Realpolitik' concern with political and moral worth being centred in the pragmatic behaviour of the self-interested individual, even if it requires that some must suffer. Obviously this attitude predates Thatcherism, and its roots lie in the consensus era (and indeed this speech, or a version of it, appears in the book). What was brought out in the Thatcher era was a high-level *enactment* of this attitude. As the neoliberal turn became the site of human endeavour and came to be seen by many as an arbiter of human moral behaviour, this personality type was highlighted: one that considers human beings as commodities, or as units of productivity, and human behaviour as a zero-sum game of resource management.

The moral ambiguity continues throughout the book and the series – Bill spends a lot of time attempting to rationalise what he should do, and his thoughts swing between a kind of altruism, and self-interest. At one point he is kidnapped by a mob led by Coker, who want him to join their salvage crew, helping out the blind by foraging for food and shelter. Despite having been kidnapped he seems to take kindly to this group and helps them out for a time. They take over an old Victorian hotel with people living in it. He explains to them that his crew are living there now, though in the series his ultimatum is a little softer – Bill offers them to take their share of the food they find, and then gently explains that if they don't comply they will 'have to find somewhere else to stay. I'm sorry, but it's the only way.' There is certainly a critique of colonialism to be read here, and it is echoed at the end when the sinister Torrence tries to take over the farm where Bill and his friends are living.

Bill's dilemma is whether to work with the initial group and try to rebuild humanity – a good, altruistic idea, but perhaps worthless or just futile – or plunder what is available while he can. This becomes something of a Realpolitik choice between 'self-interest' and community, and it serves to drive the character closer and closer to a kind of cynicism, which is later articulated in the book. This seems to chime with Boucher's description of Avon as both idealistic and cynical at the same time, without a certain grasp of his own motivations (Stevens and Brown, 1992: para 103). Avon is a character driven by a completely different set of concerns and motivations to a consensus-era character. He is pragmatic in the extreme, but mainly with regard to his own self-interest. Bill is more moderate: he is never (to paraphrase Boucher) totally cynical or selfish, but we can always detect him sliding more towards the direction of self-interest than altruism. Later in the novel Bill has an argument with Coker about humanity. Bill contends that people have 'mostly peasant minds' (Wyndham, 2016: 178), then says:

> 'You can't drive a flock of sheep to market in a dead straight line, but there are ways of getting 'em there.'
> 'You're being unusually cynical, as well as very metaphorical, this evening,' Coker observed.

I objected to that.
'It isn't cynical to have noticed how a shepherd handles his sheep.'
'To regard human beings as sheep might be thought so by some.'
(Wyndham, 2016: 179)

Coker seems to have more faith in humanity and calls Bill 'Machiavellian'. Bill therefore provides a template for future iterations of the Thatcher-era neoliberal character.

Later in the series a group, including Bill and Josella, have occupied a farmhouse and are deliberating over what to do next. Coker arrives (Bill and Josella had thought him dead) and he asks if they would join him in the Isle of Wight, where the Triffids are largely kept at bay. Coker wants to build a better world and is not interested in reproducing what was already there – a stark difference from *Survivors*, where (at least the English) characters are by and large interested in reinstating the country as it was, with all its hierarchies reproduced. Coker never makes it clear what this 'better world' will look like, but the promise of radical reform seems enough to entice Bill. However, before they can make a decision, a man called Torrence arrives in a tank, dressed in military uniform. He describes himself as the 'Chief executive officer of the emergency council for the South-East region of Britain'. He offers that they set themselves up as a kind of feudal colony. 'You're offering to make me a kind of feudal lord?' Bill asks (slightly echoing the early exchange between Anna and Wormley in *Survivors*). In the end Bill manages to deceive the military men, and the crew depart for the Isle of Wight.

The Day of the Triffids is best seen as a transitional piece – a prototype for the darker territory into which other science fiction television series of the 1980s ventured. Bill Masen is a character who is torn between the old 'consensus' methods of duty and responsibility, and the more contemporary individualist approach. Later characters such as Avon and Steel no longer entertain moral dilemmas, but merely act in ways that are largely self-centred and Machiavellian. In due course the Sixth and Seventh Doctors adopt the same method. As such, Bill provides a template for these more morally questionable characters that emerged in the 1980s science fiction television landscape.

The Tripods (1984–85)

Based on a series of children's books by John Christopher (the pen name of Sam Youd), *The Tripods* is set in England and France in 2089–90 (for the television series – the books do not specify an exact date). The original novels, *The White Mountains*, *The City of Gold and Lead* and *The Pool of Fire*, were published in 1967–68. The series depicts Earth as ruled by the Tripods: huge machines, about 80 feet high, with three 'legs' for moving around, very strongly resembling the Tripods from H. G. Wells's *War of the Worlds*. The Tripods have conquered the world and established a 'benign' dictatorship. Under their rule there is no war, and very little poverty. Children in school are taught to worship them for ushering in peace and prosperity. In an expositional scene early on, a schoolteacher tells his class:

> nature and the Tripods are the two essentials for the continuation and well-being of mankind. Nature's bounty clothes and feeds us, and by their benevolent presence the Tripods have eliminated the evil and greed of war ... Consider the unthinkable barbarity of deliberately killing other human beings and how it must've been in the dark days before the Tripods came. For centuries aggression dominated men's activities, ruining his every endeavour, and in particular making impossible any true partnership with nature such as we now enjoy in our more enlightened times.

In his speech, the teacher has more or less conflated nature and the Tripods. Both are as essential and as timeless as each other. Both represent the only possible, logical way of being. Both are, therefore, natural. Barthes, in *Mythologies* (1957), considers mythology to be that which 'turns history into nature' (Allen, 2003: 36). Barthes writes, 'myth has the task of giving an historical intention a natural justification, and making contingency appear eternal' (1991: 142). *The Tripods* enacts this sense of mythologies more clearly than any of the other series – *Blake's 7* tends to expose the constructed nature of life in the galaxy by showing it from the perspective of revolutionaries. *Doctor Who* also allows us to see 'behind the veil' of many corrupt societies. In the world of *The Tripods* the boys and the Vagrants see this world for what it is, but we are also able to experience the perspective of those who are subservient to it and its rewards. It is through these characters that the 'mythologies' of the series become evident.

In this series humans have reverted to a largely agrarian lifestyle, congregating in small villages around the countryside. Far from the trust in technology exhibited in the consensus-era series, *The Tripods* explores the 'other end' of the spectrum – the death of technology. Its loss signifies the loss of human autonomy, enterprise and hope, but only to an outside observer – those living within it have been conditioned to love it. The cities have been ransacked by the Tripods: largely abandoned, they have gone to ruin. The remnants of twentieth-century civilisation – the characters refer to the inhabitants of that century as 'the ancients' – are evident, but it is also evident that the characters know little to nothing about the technology humans used to have – Will and his friends often use naive names for obsolete pieces of technology, such as the discovery of an old car which the boys call a 'carriage without a horse', or a grenade they discover which they call an egg.

The story of *The Tripods* focuses on Will, a young resident of the village of Wherton, which is somewhere near Winchester. Will watches along with the rest of his pastoral village as his cousin is lifted into the mouth of a Tripod and returned to the residents with a Cap on his head. This ritual of Capping is undertaken when a child reaches the age of 14 (or 16 in the series), and is designed to limit one's capacity for original thought by way of a metal chip implanted in the brain (with the outer part visible at the top of the head). After Capping, a person's intellectual and imaginative horizons are considerably narrowed. Creative expression is very difficult, as is any kind of complex abstract thought. In theory the Caps should limit one's aggression, but as we will soon see, there are exceptions. It seems that one's inquisitiveness is also removed: one no longer questions the world they are living in, but simply accepts it. Perhaps the most consistent function of the Cap is to instil a devotional attitude to the Tripods themselves. The Cap serves as a kind of symbolic (or perhaps literal) 'lobotomy', dampening one's personality. Will is strongly against Capping after seeing his cousin undergo the ritual, and watching afterwards as the boy behaves in a docile manner.

Wandering around the outskirts of Wherton are the Vagrants – those who have resisted Capping, or have been rejected by the process – their chips have malfunctioned and left them permanently brain-damaged. Vagrants are treated with kindness and sympathy (at least in Wherton) but are never allowed an inclusive role in society. They are largely homeless and nomadic, and are to be pitied by productive members of society. Will and his cousin Henry come across a Vagrant who calls himself Ozymandias and quotes the Shelley poem. Ozymandias saw the evil of Capping so he pretended that he had been Capped and that it had malfunctioned (superficially attaching the Cap of a dead man to his head), making him a Vagrant. Will and Henry fall in with Ozymandias, who assures them that there are like-minded people called the 'free men' – those who do not want to be capped and ultimately want to resist the Tripods – and they are gathered in 'the white mountains' in France. So Will and Henry decide to journey there, and along the way they pick up a young French boy whom they call Beanpole (his real name is Jean-Paul, but the boys misunderstand the name so settle on the rhyming 'Beanpole' as a nickname). Ozymandias is apparently killed early in the first season, but returns in the second as one of the free men in the white mountains.

It is later revealed that the Tripods are controlled by the 'Masters', an alien species who built a domed city in the mountains in France with artificial air and gravity, and they plan to terraform the planet to their own conditions and needs, and thereby extinguish humans. In the television story we learn by way of exposition that the human 'ancestors' began to develop AI, but then a nuclear war wiped them out. The Masters arrived at this point and began to rebuild the society along feudal lines as a means of control. Above even the Masters are the Cognoscs: beings with no physical form, but closer to pure intelligence, an innovation created for the series and, like other aspects of the series, a concept that shares something in common with the Overmind from Arthur C. Clarke's novel *Childhood's End*. All of this, of course, has religious overtones – the characters see the Tripods as gods – and the means of control the Tripods exert is something akin to a religious cult.

The series (two in total) were not particularly successful, garnering disappointing viewing figures, and the decision was made by Head of BBC Drama Series and Serials, Jonathan Powell, to terminate the series, despite the third book being scheduled for adaptation. Consequently the series ends with Will, having escaped the Tripods' lair to discover he has made little difference, asking rhetorically, 'Has it all been for nothing?' Added to the insufficient ratings, Powell believed the series failed to engage substantially enough on the level of characterisation and acting (Sexton, 2016: 479). The failure of the series could also be attributed, as Geraghty and others note, to the influx of American series with superior production values. Science fiction was losing its grip in Britain, as American series with larger budgets flooded the British market, and it became cheaper for the British to import them.

Geraghty also sees the series as too pessimistic for a country in the grip of Thatcherism:

> [The series'] mediocre reception during the Thatcher era (with economic recession and rioting in the inner cities) intimates that British science fiction television in the 1980s needed to look upon a future where life was going to be better than the present. Depictions of rural countryside and pastoral villages patrolled by giant, authoritarian machines were not what audiences wanted or needed. (2011: 105)

While the series depicts a kind of feudal society quite divorced from modern economics or the 'free market', it nonetheless allegorically draws out many facets of neoliberal behaviour in Thatcher's Britain that are created by a distant authoritarian power that employs a brutal police force but remains otherwise remote. We will see that the arbitrary nature and Machiavellian behaviour of some of the characters reflects the trends that were becoming prevalent in workplaces. More centrally, I will argue that the authoritarianism of *The Tripods* mimics that of Thatcher's neoliberal society – the machines are largely unseen, and rarely intervene in human affairs. This encourages what Fisher (2009) calls the 'flat hierarchies' of neoliberalism, where there is no obvious authority and no accountability, creating a space for authoritarian personalities to intervene – an aspect that is absent from the books but is explored within the series. Alongside this analysis, I claim that the notion of Capping becomes a metaphor for a hegemonic system, also a means of control in Thatcher's neoliberal agenda. Together they form Hall's 'authoritarian populism' (1988: 28), which Thatcherite society would have recognised – the dissemination of 'populist' ideas within an authoritarian regime. I will also argue that the divisions in this society (introduced in the books and drawn out by the series) reflect many of the tensions of both the era before Thatcher and the neoliberal beginnings.

The series is inflected with the neoliberal changes to television in this era. One of the major changes is in technology. Max Sexton links the production values of the series to the commercial climate of the era, forcing the series to improve its technical competence to keep apace with not only the visual effects-laden *Star Wars* and other Hollywood movies, but also domestic competition with the newly devised Channel 4, which was created in 1982, two years before *The Tripods* began. The corporation's answer was an upswing in the quality of special effects for the series. Through a technology called Quantel Paint Box, the series was able to realise the Tripods with enough believability to convince the viewing audience of a certain verisimilitude (Sexton, 2016: 470). Much of the power of the series arises from that early sequence where the sleepy rhythm of a small village in the English countryside from a bygone era is suddenly interrupted by a giant, three-legged machine on the horizon, pressing its huge foot into the stream. This juxtaposition, of the seemingly archaic scene, and the intrusion of an incongruous futuristic science fiction element, produces an arresting contrast, though, according to Geraghty, it provided too much of a sense of confusion for some (2011: 109). The visual effects of a ruined, post-apocalyptic Paris are also effective. In Series 2, when Will and his friend Fritz make it to the City of Gold, the rendering of the Tripods' city is visually impressive for the era, using new digital technology to bring it to life (Sexton, 2016: 477).

Sarah Seymore considers the books to be products of the upheavals of the 1960s, connecting them to themes of colonialism and Empire, and notions of 'the other'. She also considers Ozymandias and the Vagrants as representatives of the hippie movement and the counterculture of 1968:

> The hippie culture, which developed mainly in the USA and in Great Britain, widely changed the Western way of living. Many young

people rebelled against those middle-class values their parents taught them, since they held that conservative beliefs impeded their freedom of personal expression and development. They also felt they had to get involved in the debates around nuclear weapons and about social and racial difficulties. (2014: 79)

Many of the ideals of the hippie era (contemporaneous to the writing of the books) were repurposed and braided into the fabric of right-wing discourse by the 1980s. Filby notes that 'those on the right would eventually come to steal the language of 'liberty' and 'individualism' from the left but would attach to it very different meanings' (2015: 84). Those meanings were all connected with the new economic liberalism of Thatcherism.

The connection between those 1960s upheavals and Thatcherism is a curious one. Many of the youth of the era were demanding changes in the areas of individual expression and personal freedoms. Famously Mick Jagger, fresh from his overturned jail sentence for possession of drugs, argued in the 1960s for individual rights, personal autonomy and freedom from State intervention – a prototype of the libertarian attitude that would emerge in the 1980s, repackaged as part of the right-wing project. Ironically it was the conservative William Rees-Mogg, then editor of *The Times* and later one of Thatcher's appointees to the BBC's Board of Governors, who wrote the editorial that changed opinions ('Who breaks a butterfly on a wheel?' from 1967), arguing that Jagger and Richards's sentences were too harsh. Jagger later became something of an admirer of Thatcher (and Rees-Mogg). To this end, in *The Tripods* the boys' bid for autonomy against an authoritarian power would, on the one hand, be recognised as a symbol of the 1960s left-wing project, but within the series, produced in 1985, as Thatcherite – the boys want autonomy from the 'State' and strongly oppose its interference in their lives, even to the point of literally invading their personal thoughts. On closer examination it becomes apparent that this 'State' behaves in a Thatcherite manner – appearing to give people that freedom and autonomy, but only in a superficial sense, masking its true effects by way of the Cap, just as the Thatcher government gave the appearance of autonomy and freedom of expression, but only in the narrow sense of economic endeavour. In transposing a story written in the 1960s to a 1980s context, the meanings of these essential terms – freedom, autonomy and others – have been reformatted into a much more complex web of relationships between power and resistance.

Seymore also considers the social stratification of the Vagrants to be prevalent in the television version. She discusses Episode 11, where the boys, having escaped a French village where they were stealing food, encounter a group of Vagrants in a forest. They are dressed as stereotypes of savages with skulls as decoration. She notes:

> Obviously the skulls symbolise savagery and superstition. What is more they are an Orientalist stereotype of primitive decoration, and frequently associated with Cannibalism. (2014: 77)

She argues that this invites a comparison with nineteenth-century colonial literature and turns them into the 'other'. This is resonant with the project in Thatcher's Britain of placing firm emphasis on the 'othering' mode when speaking of the immigrant, or indeed the British citizen who is not part of the dominant group. Chapter 4 has already discussed Thatcher's comments about being 'rather swamped' by other cultures. She also pitted the 'moral' capitalist over the 'immoral' socialist; or even more insidiously, the heterosexual over the (anti-family) homosexual (the controversial Section 28 the Local Government Act 1988 banned the promotion of homosexuality in public). This polarising attempt to foreground the essential 'British' character as coherent and of measurable qualities – white and European, heterosexual and capitalist – summons a particular, ethnically and ideologically narrow version of society and affords us insight into the presentation of Thatcherite society, with a certain type of Briton 'naturalised'.

To view the Vagrants from a complementary perspective, we return to Barthes's notion in *Mythologies*, in which the bourgeois class turns 'history into nature' by using essential types to construct a false view of society. This mimics the strategy of the Tripods themselves, who erased human history when they invaded, and instilled a new social order which became naturalised. The depiction of the Vagrants recalls Barthes's comments about the 'bastard' in the constructed sport of wrestling:

Science fiction TV adaptations of the 1980s 163

> What then is a 'bastard' …? Essentially someone unstable, who accepts the rules only when they are useful to him and transgresses the formal continuity of attitudes. He is unpredictable, therefore asocial. He takes refuge behind the law when he considers that it is in his favour, and breaks it when he finds it useful to do so. (1991: 22)

If people can be reassured, for instance, that there have always been outcasts in society, that this is in fact the natural order, then the essential quality that they represent will be more easily accepted. If this 'bastard' has always behaved this way and always will then we (the 'good' bourgeois citizens) need not think of him, or try to help him, but rather treat him with indifference, as part of an immutable natural order. We will use him as 'other', to differentiate ourselves from him, and reinforce a hierarchy of values. Barthes writes:

> The petit-bourgeois is a man unable to imagine the Other. If he comes face to face with him, he blinds himself, ignores and denies him, or else transforms him into himself. In the petit-bourgeois universe … any otherness is reduced to sameness. (1991: 152)

In the case of the Vagrants, they have become part of a social order in which the Tripods are the heroic rulers, the Capped are the free citizens, and the Vagrants are the 'Other', to be treated with kindness perhaps, but pitied and feared. The Tripods have completely erased history, and have made many artificial behaviours appear natural and immutable. Thatcher emphasised certain 'types' over others in a similarly 'mythical' manner, and the Vagrants recall this social stratification, and the acceptance (by the general populace) of nature over history.

Several important innovations have been made to the source material to bring the series into the world of the 1980s. In his preface to the first book, *The White Mountains*, Christopher discusses how the world of capitalism was in fact oppositional to his intentions. He writes:

> The chaotic capitalist system that [the Tripods] first encounter, with its emphasis on individual enterprise is not suitable for this purpose [of world domination]. So they delve into human history and find a system which is. Out go bankers and investors and those awkward types who just want to do something different; back come kings and nobles, farmers and peasants – people accustomed to

order imposed from above, in a world which only changes with the seasons. (2014c: xv)

Here Christopher is implying that capitalism and individual enterprise are conducive to personal autonomy and creative endeavour. Though his introduction was written in 2003, the novels themselves were written in the 1960s, and the capitalism of that era is one tempered by regulation and state ownership, and not yet affected by neoliberalism. The books (especially the first volume, *The White Mountains*) do indeed read along the lines of feudalism, though the society is more favourable to the 'peasants'. But the series takes these basic ideas and adds several new ingredients to position it as an ambiguous commentary on neoliberalism.

Ironically, some of the most Thatcherite aspects of the story are set up, not in the television series but in the prequel novel, published in 1988 – the Thatcher era – twenty years after the original books. It appears that Christopher was attentive to his critics, who questioned how the Tripods could have enslaved the human population when they were relatively vulnerable machines – they could be fired upon with missiles and easily subdued. In *When The Tripods Came* Christopher (2014d) outlines how the Tripods manage to take control, not by pure force, but with the art of persuasion. When the first Tripods are destroyed by military tactics they decide to beam a television series into the homes of everyone: *The Trippy Show*. This show, a mixture of music and sketches, contains a set of subliminal and hypnotic messages that compel people to worship the Tripods. Some of Christopher's book reads like satire – a parody of the theories of Marshall McLuhan and others – where people resort to violence if they are deprived of the latest episode of *The Trippy Show*. It brings to mind David Cronenberg's surreal *Videodrome* (1981) about a television station that broadcasts a cancer-inducing signal which drives people literally insane. Yet it also places us squarely inside a 1980s phenomenon: the dissemination of political messages through media outlets. Though she did use force on occasion, Thatcher understood, on the whole, that persuasion was the means by which people could be brought to a new political understanding.

We have seen how Arthur C. Clarke's novel *Childhood's End* served as a forerunner for series like *Quatermass and the Pit*, and

Doctor Who's 'The Daemons' (Seymore also connects the novel to *The Tripods*). Here another aspect of the novel is recalled in the idea of the benevolent dictators. In the case of *Childhood's End* the 'Overmind' has sent the alien race (known only as the Overlords) to Earth to watch over the humans in a way that is dictatorial, and in common with *The Tripods*, they end all wars and usher in an age of peace and prosperity. There is no necessary trade-off in *Childhood's End* apart from surrender to the Overlords. The endgame for which the overlords are preparing humanity is a relatively enlightened one – although Earth is eventually destroyed, this was apparently unavoidable, and the survivors (all children) have developed psionic powers, and are ushered to another world. They have progressed to the next stage of evolution, which they were always going to do provided they didn't destroy themselves first with a war or some other catastrophe. The Overlords were merely overseeing and facilitating this event. In *The Tripods*, although the machines also usher in an age of peace, the goal is very different: the Masters, aided in the series by the Cognoscs, have used Capping to create an age of ignorance, regression and conformity, in preparation for the annihilation of humankind.

The recipients of the Capping – that is, almost the entirety of humanity – accept and even welcome this process and look on The Tripods as their benefactors. Once Capped, an entire community is safe and secure, and able to live a simple but fulfilling life without fear of war, disease or poverty. Whatever yearning an individual might once have experienced is replaced with a contentment and sense of conformity. According to Ozymandias, a Cap robs one of a 'sense of wonder, curiosity, feelings of aggression and rebellion'. The trade-off made is a degree of freedom or autonomy for security and peace of mind, but like *Sapphire & Steel* it is ultimately an illusion. The reality – a brutal conquest of the entire human species – is seen clearly through the eyes of Will and his companions. Will's constant determination throughout is to resist at all costs. He sees the authentic road as the right one to take despite its difficulties. At one point in the first book, *The White Mountains*, he narrates: 'Nothing mattered, nothing was of value, without a mind that challenged and inquired' (Christopher, 2014c: 145). Similar territory is explored in Anthony Burgess's dystopian novel, *A Clockwork Orange* (1962), in which Alex, a violent and antisocial youth, is given a new drug and therapy which curtails his violent impulses, but in the process turns him into an automaton – a 'clockwork orange'. The message that it is better to be 'free' despite its many challenges and hardships is one that resonated with a great many young people at whom the books were aimed and, to reiterate Seymour's point, chimed particularly with 1960s youth.

The key to this trade-off – what we might consider the 'novum' in this story (along with the Tripods themselves) – is the Cap. The Cap serves as a metaphor for the many ways that societies have been controlled and regulated throughout history. The metaphor stands just as effectively for communism and dictatorships as it does for feudal societies. In each case a ruling power exerts its influence over a populace and demands devotion and loyalty. In some cases (such as North Korea) the populace is expected to show its joy and elation at being governed and controlled by this power. Every society under the regime of a dictator or pseudo-dictator has had its dissidents – those who speak out against the conditions under which they are subjugated. The more complex project is the hegemonic one: a society managed by a hegemonic power surrenders its autonomy to some extent, and does so willingly, usually because of perceived benefits. People are not subdued by military power, but by ideas. Messages are circulated around the media and other 'authoritative' sources which encourage citizens to conform in exchange for greater power or autonomy, or financial freedom. Gramsci was the first to posit that the ruling classes mobilise ideological views in their favour, in order to negotiate their position and to win consent over those whom they dominate. Thatcherism seized on this function of hegemony, masking and muting the contradictions of late capitalism and broadcasting her message through the institutions – the churches, the educational establishments and the media. Harvey comments on how the message in Thatcher's Britain eventually spread 'through the networks of class and privilege that had long connected government, academia, the judiciary, and the permanent Civil Service' (2005: 55), in a hegemonic process that he calls the 'construction of consent' (2005: 39). As a comparison to this contentment in Thatcherite society, the 'Capped' characters in *The Tripods* are happy, sometimes overjoyed, to surrender their autonomy to the Tripods for the 'utopian' lifestyle it affords them. Although the Cap becomes a kind of 'empty signifier' for the many ways people adapt and manage to live within a corrupt, mismanaged or unequal system, even coming to love and appreciate its benefits, the series, broadcast in the mid-1980s, makes itself most readily available for interpretation as a satire on Thatcherite society because the characters are only too happy to 'buy into' the means of their oppression.

The connections to the other series of the era become apparent as the series continues. The authoritarian power – the Masters themselves – deploy 'Black Guards': human representatives, to lay down a brutal form of social order. The Black Guards were created directly for the series, presumably to add a level of jeopardy absent in the books (they are often on the trail of Will and his friends). The Black Guards share some similarity with *Blake's 7*'s Federation Troopers, both visually (black-clad troopers) and metaphorically as a symbol of blunt, authoritarian power, redolent of Thatcher's enthusiasm for deploying the police. But the Black Guards are also, arguably, an extreme addition to what is advertised as a 'free' society. People are generally happy with their situation, yet they are occasionally faced with these neofascist enforcers. There is a contradiction here, but it's one that is similar to Thatcherite society, which advertised itself as a 'free' society despite the occasional appearance of police in full combat stance. Indeed, John Stalker, the Former Deputy Chief Constable of Greater Manchester, claimed in 2013 that in the 1980s Thatcher 'turned the police into a paramilitary force and put us on to a war footing' (para 1). Stalker claims that this war footing 'was never more clear than during the miners' strike in 1984 when I believe Margaret Thatcher took Britain to the brink of becoming a police state' (2013: para 6). In the world of *The Tripods*, there is certainly a hint that the free men are known about and must be stamped out, but it seems the level of menace and blunt power (as well as the aesthetic choice, to make them appear threatening and imposing) invested in the Black Guards is disproportionate. Through the Black Guards a dichotomy is made to which the series continually returns – that there is 'actual' terror, depicted through the Black Guards as a parody (or perhaps merely exaggeration) of the worst forms of authoritarianism – and there is 'soft' authority delivered by way of an apparently benign power. *The Tripods* invites us to see one (actual terror) as merely the visible face of the other, but the distinction would be lost to people in this world. They would see the Tripods as their benefactors and the Black Guards, separately, as merely the 'authorities'. This allows for both an apparent lack of authority (which leads to personal conflict) and authoritarianism at the same time.

In the middle block of episodes of the first season (episodes 5–8), Will and his friends are taken to Chateau Ricordeau, a French estate where people live a lifestyle somewhere between medieval and Napoleonic. The residents of the chateau – the Count and Countess, their staff, family and friends – take Will and his friends in and behave kindly towards them. In the television series Will and their daughter Eloise fall in love after she falls in the water and Will rescues her. Her parents are so impressed that they immediately decide Will (whom they rename Guillarme) should marry Eloise. This causes much discontent between Will and the Duc de Sarlat, Eloise's cousin and erstwhile suitor, who is suddenly deemed unworthy for her hand in marriage (the reasons for this sudden change are sketchy at best: he insisted they report the visitors to the Black Guards when they first arrived, which the Count considered a violation of his hospitality). Later Will discovers that Eloise has been Capped, and he is torn between love and disgust. He nonetheless stays, and the Count and Countess hold a party where they reveal Will and Eloise are betrothed. The events that follow demonstrate a neoliberal approach to human relations: chiefly the arbitrary nature of the 'workplace', and the Machiavellian behaviour of those pitted against each other.

The chateau holds a tournament – an annual event, which the Tripods sometimes attend. The Duc de Sarlat wins the tournament, earning him the right to name the 'Queen of the Festival', an honour which he bestows on Eloise. Will soon discovers that this means she is to serve the Tripods in 'The City of Gold', their mysterious purpose-built base. Eloise is euphoric about this development, despite the fact that it means she and Will must part. When she relays this information to Will she is in a state of transfixed and docile ecstasy, almost completely oblivious to the emotions that were strongly felt only moments earlier: their apparent love for each other. This honour of serving the Tripods is apparently so much more meaningful to her than their love, and completely eclipses any thoughts of marriage. She is taken up into the Tripod, and Will is left watching in despair. The Duc de Sarlat later admits to Will, 'What I cannot have, no one else shall have', and that he deliberately named her Queen of the Festival so that she and Will would have to part. He also admits that he never really loved Eloise – rather, his actions were motivated by pure envy and spite. He is not an ideological 'villain' or an arch manipulator with a grand scheme; he is simply concerned with his individual standing and egotistical self-interest. He is the 'worker' whose 'bonus' was promised and then, due to an arbitrary restructure, was lost, and so he resorted to Machiavellian tactics to ensure his own continuity. He even wishes Will a happy life with someone else and leaves their quarrel at that.

The novel does not present the above romantic triangle. There is in fact no love story at all, though Will and Eloise are very friendly. When Eloise is named Queen of the Festival in the book, she is equally happy, but has less to lose. She and Will are already drifting apart (as soon as Will notices her Cap he is horrified, and can no longer view her wholly as a friend) and there was never any love story as such, or rivalry (the Duc de Sarlat was a character created for the series). The series, however, confuses and fragments the narrative by artificially introducing a love triangle in an absurdly short space of time, rendering many of the exchanges incoherent. There is no obvious reason why the Duc de Sarlat is not worthy as Eloise's suitor, and yet he is cast aside as soon as Will arrives on the scene. Indeed the Duc is the champion of the tournament, and though he cheats slightly Eloise doesn't seem to mind – she even commends him for it. There is even less reason, from the Count and Countess's point of view, why Will should be her suitor – he saves her life, and she falls in love with him, but from her parents' point of view he is merely an English 'commoner'. Nonetheless they name the two as betrothed without even much regard to their own feelings about it. Finally when she is named as Queen of the Tournament, Eloise has no compunction about abandoning any plans of marriage to Will in order to serve the Tripods.

Eloise's brainwashed joy at being chosen as a servant of the Tripods is more pronounced in the series than the book. In the book she appears to Will before being taken away by the Tripods and tells him what this 'honour' means, to Will's complete incomprehension:

> She said, 'When you are called you will understand.'
> 'I will not be Capped!'
> 'You will understand' (Christopher, 2014c: 158)

In the series, Will must procure his information while chasing her and a procession of admirers towards the Tripod itself:

> ELOISE: The tournament Queen must serve the Tripods. It is always so.
> WILL: How? Where?
> ELOISE: In the City of Gold. It is the supreme honour ... goodbye Guillarme. You will understand ... when you're Capped you'll understand.
> WILL: No!
> ELOISE: I'm so happy. Remember me.
> WILL: No, Eloise!
> ELOISE: I will remember you.

In many ways the television version of events mimics the neoliberal tendency to encourage Machiavellian behaviour, and to fragment daily existence and 'rewrite the script' on a regular basis. The workplace has become a site of discontinuity, to which employees have simply had to adapt, and while the maximisation of profit is the original goal of neoliberalism, this behaviour bleeds into everyday existence. Von Dirke discusses the loss of traditional authority in a neoliberal environment, replaced with authoritarianism. This is all for the maximisation of profit – workers are replaced as their existence becomes too expensive, sometimes rehired on temporary contracts, and the instability created promotes duplicitous behaviour (2017: 330). Fisher describes how, in the neoliberal environment, 'no decision is final, revisions are always possible, and any previous moment can be recalled at any time' (2009: 40). He then discusses a middle manager who

> turned adaptation to this 'fungible' reality it into a fine art. He asserted with full confidence a story about the college and its future one day – what the implications of the inspection were likely to be; what senior management was thinking; then *literally the next day*

would happily propound a story that directly contradicted what he previously said. There was never a question of his *repudiating* the previous story; it was as if he only dimly remembered there ever being another story. (2009: 40)

Promises made in the morning are ignored in the afternoon. Enemies become friends with little rationale, and vice versa. Relationships shatter in seconds for reasons that appear to be arbitrary. This leads to a fragmentary mode of living, where there is no continuity, only the illusion. To underline this point, after Eloise is taken by the Tripods her parents seem almost unable to even recall her existence. Will tries to extract answers from them – what they feel about her loss – but only receives a kind of dull pride in their departed daughter. They insist all the same that Will stays, despite the reason for his staying now having been removed.

While sexual rivalry and competition are nothing new, and certainly can exist in a feudal society, there is a marked difference here: the Duc de Sarlat is motivated by jealousy – not necessarily jealousy of Will per se, but of what Will represents: the illogical and unfair manner in which he, the Duc, has been usurped. The arbitrariness of both the Duc's loss of position and his solution to the problem, and of Eloise's willing acceptance of her new role as a servant of the Tripods (and indeed her family's submission, even joy, at this development) tends to mimic the arbitrary nature of neoliberalism. The Duc's anxiety at his loss echoes the neoliberal tendency, which puts 'each individual "at persistent risk of failure, redundancy and abandonment through no doing of its own, regardless of how savvy and responsible it is"' (von Dirke, 2017: 329). The logical response is jealousy, and that jealousy spurs a sense of unhealthy competition and duplicitous behaviour. With a lack of regulating authority to curb this behaviour, it is allowed to run riot.

But this behaviour also runs counter to the logic of the series. Ozymandias claimed in the beginning that the Caps limit one's aggressive behaviour, yet the Duc de Sarlat, who must have been Capped himself, displays highly aggressive behaviour. In displaying his Machiavellian tendencies, the Duc de Sarlat is demonstrating an (albeit sinister) degree of creative thought in his scheming to deprive Will and Eloise of their love. The tournament itself, while remaining within the confines of a game, is a rehearsal for war, so the Caps seem not to have curtailed the human tendency for conflict. Later, when Will and his friends go to the White Mountains, they are trained up to compete in the tournaments, which involve aggressive sports like boxing. Will trains in boxing, then gets into a fight in a tavern. So it seems once again that the caps serve here as a metaphor for not only hegemony but some of the excesses of capitalism and its effects on the mind. One sees the way the people are adapting to their new reality and all its inconsistencies, and some are turning it to their advantage. Their Caps may limit them, but they have turned their attention (and aggression) to more petty and selfish endeavours.

To some extent the abrupt changes in the story may be ascribed to the Caps which all characters wear. Perhaps their minds are conditioned to place less value in love than service, or to ignore tradition (or accept the Tripods' reconstructed 'official' version of history) for the sake of contentment. It is never clear what the parameters of the Caps are. Presumably their two basic functions are to limit aggression and produce a sense of overwhelming devotion to the Tripods, necessitating a complete ignorance of history. Yet when Will is at the engagement party he is reminded by a nobleman, the Compte de Saclay, 'Your origins … were humble in your native land … I applaud your greater fortunes.' He later discusses his delight that the Tripods destroyed the 'evil' city of Paris, reflecting his absorption of hegemonic ideas that have drifted down from the Tripods themselves. On the one hand tradition is of little to no significance to the Compte, and on the other his 'breeding' and 'class' still matter to him, even though the roots of this breeding and class are now lost in time, belonging to a world he condemns. This is another example of hegemony: he has bought into the rhetoric of liberation from evil and given his tacit consent to the Tripods to rule, ingesting and reproducing their ideas. This is achieved in part by the Compte's sense of belonging. There is a kind of 'common sense' at play here in the Gramscian form: a cementing of cognitive dissonance. The characters in *The Tripods* retain what they consider to be 'titles', evidence of an aristocratic past. This past has been manufactured to fit a certain narrative, as the Tripods here have literally erased the original past. The Tripods seldom interfere directly in human lives, leaving a gulf of authority and meaning, which is filled, at least in the television series, by adherence to meaningless shards of 'tradition'.

When Will (and his friend Fritz, the name perhaps deliberately echoing Fritz Lang, director of *Metropolis*) enter the City of Gold in Season 2, they discover a world that is a much more explicit mirror of fascism, but also has strong neoliberal tendencies. The City of Gold is the power centre of the Tripods, and it's here that a social order has been created which is entirely absent from the source material, Christopher's book, *The City of Gold and Lead*. The series has invented a kind of stratified reality of bourgeois oppression. Inside the city, young people are selected to be 'slaves': sent there to serve the Masters. Down in the pits the workers are brutally supervised by the Black Guards. Many of these young people are forced to carry out back-breaking labour, and are whipped by the Guards if they falter. It is never explained to what extent their Caps allow them to believe they are enjoying what is blatant torture.

The Masters are in fact closer to white-collar employees. They are assigned jobs which, to Will, seem entirely futile. Their 'employers' are the Cognoscs. Some exceptional humans have been assigned to maintain a defunct power station, which the Masters are trying to utilise as their power source. They are allowed to frequent a 1980s-style night club with disco lights. The Masters and these power station employees, then, are the professional class – the bourgeoisie. Von Dirke discusses the idea posited by Mark Siemons, that the bourgeois workers in a neoliberal environment are similar to the demiurge in Greek mythology:

> the demiurge is only a half-god who is never the creator of matter but only a facilitator or, in other words, a technical virtuoso who orders and shapes the universe from the already existing matter according to another authority's design. (von Dirke, 2017: 336)

In other words, the white-collar worker is always subject to a higher authority – the disembodied marketplace itself. In the series, the disembodied 'marketplace', the regulator of ideas, are the Cognoscs, which are the true power. Will is taken to meet the Cognosc, and is on good terms with it (for reasons that are somewhat illogical). This disembodied authority at the top of the hierarchy is literally a nonentity, without corporeal form but at the top of the neoliberal ladder.

There is still a kind of feudal structure in the series, but by the time the series comes along it is more subtle than Christopher outlines in his original books. The kings and nobility are not authoritative powers in this world – they are as remote as anyone else. Like our world they have been reduced to mere symbols of authority and order, their titles honorary only. There is much more apparent prosperity than in a feudal society. There are peasants, but they tend to live well, and all are equally subjugated to the power of the Tripods. There is a sense, too, of fascism, as represented by the Black Guards. But what makes it resonate with a neoliberal world is that the Tripods' control is welcomed, and within their narrow parameters the people feel themselves to be free. The Tripods behave, not as an authority in the interventionist sense, but as authoritarian – rarely physically there but always present, literally controlling the thoughts of the populace from a distance.

In updating the series to a Thatcherite context, the writers (Alick Rowe for Series 1, Christopher Penfold for Series 2) have added many new plot elements. In some cases these new elements complement the source material, but in many cases they confuse it. The new material emphasises the trends that had become apparent in the neoliberal Thatcher era: fascistic guards, noncorporeal entities that resemble the neoliberal marketplace, and a fragmented and illogical sense of time and place, echoing the neoliberal tendency to create an incoherent reality comprised of shards of one's life without an overarching or regulating authority.

6

'It Won't be Easy': original science fiction series of the 1980s

The much-maligned title sequence for *Star Cops* (1987), Chris Boucher's ill-fated space-detective series, features a pop song: 'It Won't be Easy', by Justin Hayward of the Moody Blues. It was increasingly difficult in the 1980s to produce original content, written directly for television, especially science fiction. Market forces and Thatcher's interventions combined with a general lack of faith in the genre (at least in the British context) and resulted in a dearth of original content. The previous chapter briefly discussed the way in which science fiction television (and all television) was compromised artistically in the Thatcher era because of the move towards privatisation, the relatively cheap access to American-made series, and the artistic constraints applied to writers, producers and directors. This new environment was particularly difficult for science fiction.

As such, in that era there were only two notable science fiction drama series written directly for the British screen: *Star Cops* (1987) and *Knights of God* (1987). The two series, broadcast on the BBC and ITV respectively, are nearly polar opposites of each other, and both present a very different engagement with the Thatcherite landscape. But in a sense both series are reflections of each other. One is steeped in mythology, fantasy and allegory, while the other is apparently stripped of any. One embraces the neoliberal fantasy of the hero narrative, already drenched in imperialism, while the other pushes for the postmodern world view of 'a return to the real'. Both are informed by a certain neoliberal world view. Neoliberalism (especially in the Thatcher era) trades both in fantasy – the fantasy of the individual hero called to greatness – and also strips away fantasies and delusions and attempts to present the world 'as it really is'. These series attack both ends of this spectrum.

Knights of God (1987)

Apparently produced for children, *Knights of God* contains disturbing and arresting images and ideas more appropriate to adults. It deals with the neoliberal challenge by resorting to symbolism and fantasy, and locating its struggle at least partly in ecclesiastical terms. It deploys the myth of King Arthur to advocate for the traditional values of Britain – the Church, the military and the monarchy – and suggests that Britain's social problems can find their cure in a return to a conservative past. Similar to *Survivors*, but with much greater emphasis on tradition, the series strongly venerates the benign leadership of a monarch, bolstered by a robust Church, and with the armed forces at that monarch's command. The series trumpets a loud and unapologetic nationalism that a strongly traditional Tory would find agreeable. Thatcher herself was ambivalent about the Royal Family, uncomfortable with the contemporaneous Church, and if anything she was radically modern in her economic outlook. On the other hand, she was deeply religious, and a supporter of Victorian Britain and its 'moral virtues'. *Knights of God* is somewhat unambiguous, but because of the ambiguities and tensions of Thatcherism and neoliberalism there is a sense that both sides of the argument – the clash between the authoritarian Knights and the traditional values used to push back against them – are mobilised to produce a contradictory engagement with Thatcherism and neoliberalism.

The series was produced by Southern Television (TVS). It was shown only once, in 1987, before the regional company was absorbed into ITV. There are various possible reasons why it was not repeated. The website Pop Culture Retrorama suggests:

> The late '80s saw something of a surge of Welsh nationalism, with some proponents advocating a complete split from the UK. It's possible that TVS opted not to repeat the series in this environment, where scenes such as Gervase Edwards (Owen's son) being prodded through

a prison camp and being called a 'Welsh git' might have inflamed sensibilities. (Green, 2020: para 5)

In any case, the series was no doubt designed to be repeated. The production values are high: it is shot entirely on film, lending it a cinematic quality, and avoiding the feel of a studio. There is a very strong aesthetic sense which anchors the viewer in the dystopian world. A burning Union Jack is the first image of Episode 1, followed by rows of jackbooted 'Knights' marching in sync. The Knights are dressed in black uniforms, similar to the Black Guards in *The Tripods* and the Federation troopers in *Blake's 7*, and sometimes wear long flowing capes. Even in the Knights' headquarters, full of stone and metal, there is a foreboding sensibility that would work only on film. This effect would have been lost had video been used, enhancing reflective surfaces so that studio lights bounce off them. There are many realistic scenes of armed fighting, involving machinery and explosions. In terms of verisimilitude this elevates the series above the majority of British science fiction television.

It is set in a radically altered England (now called Anglia) in 2020. At the helm is the fanatical Prior Mordrin. His second-in-command is the treacherous Hugo (played by Julian Fellowes, who would later create *Downton Abbey*). Even more of a psychopath than Mordrin, Hugo is responsible for the execution of the Royal Family. They call themselves the Knights of God because they have adopted a fundamentalist version of an Old Testament-inspired religion to counter what Mordrin views as the 'weakness' of Christianity. They have managed to secure most of what was England except for some of the north, which they call the wastelands. In Wales, which hasn't yet been conquered by the Knights, there are several factions of rebels, overseen by the mysterious Arthur. One faction is led by Owen Edwards. Owen's son Gervase is apprehended by the Knights and sent to their re-education camps. There he meets Julia and they become a couple.

Early on it becomes reasonably clear to the viewer that *Knights of God* is a modern version of the King Arthur myth, with a few alterations: Mordrin is Mordred; Arthur is not the titular king: in this version he is elderly, and more like a Merlin character. He is indeed Mordrin's father (though John Woodvine, who played

Modrin, and Patrick Troughton who played Arthur, were only nine years apart in age and looked like contemporaries). There is a strong suggestion that the symbolism of the king returning to his people is enough to restore order. Gervase reluctantly, and then enthusiastically, accepts his fate as the king. Late in the series he is sent (by the Archbishop of Canterbury) to an island not unlike Avalon, where monks confer upon him the title of King and explain that when his family was slaughtered by the Knights, Gervase was spared and given to Owen to raise. Gervase and Julia sail back to the mainland on a boat with a Union Jack flapping in the wind, gifted to them by the monks. Upon his return to Wales he delivers a rousing speech at the rebel base, introduced by Julia's father, the Brigadier, and broadcast on the radio to all the land. After the speech, the assembled all sing 'God save the King' with reverence. By this stage, in the Knights' headquarters, Hugo has betrayed Mordrin and is mounting his own attack, but he finds it is too late – the people have learned that the king is alive, and almost the mere fact of this seems to be enough to destroy the Knights. The rebels mount an attack on the base, which, coupled with the Knights' own internal power vacuum, is enough to defeat them. There is no critique of the idea of the king as a figurehead around whom the nation can unite, and the one who will overthrow tyranny. Gervase does little more than deliver a rousing speech by the end of the series, and yet the symbolic weight of his return as the king sends the Knights into irreversible disarray.

Although the series begins by presenting a revolutionary world of armed resistance against an authoritarian power, calling to mind the same kinds of struggles that inspired *Blake's 7* (and indeed Gareth Thomas, Blake in *Blake's 7*, plays Owen, which tempts the viewer to imagine this series as a kind of prequel to *Blake's 7*), it soon devolves into a deeply conservative fantasy. The King Arthur story forms a nationalistic view of Britain. Its use as a story of the individual who united a nation is all too easy to absorb into a narrative that is suffused with conservative and right-wing elements. There are aspects of other influences too. There is an echo of the English Civil War, especially in the fact that after winning the war, Cromwell died and his son was not equal to the task of governing England. Consequently Charles II, in exile in France, was reinstated as the King, inserted retroactively into the history of England as if the war never took place. This of course furnished the nationalistic myth that England cannot survive without a monarchy, something that *Knights of God* treats as axiomatic: a natural fact. There is also a hint of the Russian Revolution in the sense that the Russian Imperial Family were executed but the legend persisted that Anastasia, the young daughter, escaped. All of these influences come to bear on what is essentially a neoliberal British hero-myth – a tale of the gifted individual, the 'chosen one', imbued with near-mystical powers who takes on the weight of an entire nation. These overtones make *Knights of God* a fascinating, if disturbing, study in the way that Establishment forces, Thatcherite policies and neoliberal ideas cohere into a grand metaphorical statement about British (or perhaps merely English) nationalist superiority in the face of traumatic social change. In calling on these forces to vanquish the onslaught of darkness, the series becomes a straightforward Manichean story of good and evil, while providing a somewhat ambiguous commentary on Thatcherism and neoliberalism. This section will discuss the way the series, through a relatively simple storyline, throws up several contradictory positions.

This basic hero-myth structure draws from a more generalised sense of mythology derived from Joseph Campbell's writings in *The Hero with a Thousand Faces* (1949). Campbell called himself a 'mythologist'. Informed by Jung's studies of the collective unconscious, he studied the world's myths and discovered to his satisfaction that they all exhibited strong similarities. He combined them into what he called the 'monomyth'. Campbell, building on the work of Jung and others, posited that all myths and religions are merely expressions of archetypes contained within our subconscious, and these archetypes are largely the same for all of us. He said to Bill Moyers, 'Essentially it might even be said that there is but one archetypal mythic hero whose life has been replicated in many lands by many people' (qtd in Lefkowitz, 1990: 430). As well as drawing admirers, Campbell's work has been much criticised for its shortcomings. For one, Campbell's reductive notion of the monomyth seeks to collapse all myths into one, and in doing so ignores the central importance of the specificity of culture (as evidenced by the quote above). There is indeed a strong Western (imperial) bias to his view of mythology. Koven writes, 'while superficially appearing to be egalitarian, [it] is in actuality, purely colonial: only from a point of cultural hegemony can one hold one's culture up as a template for other cultures and say that they are more or less the same' (2007: 9). Campbell has also been criticised for the implicit neoliberal tendencies of his work – the glorifying of the individual. Lefkowitz expresses this concern when asking, 'Wasn't Campbell really endorsing selfish materialism when he recommended to his viewers that they each "follow their own bliss"?' (1990: 429).

Perhaps because of the above reasons, Campbell deeply influenced George Lucas, whose *Star Wars* trilogy presents its own hero-myth, with many Arthurian themes included, and the success of *Star Wars* (1977) led to Hollywood's near-universal embracing of Campbell's work, a short version of which became known as 'The Hero's Journey'. This gave rise to what is now the standard neoliberal Hollywood narrative – the exceptional individual, the 'chosen one', who stands above governments to contend with higher forces, taking authority into his own hands, while leaving the basic social order unchanged. The neoliberal story is often Manichean: in many versions the villain is so comically evil that it would be impossible to compare it with real-world situations – see the Empire in the *Star Wars* universe, or HYDRA in the Marvel Cinematic Universe. This allows for an individualistic hero to exemplify everything 'good', while exhibiting his own 'tragic flaw'. This storyline provides the spine of action movies ranging from *Die Hard* (1988) to *The Matrix* (1999) to the *Harry Potter* film series (2001–11) and beyond.

Another reference that *Knights of God* makes is to Frank Herbert's *Dune* (1965), which presents the story of a boy from a royal house who has been displaced, exiled from his home and stripped of his title, and must fight to emerge as the true king (importantly, Herbert went on to apply critical pressure to the concept of the hero and the chosen one in later books). This, and the other reference points, rest on the neoliberal notion that the people are in need of an exceptionally talented individual, and this individual is more important than governments or the people (see Spencer, 2018). However, *Knights of God* does depart from the classic neoliberal tale in two respects. Firstly, the hero in Campbell's formulation has been so altered by his journey that he can never 'return' to his original state or physical home, and must leave. It's clear that Gervase will stay and reign over his people as king – but it is also clear, as in 'The Hero's Journey', that he can never properly return to his small Welsh village in an emotional sense. Secondly, the neoliberal hero usually does little or nothing to change the social order or to participate in political movements. Gervase claims in his speech that he believes in democracy and will reinstate it when he is King.

Even more so than *Survivors*, symbolism plays a vital role in the series. Towards the end, Hugo betrays Mordrin. In the final confrontation between the two, cinematically lit and framed, Hugo is reaching for the crown (that presumably once belonged to the monarch) when Mordrin throws a knife in Hugo's back before he can seize it. His shadow dances around the stone background, lending an operatic sense to the melodrama. As he dies from a knife in the back, Hugo says to his assassin, 'I told you: the boy would kill us all.' Mordrin, now driven half mad, takes the crown out of his dead lieutenant's hands and says, 'Not for you. You aren't worthy.' None of this makes sense on a literal level: the boy, Gervase, has not killed them except in the sense that his very appearance as King has driven them mad. The crown is merely a symbol here: all is lost, and the only utility the crown itself has is to confer a kind of metaphorical power on its wearer. Mordrin is denied even that, as he is later killed by his own father Arthur before he manages to place it on his own head. Had he managed, of course, nothing would have changed, as the crown is merely symbolic. *Survivors* also suggests that the power of the King lies not within the man, nor is it even contingent on him remaining alive. The power rests on the symbolic status of the office itself: the fact that Britain has a king is more important than any qualities (including breathing) that the King possesses. In Lacanian terms, the symbolic refers to the world of language, where language shapes meaning. Fisher references Žižek's example of the judge who speaks, and 'when he speaks, it is the Law itself which speaks through him' (qtd in Fisher, 2009: 48), so that we are encouraged to accept the authority, not of the man who is flawed and weak as any other man, but of the authority – the symbolic power – of the idea he represents and mediates through himself. When Gervase speaks, the ancient tradition of British monarchy flows through him, but in a way that feels especially contrived, as Gervase is effectively transformed simply by the revelation of his identity. The institutions of British power, through Gervase, are contained within talisman-like objects like the crown and the flag, imbuing their owners with symbolic power. This contrasts somewhat with the controversial ending of the hugely successful television version of *Game of Thrones* (2011–19). After years of fighting for the throne of Westeros, Drogon, the pet dragon of the now dead Daenerys, melts the throne with his fire-breath. The destruction of that throne, for years the very symbol of the highest monarchy in the land, indicates the futility of the quest for its domination. In *Knights of God* the crown has the opposite quality: it is an object so sacred that its proper use encapsulates everything important about monarchy.

Thatcherism, as we know, rests on contradictory assumptions. On the one hand it is a return to traditional Victorian morality. Thatcher was constantly calling to mind the Victorians as her models of British 'greatness'. She certainly understood the value of symbolism. She was religious herself, and approved of the Church, but criticised it around several social issues (and that criticism was returned, as this chapter will soon discuss). On the other hand, she was nothing if not a radical force for change, and her neoliberal tendencies contradicted the traditionalist aspects of her policies. Through her Realpolitik approach (earning the moniker 'The Iron Lady', which she relished) and her mobilisation of the police and military, Thatcher came very close to authoritarianism. But she also carefully positioned herself as the *antidote* to authoritarianism, especially during the Falklands War, which will be discussed shortly. Thatcher's contradictory political 'philosophy' is played out, to an extent, on both sides of the debate found in *Knights of God*, which is at core a contest between two different modes of right-wing authority: the deeply authoritarian and the traditional. Thatcher drew a little from both stalls, but also added economic radicalism, which this series does not discuss. But inasmuch as Thatcher is 'represented', Gervase proves himself to be the 'ideal' Thatcherite hero. Something of a synthesis of various right-wing positions, Gervase is a strongly individualistic hero in the neoliberal mould, but he also advocates for traditional values.

The writer, Richard Cooper, was himself a deeply committed Catholic. Although it seems that the series, with the Knights of God themselves fuelled by a religious dogma of firm authoritarian leadership, might be a comment on the oppressive nature of religion, it ends with a simple assertion that religion is not itself the problem, but in fact the solution. Rather than replacing religion with a new order, it proposes to replace a domineering, oppressive religion with the more civilised, embracing and perhaps even liberal religion of High Anglicanism. Early on, the children of Welsh rebels are rounded up by the Knights and taken to re-education camps. In an echo of the school scene in *The Tripods*, the children are subjected to a lesson by one of the Knights:

> The year 2000 – twenty years ago: a momentous year, when the great revival in religious belief reached its climax. We now know that most Christians were very mistaken, misguided people. But it took one man to show us this. One great man. Our inspired leader: Prior Mordrin. He saw that Christianity was a religion for slaves, for weaklings, and he founded a true religion: worshipping a god of power, strength, and vengeance ... at the end of the 20th Century there was massive unemployment and a deep, bitter envy of the North for the South, and this led to unrest and riots, violence, arson and murder in those northern cities. It was Prior Mordrin and the men who gathered round him who fought to restore law and order. And when the civil war broke out, it was Prior Mordrin and his knights who defeated those forces and provoked an insurrection. Every day you should go down on your knees thanking God for that man.

It is not entirely clear which God Mordrin worships, but it is most likely the Old Testament version of Jehovah/Yahweh. Tim Munro, in an early review, writes, 'Cooper calls it a warning against rightwing, "God-is-on-our-side," religious cults, and the Knights are such a body' (1988: para 16). But the series is itself right wing – perhaps centre right rather than hard right – with its recommendation of a return to a highly traditional country, its Manichean world view and its central Arthurian hero-myth. Cooper's position – that the traditional (Christian) God is a bulwark against the dark forces of fascism – can be discerned by Gervase's rousing speech, broadcast to the country as his maiden speech as King: 'I'm praying very hard that the good loving God will bless us in all the things we have to do in this, our great hour of need.' The speech has some of the cadences of Churchill, Thatcher's great hero, and also foregrounds the 'loving' God as the antidote to the wrathful god of the Knights.

The strong advocacy of Christianity in the piece points to debates that were prominent in the 1980s around the role of the Church. Cooper's approach to these issues lies in the Knight's words: 'Christianity was a religion for slaves, for weaklings.' This reflects, to an extent, the perceived 'weakness' of the Anglican Church in the view of moral campaigners of the 1980s. The implicit suggestion is that when the Church is weak on social issues, it creates a space for a dictator to step in. What is needed then is a reform of the Church along more traditional lines. Though in reality the Church's influence had been waning for decades, it nonetheless became the site of various political altercations in the 1980s. The Anglican church was never particularly supportive of Thatcher, who did indeed perceive weakness in its ranks. Early in her tenure the Church published a document called *Faith in the City* (Central Board of Finance of the Church of England, 1985), implicitly criticising Thatcherite policies. The tension rarely wavered. As the 1980s rolled on, the Church was criticised by socially conservative commentators (including Mary Whitehouse, the infamous campaigner for moral decency in the media) for its moral laxity. It appeared to relent on issues of divorce and remarriage and women in the clergy, and it became very confused over the issue of homosexuality (see Filby, 2015: 223–5). In the storm of the AIDS pandemic, this became a prominent social issue. In all these areas the Church had become something of a scapegoat – Thatcher targeted it, blaming it implicitly for not providing adequate leadership and allowing for moral lapses. As Filby writes:

> The moral lobby fuelled the right-wing notion that collectivism, liberalism and moral breakdown were inextricably linked when they were noticeably silent on the pernicious forces of consumerism, the free-market and the culture of individualism which arguably were as much to blame. (2015: 208)

The Church then, (along with other institutions), became an easy target to mask the more deleterious effects of capitalism.

In the later years of her administration Thatcher began to understand the accusation levelled at her government, that monetarism could be perceived as leading to amoral outcomes. She had always maintained that neoliberal practices are deeply moral, even resorting to scripture to illustrate her point. As many others have pointed out (see for example Filby, 2015: 85), she often recited the parable of the Good Samaritan in service of this very point. As early as 1968 she gave a speech which included the claim:

> Even the Good Samaritan had to have the money to help, otherwise he too would have had to pass on the other side. (Thatcher, 1968: sec. 6, para 42)

She clarified this point in an interview in 1980, in which she said:

> No one would remember the Good Samaritan if he'd only had good intentions; he had money as well. (Thatcher, 1980b: sec.1, para 116)

To strengthen her personal resolve she turned to various authorities, including her adviser Brian Griffiths, who made a somewhat confused case for monetarism as the most morally upright ideological position (in opposition to socialism). Filby notes, 'Griffiths was not simply forwarding an ethical case for capitalism, but an explicitly Christian one' (2015: 236). Griffiths made a distinction between the accumulation of wealth (which was a moral good) and the worship of wealth (which was a sin) (see Filby, 2015: 236–7). Another writer to whom Thatcher turned was the American theologian Michael Novak, who also saw morality in capitalism. Filby writes that Thatcher was most taken with 'Novak's contention that the Democratic capitalist system was not just an economic system but also a moral one which encouraged both individual virtue and crucially mutual cooperation' (237–8). All of this speaks to an uneasy and contradictory alignment between religion and the marketplace, and the relationship between the players on either side was in many instances contentious.

Thatcher had an antagonistic relationship with the then-Archbishop of Canterbury, Robert Runcie, who occupied the post from 1980–91. In a documentary made by his son James, Runcie claimed, 'For me there was a government that was successful in strengthening the economy and dealing with the unions and yet at the same time I could look out of the window at Lambeth Palace and see the fires of Brixton burning' (qtd in Bates, 2000: para 8). In *Knights of God* the fictional Archbishop is something of a hero. When he meets Gervase and Julia he asks, 'Tell me: do you believe in the real God, before the Knights perverted the meaning of that word?' Gervase replies that he does. Later, when Gervase is attacked by some of Hugo's thugs, the Archbishop intervenes and rescues him, but dies in the process.

In a sense the series' advocacy of Christianity is an empty signifier: it does not specify what the connection may be between the Church and society's problems, nor does it examine the Church's approach to neoliberalism. It never makes any claim about the Church as a liberal or conservative force. Instead the Church stands in the abstract as a signifier of decency and social cohesion, and a balm against the forces of evil. The Archbishop's direct question about belief may be the exception – in this case the series seems to be stating very clearly that a sincere belief in God is an essential foundation for a good society (a position taken by Edmund Burke [1729–97], who is often regarded as one of the primary shapers of conservatism). The Archbishop's strong opposition to the Knights could simply be read as a reflection of Runcie's critical attitude to Thatcher. Nonetheless there is no discussion about how belief is translated into social action, and thus the series can sidestep the more difficult questions that were appearing in Britain at the time, around the Church's waning leadership over important social issues, and Thatcher's disapproval of Runcie and what he stood for – an increasingly liberal and inclusive approach to social issues.

The Knight's 're-education' speech is notable for other reasons, related to authoritarianism. He teaches, 'at the end of the 20th Century there was massive unemployment ... and this led to unrest and riots, violence, arson and murder in those Northern cities'. The riots that took place in the 1980s were not confined to the northern cities, but some of the issues raised in the speech are approximations of the reality of Thatcher's era. The cause that the Knight proposes for all this is Christianity. The real-world riots were in fact much more closely connected to the

Thatcher administration's many neoliberal changes, which left people unemployed and socially disadvantaged.

The 1981 riots, in Brixton (South London), Birmingham, Leeds and Liverpool, were undertaken by largely ethnic minorities – either immigrants, or children of immigrants – from the Commonwealth. In each case, the riots arose from a base of people who lived in poor housing areas and undertook low-paid manual jobs. The Scarman report, commissioned to enquire into the causes of the Brixton riot, concluded that 'racial disadvantage' and 'racial discrimination', mainly from ethnic minorities from the Commonwealth, were the cause (John, 2006: sec. 2, para 18). Thatcher's response to this crisis, similar to Mordrin's, was to reinforce the authoritarian aspect of her administration, praising the police as the antidote to violence and disorder. Later, in 1985, there were more riots in Brixton and other parts of London, with many of the same themes around disaffected immigrant communities.

In *Knights of God* the Knights represent authoritarianism and tyranny, while the 'good' rebels are almost flawless in their pursuit of truth and freedom, and they have the forces of traditional British Establishment on their side. Thatcher too recreated Britain in Manichean terms, with some of the same heroes and villains. O'Shaughnessy writes:

> Thatcherism rewrites the language of politics, renarrates the national past and disqualifies all other voices. Thatcherism presents itself as a Manichean battle for freedom and truth. (1996: 297)

In her rhetoric, she changed the terms of debate from the Consensus era, and in doing so constructed the myth of the 'good' citizen and 'evil' enemy. As O'Shaughnessy writes, 'The social democratic period of compromise between labour and capitalism between 1945 and the 1970s is renamed socialism' (1996: 297). Together with the socialists are the Soviets, engaged in their evil and undemocratic pursuit of power. The antidote to socialism is what Thatcher calls freedom, which is only realised in economic terms. O'Shaughnessy notes:

> This linkage of individual freedom with free enterprise and labelling of the post-war period as anti-enterprise state socialism is crucial to

the Thatcherite reordering of national history. It allows a campaign for free market liberalism to present itself as a war of national liberation, an attempt to restore freedom to a freedom-loving people (1996: 297)

Thatcher, therefore, would not have identified with Mordrin, the dictator who is seeking to rob people of freedom. She was especially careful to distinguish herself from a tyrannical figure, and align herself to Churchill and other 'emancipatory' figures. In mythologising the Falklands War, Thatcher exercised what Monaghan calls 'the rigid polarities of such moral absolutes as good and evil' (1998: 7). In her rhetoric Thatcher managed to characterise Galtieri's Argentinian junta as 'evil', with the British forces as the good necessary to dispel them. She even went so far as to compare Galtieri to Hitler, and therefore implicitly to compare herself to Churchill: 'When you stop a dictator there are always risks, but there are great risks in not stopping a dictator. My generation learned that a long time ago' (Thatcher, 1982: sec. 1, para 18; also see Monaghan, 1998: pp 15–26). In running the Falklands campaign, Thatcher was in some senses framing herself as the successor to Churchill. In doing so she was able to evoke the images of the Second World War and the sense of Empire and patriotism inherent. Procter comments:

> Through the image of Churchill, Thatcher evoked Britain's earlier 'principled' battle against Nazi Germany and along with it connotations of the nation's past imperial greatness: Britain as a bulldog breed that could once more rule the waves. The nostalgic language of Empire within which Thatcher couched the Falklands campaign was resoundingly popular with the British electorate. (2004: 100)

Once again recalling the past and pressing it into service in the present, Thatcher rendered the myth of 'Great Britain' alive again, and stripped it of historical context.

Thatcher's process of reaching back into the past to evoke a kind of nostalgia was an effective strategy during the Falklands. Her embrace of Victorian ideals has been discussed already, including the associated ideas of Britain's chivalric past. Monaghan calls to attention her speech to ITV in April 1982, where she said, 'We must go out calmly, quietly to succeed' (Thatcher, 1982: sec. 1, para 24), pointing out that she even 'loosely paraphrased' Queen Victoria in her speech about the Boer War (despite the fact that they were defeated) (1998: 11). Monaghan notes that Thatcher created 'a discourse constructed around phrases such as "our heritage" and "our great past", so the real world gave way to myth, the secular to the sacred and history to essence and timelessness' (1998: 3). Thatcher aimed to create that sense of 'nostalgic tradition'. The 'contemporary state ... dissolves into the "ancient nation". Britain, a rural paradise, [is] structured around the patriarchal family and a well-defined social hierarchy' (Monaghan, 1998: 3). In using terms like 'our heritage' and 'great past', as Monaghan comments, 'Thatcher could rely on conjuring up a network of images' (1998: 18) but in an abstract way (an 'empty signifier' into which people can project their own visions). These images of Victorian heroes are again archetypal, calling upon a collective memory and tapping into deeply held convictions of nationhood and identity.

A straightforwardly conservative fantasy about the vanquishing of 'evil' in the person of a neofascist dictator, and a return to a more traditional England flooded with mythical symbolism, would then appear to be a ringing endorsement of Thatcherism. Thatcher was certainly a proponent of the Victorian era, and this series in a sense advocates for a return to that form of social structure. But Thatcher worked hard to distance her administration's aims from the version of conservatism that had preceded them. She had little interest in preserving what she saw as a calcified class structure. Her introduction of economic liberalism was designed, in part, to free Britons from the generational patterns of enslavement to certain types of work based on class background. Her 'vision', it must be remembered, was

> a man's right to work as he will, to spend what he earns, to own property, to have the State as servant not as master: these are the British inheritance. They are the essence of a free country and on that freedom all our other freedoms depend. (1975: sec. 4, para 72)

This vision is of course one of economic freedom only, but certainly light years away from Mordrin and his Knights.

Thatcher also had an ambivalent relationship with the monarchy, and the Queen in particular. Though she always publicly displayed the utmost respect for the Royal Family, she differed with the Queen on many subjects, including (reportedly) the issue of apartheid in South Africa (to such an extent that many papers reported the Queen calling her 'uncaring'). So although she proclaimed the Victorian era to be the one in which 'Britain became great', it would be a mistake to call Thatcher a traditionalist. It is true, of course, that the different aspects of her political project were contradictory, but they were not advocating for a wholesale return to a Victorian world, where the traditional monarchy ruled, and presumably by extension the class system would be firmly entrenched. *Knights of God*, then, both plays into Thatcher's hands, as well as presenting a covert critique of her administration. All of this represents that nostalgic dream of a 'return to greatness'. *Knights of God*, too, embraces that dream. Far from the blunt and oppressive power of Mordrin, Thatcher's strategy managed to clearly delineate the difference between herself and an authoritarian – indeed, she imagined the two as polar opposites. What she was promoting, after all, was a wholesale embrace of the global free market, the decider of opinions, the arbiter of tastes and social mores. The global market works as an antidote to moral principles set down by any particular government. This was anathema to the small-minded (and murderous) nationalism of Hitler, Galtieri or Stalin. But of course Thatcher's project was contradictory, poised between the present of the free market and the past of the Victorian ideal. Added to that is the spectre of Churchill and what he represented, and the authoritarian appeal to the police and military.

Despite her stated loathing of dictators and her dream of a Victorian ideal, there is nonetheless a trace of Thatcher in Prior Mordrin and his Knights. They are uncompromising, militaristic, and look for iconography and symbolism that reinforces a message of strength. They are quick to deploy their armed forces to stamp out opposition just as Thatcher did with the police. Crucially, they appear to be offering a kind of freedom, but are in fact deeply authoritarian. In the first episode Mordrin appears on national television and appeals to the nation to join together to rebuild 'our great nation'. In that broadcast Mordrin assures the people, 'We, the Knights of God, will rule you with strength, with wisdom, and with justice.' Thatcher too tended to use absolutes – instead of justice or wisdom she favoured freedom – but that is where the similarities end. Thatcher was obviously never a dictator. Her show of force was never so blunt and brutal as Mordrin's, nor was she ever so oppressive in her ambitions. Thatcher was more skilled at using messaging, rhetoric and persuasion to achieve her ends. The Knights of God, in that sense, are nothing more than a parody of Thatcherism, comparable with Thatcher only in the sense that both used symbolism to exercise authoritarianism with varying extremes.

By remaining ambiguous about the parameters of authoritarian power, *Knights of God* manages to celebrate a certain form of conservatism. It provides a searing indictment of fascism, which is a relatively safe position, and offers a conservative alternative. It is a critique of Thatcherism in the sense that it equates Thatcher's 'conviction' brand of politics – uncompromising, strong, authoritarian, with firm advocacy of the police and military – with the Knights, even if they are merely a caricature of Thatcherite government. It also compares the stated 'new beginning' of the 1979 Conservative manifesto with the 'beginning' offered by Mordrin in his television broadcast. It condemns the Knights' position using the touchstones of conservative British governance – the Church, the monarchy and the military – and advocates for a return to that state of affairs. Thatcher would scarcely have recognised herself on either side. She always posed herself as the antidote to dictators, setting up a strong binary between herself and Galtieri, for instance. But she also would not have seen herself as a traditionalist, desperate to return wholesale to the Victorian era. Nonetheless, *Knights of God* could not be considered in any way progressive. Its vision is traditional and backward-looking, and for that reason it must be considered a pro-conservative, if not pro-Thatcher, piece.

However, as a neoliberal fantasy, *Knights of God* slots itself into a tradition alongside *Dune*, *Star Wars* and other similar stories. Though both of those stories predated the neoliberal era, their essential storytelling elements were ideal for the time. In utilising that story structure – often called 'The Hero's Journey' – *Knights of God* becomes another story that venerates the individual hero of noble birth, and his personal struggle. It is true that Gervase advocates for the restoration of democracy as soon as Britain is returned to its 'rightful' governmental structure, but there is still a sense that the neoliberal world view has taken over as the guiding logic of this story.

Star Cops (1987)

As an almost total departure from *Knights of God*, *Star Cops* presents itself as perhaps the most 'contemporary' example of British science fiction television produced. Though set in 2027, it is the series that carries the most obviously 1980s influence, both in its aesthetic style and in its neoliberal world view. Far from embracing grand narratives or mythologies, *Star Cops* operates with an air of resignation. The protagonists of the series no longer resist the world in which they operate, but neither do they embrace it. Rather they simply accept it. Here, to paraphrase Barthes, history has been thoroughly turned into nature. The world that the characters operate within is so completely naturalised that a sense of apathy has been allowed to set in: no one can see any alternative, nor can they muster the enthusiasm to try. There is no mythology to speak of, but there is a strong sense of *Mythologies*. As we will discover, a new myth has taken over this series: the 'myth of mythlessness'. The series is an attempt to 'stare reality in the eye': to navigate the now unmistakably neoliberal world and exploit the system wherever possible.

Star Cops began in Chris Boucher's mind as an idea for a radio series. He attempted to sell it to the BBC as such, only to be told that his idea had been beaten by James Follet's *Earthsearch*. He repackaged it as an idea for a television series, and it was pitched to Jonathan Powell, the Controller of BBC 1. Powell was aware of Boucher's work on *Blake's 7* and believed the concept had momentum. But the resulting series was beset with problems, including differing aesthetic approaches from different producers and designers, strained relationships between writers and producers, and inconsistent broadcast times. Michael Grade, the Director-General of the BBC, was already finding science fiction distasteful and unprofitable (in a couple of years he was to retire the original series of *Doctor Who*). Added to this, the working relationship between

Boucher and his producer Evgeny Gridneff was always strained, with Boucher saying in 1992, 'Some producers you get on with and some you don't, and unfortunately Evgeny Gridneff and I just didn't' (Stevens and Brown, 1992). Gridneff insisted on changes, such as shooting the whole series on video (Boucher wanted the traditional mixture of film and videotape) and ordering Boucher to rewrite scripts. All this led to the series' cancellation after only one short season.

Star Cops can be viewed as a victim, in part, of the BBC's attitude to science fiction at the time. As with the other shorter series of the 1980s, there was too much pressure to compete with American imports and their superior production values. It was clearly made on a tight budget, highlighting its aesthetic limitations. The camera, set, props and lighting are barely adequate for conveying space and its environs (and much of it is stock footage). But more importantly there was a disparity between what Boucher wanted for the series and what the producers at the BBC saw in his idea, which contributed to an aesthetically, tonally, and often narratively confused result. Watts writes:

> The difficulties for Boucher began early when he delivered a two-part opener to the BBC, that essentially laid out the concept and characters for the rest of the series to follow. The initial script reveals a different character dynamic to the one that made it to the screen, with the emphasis placed more upon the traditional detectives' double-act as opposed to a team. Originally the series was structured around … the formulaic approach to a buddy partnership as seen in hugely popular crime dramas such as *Starsky & Hutch* (1975–79), *The Sweeney* and *The Professionals*. (2020: 39)

However, Boucher was told by the producers that they did not want two-parters and he was forced to rewrite, condensing the first two episodes into one.

The series follows Nathan Spring, a chief superintendent in the British police in 2027. By this time there are various bases on the moon as well as satellites orbiting the Earth. Nathan is urged – more or less ordered – by his superior to take on a new position as Commander of the International Space Police Force, nicknamed the Star Cops. Nathan doesn't want the job – he is so adamant that he says he will withdraw his name, but is advised that this is a bad idea. When asked why, his supervisor says, 'Well in the first place, you're the only Brit left. It wouldn't look good to pull out before the final adjudication.' Nathan replies, 'Well I didn't realise it was an event in multimedia sport – tell me, do I wear a sponsor's logo?', and indeed there is a strong element of the corporatisation of Britain (and the world) right from the outset, which will be discussed. This arbitrary reassignment demonstrates the capacity for the 'post-Fordist society to periodically reskill as they move from institution to institution, from role to role' (Fisher, 2009: 40). The only apparent reason that the Commander has pushed Nathan so adamantly to apply is seemingly because of the embarrassment it will cause if the only British candidate withdraws. There is also a sense that Nathan is being extracted from his present case because he insists on more traditional methods of detection – in 2027 most of the detective work is carried out by computers, and Nathan is presented right from the start as an old-fashioned man: a gumshoe in the world of technological solutions.

The series had two distinct aims in order to position itself as unique and worthy of a large viewership. The first was that it would be more 'realistic' than most other science fiction television. It is an attempt at 'hard' science fiction, aligned with contemporaneous ideas about space travel. This desire to replicate the conditions of space even resulted in a visit to the set from Pete Conrad, the American NASA astronaut. Among his recommendations, according to the actor Trevor Cooper who played Colin Devis, was to replicate the conditions of weightlessness aboard the ship from the Earth to the moon. This involved having the characters' hair stand on end and arms wave in the air if they were asleep. Actors were also held into harnesses to replicate floating in low-gravity environments on space stations and the moon. Many of these details were dispensed with as the process became too logistically difficult, but this level of detail and desire to conform to the science in science fiction demonstrates a commitment absent from much else in the genre. Secondly, it was an attempt to blend genres. Boucher was experienced in both science fiction and the detective genre, having written for detective series like *Bergerac*. It was hoped that this blend of genres might draw viewers from both stables. The effect seems to have been the opposite – science fiction viewers did not appreciate that the series was devoid of the usual trappings of science fiction – aliens, monsters, outlandish technology – and fans of the detective genre were discouraged by the science fiction setting (see *Cult of ... Star Cops*).

The series made attempts to guess at the level of technology in 2027. Perhaps one of the more accurate innovations within the series is the prevalence of screens in Nathan's house (and everywhere else), which Nathan uses as communication devices. As mentioned, Nathan resents the amount of police work done by computers and remotely over screens, and this seems to be one reason why he is taken away from his current assignment and redeployed to the Star Cops. He also has a companion: Box. Box, given to Nathan by his father, is an AI unit inside a case, which speaks to Nathan with his own voice. Box is, in a sense, the successor of *Blake's 7*'s Orac, but less opinionated and sarcastic. The writer Philip Martin, who wrote two of the episodes, comments, '[Box] now looks rather large given the size of our mobile phones' (*Cult of ... Star Cops*), but that was in 2006. Interestingly, Box now seems redolent of a version of Amazon's Alexa, and the amount of knowledge it can access suggests a connection with the internet, or something very similar, so that it appears more contemporary now that it would have in 2006.

Star Cops draws us into a 1980s future: very different from previous British attempts to depict a future with moonbases and space activity. *UFO* depicted a psychedelic 'swinging' version of the Earth and the moon in which there was a clear hierarchy between both. *Moonbase 3* attempted to do something similar to *Star Cops*, but depicted a future that was in many ways a projection of the 1970s, with sombre tones and dour characters. In that series David Caulder (coincidentally the name – with different spelling – of the actor who played Nathan Spring on *Star Cops*) was a scientist and a leader, who relied on the expertise of his team. The series took great pains to present him as a 'middle of the road liberal', another manifestation of the BBC's general policy of the era. The stories in *Moonbase 3* were ensemble efforts, with everyone bringing their expertise to bear on the problem, and refreshingly, Caulder would often appear vulnerable in front of his colleagues when asking their advice. Nathan Spring is much more of an individualist than Caulder. Conforming more to the neoliberal model of an individual player who is a law unto himself, Spring hires and fires people without consultation, enacts theories and 'hunches' without warning, and rarely allows others insight into his plans on a substantial level. In some ways a comparison could be made with the Seventh Doctor: though that character is in possession of aeons of knowledge, and sometimes borders on a command of supernatural powers, he too enacts his plans in secret. In the first episode of *Star Cops*, someone is accepting money to 'look the other way' while faulty space suits are provided for unfortunate members of staff. In order to flush out the guilty party Nathan hides in a spacesuit and attacks the culprit when he attempts to send off the next victim. He explains to Theroux, his eventual second-in-command, that he had to be sure he could trust him before sharing his plans. This positions Nathan as a neoliberal hero – a man of action who largely works alone and takes authority into his own hands.

Star Cops is aesthetically, thematically and indeed politically, a product of the Thatcher era, and it would be difficult to imagine the series being produced in any other era than the late 1980s. Its primary concerns are often related to issues around privatisation, nuclear waste, assisted reproduction – all issues that had come to the fore in the era of Thatcher and Reagan. Reagan's 'Star Wars' defence system is recalled in the American space station's name: the Ronald Reagan. Indeed, Thatcher assured Reagan on more than one occasion that the relationship between the two countries was a close one, with Thatcher saying to Reagan in 1981, 'Your problems will be our problems and when you look for friends we shall be there' (Thatcher, 1981b: sec. 1, para 4). Nathan, as we will soon see, is more ambivalent about his American counterparts, but there is still a strong sense of cooperation between them.

The series is so anchored in 1980s style, decor and fashion, as to be alienating for that very reason, as if Earth (or the UK at any rate) has reverted to a retro-1980s aesthetic in 2027. Ellis discusses 'both nostalgia and unease' (2007: 19) generated from watching a television programme firmly grounded in its era. It estranges and appeals at the same time because of the very specificity of its aesthetic. That is certainly true of *Star Cops*. On Earth, people wear loose and baggy clothes, often with shoulder pads. Women wear their hair teased, or in the case of Pal Kenzy, one of Nathan's team, a kind of spiky pixie cut redolent of one of the (roughly contemporaneous) guises of Madonna. The police wear an apparently standard issue 'gumshoe' trenchcoat when on Earth. This all combines to create a jarring effect when viewed from the vantage point of decades later, but also reveals how closely aligned the series is with the concerns of the production's immediate environment. Even the theme song is a recognisable 1980s product – the song 'It Won't be Easy', which polarised opinion.

Unlike most other British science fiction series of this era, *Star Cops* is not 'dystopian' in the sense of depicting a world under the grip of an obviously authoritarian ruler, or a post-apocalyptic event. Rather it presents a business-as-usual world where space travel has become naturalised, and the corporate management structure of the world has seeped into the outer regions of space. The signature of neoliberalism – an absence, or paucity, of traditional authority, has left open a space for the Machiavellian character to thrive. Wright notes that the series 'appears to reflect a burgeoning mood of contemporary optimism as the British economy improved and the worst excesses of Thatcherism seemed in remission' (2005: 300). Yet *Star Cops* is still grappling with a world of Thatcherite excess and neoliberal economics, extrapolated into the interstellar setting. Unlike the other series in this book, which use science fiction scenarios to explore the relations between power and subjugation and the growing Machiavellian character at the centre, *Star Cops* depicts a world that is free from authoritarianism, at least in the conventional sense. Unlike the other series, the characters in *Star Cops* have accepted their fate as neoliberal subjects. They do not attempt to fight against it because it has become so completely normalised as to appear invisible. Thatcher's 'no alternative' has become crystallised into the dominant mode of operation, a triumph of 'nature' over 'history'. Instead, the characters adapt (once again recalling Suvin) learning to live within the system.

Space has been largely privatised, and this leads to a different response to the work environment than has been seen in British science fiction television before. Everywhere there are logos, from the screens on which the characters communicate to the jets that transport them back and forth to the moon. Medical companies vie for contracts; nuclear waste is privately disposed of, and even some of the satellites are privately owned. In the first episode it is established that space suits are issued by private companies competing for contracts. Some of the orbiting space stations are government owned, and some are in private hands. Many of the plots revolve around the clash between corporate and public interests.

Consistent with characters from the other shorter and less successful series, Nathan himself is not Machiavellian. He is authoritarian to a degree, in that he sometimes enacts his plans without regard for the 'chain of command'. Nonetheless, he is a far cry from Avon (a character whose arc was deeply influenced by Boucher) and the others in the major series. In similar vein to other shorter and less successful series of the era, Nathan is a reasonably uncomplicated hero – he is resourceful, he is somewhat loyal; he's intelligent and morally uncompromised. He must deal with the characters around him, who are much more insidious, or just plain incompetent, in their behaviour. The 'positive vision' of the era, Wright claims,

> is tempered ... by showing the greed, distrust, manipulation, and ambition characterising human interaction on Earth transferred to space. The series' cynicism, profanity, and jaded perception of international and personal relationships indicate a loss of faith not only in humanity but also in humanity's capacity for change. (2005: 300)

Some of these specimens of humanity are part of Nathan's crew. The most compromised, perhaps, is Pal Kenzy, the Australian officer. In many ways Kenzy is the series' answer to *Blake's 7*'s Avon. Though not operating quite at that level of misanthropy, Kenzy is a self-interested Thatcherite character, determined to exploit the system in whichever way she sees an advantage. The first time Kenzy arrives on the base, she attempts to persuade the others that they should be armed with laser weapons recently developed in Australia. When Nathan informs her that the police don't use guns on the moon, she replies, 'Well that'll be good news to the scum who'll be pouring out here', revealing a peculiarly 1980s form of xenophobia. This scene sets Nathan in opposition to his counterparts in American generic police television – the celebration of guns and violence that is apparent in any number of US action series: *The A Team, Magnum, PI* or

Miami Vice. Kenzy's comment, especially with the word 'scum', is more likely to issue from the mouth of Clint Eastwood's Dirty Harry than a British hero or heroine, even if she herself is Australian. This aligns her with the emerging authoritarian mentality of the 1980s neoliberal environment – the individual of dubious moral standing who takes the law into their own hands. Of course the debate in 'the real world' about police carrying guns has only intensified since then, lending the scene a certain authenticity.

In that episode, Nathan and Devis have created a kind of entrapment scenario for Kenzy and filmed it. In the footage, played back to her in the presence of the others, Kenzy believes she is sending a small-time criminal back to Earth, thus depriving him of his livelihood, unless he pays her for 'protection'. The 'criminal' turns out to be Devis. For this 'hustle' she is summarily dismissed from her position by Spring and sent back to Earth. Later she is aboard a ship travelling back to the moon and she finds herself seated next to Devis. This doesn't seem to cause the animosity it should – they get along well, even flirting slightly. There is an incident aboard the ship – terrorists threaten to use a bomb to blow it up. Kenzy manages to 'save the day' by catching the bomb. She uses this newfound hero status to her advantage, appearing on the media and jostling for her reinstatement. In a television interview, supported by Devis, she discusses her heroic acts. Because of the media exposure Nathan is forced into a position where he must rehire her.

As in the events of *The Tripods*, what happens here is arbitrary and fragmented. To recall Fisher, in a neoliberal environment, decisions are made one day which are entirely reversed the next, with no apparent lack of continuity experienced by the players involved. In addition to that, there is a thoroughly 1980s scenario of media manipulation. Kenzy and Devis are quite comfortable in each other's company, despite his successful bid to have her fired only days earlier. Kenzy's reassignment to Spring's Star Cops causes little to no animosity, and Spring seems to accept it with an ironic shrug: when asked if he will reinstate her he replies, 'Reinstate her? Listen to the bloody woman – she's reinstating herself!' Even Nathan's wry acceptance that Kenzy will have to be reinstated because of her media appearance speaks to this neoliberal environment where the image and the presentation of that image tends to eliminate the need for any nuance. Hall makes the claim, 'Our culture is saturated by the image in a variety of different forms ... The image itself ... seems to have become the privileged side of late modern culture' (2005: 5). Through the image, the late twentieth-century subject has learned to understand itself. Part of the reason Kenzy is reinstated is because she exploits the image. There is a thoroughly modern sense, then, that media manipulation is the modern way to engineer any situation to one's advantage, to almost erase history and create a new narrative. Kenzy is a thoroughly 1980s character who would've been at home in any television corporate office of the era. She is cynical; she exhibits an unhealthy interest in money and image, and little in justice. Nonetheless, the 'relationship' between Kenzy and Spring, by the end, develops into one that could become romantic, and this is designed to illustrate an evolution of both their characters – she the hard-bitten cynic and hustler-turned-romantic, and he the honest broker, intolerant of corruption, who falls for the 'bad girl'. But its side effect is to highlight the capricious nature of the neoliberal environment, where people are thrown together into work situations with no overriding authority or continuity and simply develop something resembling affection for each other based on circumstance – and even the 'affection' could be merely another effect of the ironic personality traits necessary to survive in a neoliberal world.

Nathan's ironic attitude is symptomatic of the new neoliberal character. Much of the survival mechanism of late capitalism was an attempt to 'look reality in the eye', to dispel utopian myths of progress and change, and accept the world 'as it is'. Fisher calls this an 'anti-mythical myth', described as the acceptance of life as 'a Hobbesian war of all against all, a system of perpetual exploitation and generalised criminality' (2009: 12), which of course is merely a new kind of mythology. Fisher writes of the hip-hop genre in the 1990s, that it sought to dispel myths, so that 'any "naive" hope that youth culture could change anything has been replaced by the hardheaded embracing of a brutally reductive version of "reality"' (2009: 11). This of course, leads to an attitude of cynicism which we can detect playing out in Nathan's ironic attitude. Much of the project of writing in the late twentieth century was an attempt to see beyond fantasies. Fisher discusses Badiou, when he writes:

> Capitalism is what is left when beliefs have collapsed at the level of ritual or symbolic elaboration, and all that is left is the consumer-spectator, trudging through the ruins and the relics. Yet this turn from belief to aesthetics, from engagement to spectatorship, is held to be one of the virtues of capitalist realism. In claiming, as Badiou puts it, to have 'delivered us from the "fatal abstractions" inspired by the "ideologies of the past"', capitalist realism presents itself as a shield protecting us from the perils posed by belief itself. The attitude of ironic distance proper to postmodern capitalism is supposed to immunise us against the seductions of fanaticism. (2009: 10)

Once we are inoculated against ideologues and their fantasies we adopt an ironic attitude as a survival mechanism. Because there is nothing left to believe in, there is only the cynicism of non-belief in anything. This leads to what Fisher calls 'a detached spectatorialism, [replacing] engagement and involvement' (2009: 6). According to Sennett, 'an ironic view of oneself is the logical consequence of living in flexible time, without standards of authority and accountability' (qtd in von Dirke, 2017: 116). Von Dirke goes on to say,

> white collar employees see through neoliberalism's false claims but instead of dismantling them, they accommodate them within their ironic world view and do so willingly. (2017: 333)

The worker, then, is aware of the absurdity of the system – its instability, its caprice, its lack of regulation leading to a void of authority; perhaps even the 'myths' the workplace might attempt to proliferate about its own aspirations and values; and simply learns to work within its parameters and adopt an individualistic 'survival mechanism'. This appears to be how Nathan operates – he is moved around departments against his will, he is forced to accept as an employee someone he recently fired for misconduct, and he does so in each case with little more than a knowing shrug and a quip. This would all suggest that Nathan then is forged in the flames of neoliberalism and uninterested in moving beyond it.

That is not to say that Nathan has 'fallen' for the neoliberal world. He is not as morally black and white as his American generic contemporaries, at least in the detective genre. He is certainly more weary of his milieu than they are of theirs – Thomas Magnum lives a life of luxury in his neoliberal paradise in *Magnum,*

PI (1980–88); Tubbs and Crockett revel in consumer culture in *Miami Vice* (1984–90). There is little in the way of social critique in these American series and others like them: the characters live within a system that they tacitly celebrate, or at the very least naturalise. There is seldom an opportunity to explore the 'dark side' of this consumerism. Nathan, on the other hand, is cynical, jaded, world-weary. He is highly critical of the privatised world around him, though his criticism comes across as ironic and cynical rather than productive. Like the neoliberal workers described above he is a spectator, he's not a revolutionary, though he may have been in the past (I will return to this point shortly). He does not allow that cynicism to creep into his detective work or his romantic life, but he does apply it to what he clearly views with distaste as an ever more commercialised and privatised world. Nathan, then, is poised between British and American modes of operation. He is carved out of the 1980s landscape of individualistic action heroes. In some ways he might resemble the titular hero of the American series *MacGyver* (1985–92). Attached to the non-profit government organisation the Phoenix Foundation, MacGyver operates largely alone and is similar in many respects to the standard neoliberal American action hero, but his characterisation is less infused with machismo in the 1980s sense – he shows pain when he punches someone, only uses violence in self-defence, and he abhors the use of guns. But MacGyver's world is another Manichean one, where there are heroes and villains, and most of the stories portrayed are melodramatic in nature. Spring is more complicated than that – alongside his individualistic traits he is also somewhat traditional. He does not operate as a maverick attachment to the police, but as a police officer, and he still, on some level, has faith in police work, though tempered by cynicism and ironic detachment. He operates in an environment that is more morally complex. He is also no fan of American consumerism, as will be seen. These traits separate Spring from most American heroes of 1980s television. Spring is merely resigned to the world he lives in, lethargically accepting its inconsistencies and working within it to accomplish his goals.

In Episode 4, 'Trivial Games and Paranoid Pursuits', Nathan goes to the Ronald Reagan station to investigate a disappearance. Inside Nathan meets Commander Griffin, an American stereotype who wears a baseball cap and a Dallas Cowboys T-shirt. He plays pool, chews cigars (always unlit), and displays an arrogant 'yankee' attitude. His quarters are decorated with sports flags and Coca-Cola signs. The two of them are extremely antagonistic towards each other, reflecting a clash of both personal and ideological positions. They have a conversation about patriotism that springs from a discussion about Spring's sacking of Hubble, an American in the Star Cops:

> GRIFFIN: He was a son of a bitch, but he was *our* son of a bitch.
> SPRING: My country, right or wrong, eh?
> GRIFFIN: There are worse philosophies.
> SPRING: Yes, most of them begin with that.
> GRIFFIN: You and Theroux [Nathan's American lieutenant] should be getting on real well.
> SPRING: Why do you say that?
> GRIFFIN: Your second-in-command's a little short on patriotism.
> SPRING: I knew there was something about that fellow that I liked.

It is possible that this exchange betrays Nathan's dislike of American nationalism, or perhaps any nationalism grounded in an irrational devotion to country placed above international cooperation. Nathan appears here to be a globalist with a traditionally British attitude – someone navigating the neoliberal changes of the 2020s: modernising but attempting to retain a national identity. That struggle – between a global and a national identity – became ever more familiar as the 1980s transitioned into the 1990s and global capital redefined the boundaries between 'national' and 'international'.

The blatant capitalist principles of the American contingent have resulted in a more technologically advanced station – the pool table on which Griffin spends his free time is made playable by way of technology that compensates for the lack of gravity. Nathan does not appreciate all this, nor does he approve of the private funding that runs the machine of the American station. He later comments that he can't get used to sleeping weightless on the station:

> GRIFFIN: We got a couple o' guys workin' on that problem right now.
> SPRING: Government research?

GRIFFIN: Hell no, they're both from pharmaceutical houses. They're probably duplicating each other's research, but what the hell? They got the funding, huh?
SPRING: Do you have any government research?
GRIFFIN: (*Throwaway*) There's some funding ...

When later quizzed about the funding, he does not answer. It suggests that Griffin cares little if the competing companies are cheating – it's all part of the capitalist game. It is clear that private funding is the means to get anything done in the American context, which would have been increasingly true in the real world too, reflecting the era in which Reagan was increasing privatisation, particularly in the pharmaceutical industry. Thatcher too, in 1988, embarked on a review of the NHS, and confessed that she herself had private health insurance.

Nathan is a traditionalist in many ways: a cop who believes in standard British methods of law enforcement including the lack of guns; a believer in a certain kind of restraint and stoicism compared with the garish American station; and a believer in a more interventionist government. It's also revealed that he was a student radical, as was Theroux:

GRIFFIN: Did you know [Theroux] was a student radical?
SPRING: (*Holds up peace sign*) Weren't we all?
GRIFFIN: No.
SPRING: Oh. Well if you're not radical as a kid, where is there to go in your reactionary old age?

Presumably this radicalism, if it really occurred, was something left wing in nature to counter his middle-aged reactionary status (and to explain the peace sign). This is all devised as a contrast to the American attitude of nationalism. In any case Nathan has moved beyond any cause, and on the only occasions where he displays a belief in anything, it is laced with knowing irony. Perhaps this positions *Star Cops* as the darkest of all series. The protagonists of *Blake's 7* at least believed in something – enough to die for. Even Avon, in the end, believed in Blake. Nathan and his colleagues have been conditioned to believe in nothing, thus aligning them with Fisher's 'capitalist realism', an attitude of jaded myth-shattering. When Britain was drowning in Thatcher's symbolic rhetoric, attempting to resurrect the myth of 'Great Britain', this cynicism is a telling attitude.

What all these instances show is a largely disapproving engagement with the tropes of Thatcherism and the now embedded neoliberal environment. In a very short space of time – roughly between 1983 and 1987 – Thatcher and her contemporaries had managed to rewrite the terms of engagement around the 'new' system of monetarism, so that when we arrive at *Star Cops* it is almost unconsciously ingrained in every frame of the show. Whereas in *Blake's 7* the new system was beginning to emerge, with Blake representing the resistant left-wing fighter against the rising tide of neoliberalism and its Machiavellian tendencies, *Star Cops* accepts the new environment as natural. Spring phlegmatically gestures against its excesses, but largely tolerates it. There is no great power to vanquish, nor any real resistance to the dominant system. The characters of *Star Cops* exist within the parameters of a system that is natural to them, as it would be, because they would have been born into it.

The two series assessed in this chapter, then, are radically different from each other, but both engage in the new neoliberal mindset. *Knights of God* explores the myths of nationalism – right wing in nature – and connects them to the neoliberal 'hero myth' propounded by Joseph Campbell and popularised in texts like George Lucas's *Star Wars*. It rises to a crescendo of nationalistic rapture which, in the end, is supportive of a certain type of Thatcherite world view, reverting to the promise of a neo-Victorian world, even if it rejects the more modernising influences of Thatcherism. *Star Cops* moves beyond the paradigm of this kind of mythology and explores an even more pernicious myth: that of what Fisher calls the 'antimythical myth' of looking life 'in the face', and seeking to embrace the reality of the world, which is exploitative, cruel and selfish, and indeed participate in it, unburdened of any naive fantasies. *Star Cops* (and its protagonist Nathan Spring) does not condone this world view, but accepts it as part of the fabric of life, and accepts its corollary: that the only logical response – as in the neoliberal world – is to adopt a posture of indifference or irony.

Conclusion

The Thatcherite blend of social conservatism and economic liberalism was always incoherent, but Thatcher (along with her speechwriters) was expert at masking its contradictions with rhetoric. She would release the constraints of regulation, and allow the market to decide on almost all economic matters. She sold this as an emancipation of the (usually male) individual, who was now in control of his finances, his ability to generate personal wealth without the usual interventions from the state by way of taxation and regulation. But to square this with her social conservatism she would remind the new subject that they were responsible – for themselves, their families and their communities. In practice this often translated to selfish and Machiavellian behaviour, and Thatcher attempted to redress this balance by resorting to philosophers and theologians who claimed that monetarism was in fact the most moral position.

The Victorian ideal as Thatcher saw it has ebbed away, but neoliberal economics remain, and have been amplified and intensified in the years since Thatcher was Prime Minister. The world is currently in a state of crisis, with neoliberalism responsible – either explicitly or implicitly – for some of the paradigm shifts in recent history. Issues around climate change, the global financial crisis and economic collapse in other countries such as Greece and Spain are at least in part connected with the ever pervasive influence of this economic system, which creates its own logic. It seems the human has been remoulded as a subject of capitalism. Few in the West can conceive of a system to replace this dominant mode. Fisher goes further, calling this state 'capitalist realism': a new myth to replace the old ones; a way of life that has been naturalised.

There is some reaction on both the left and the right against the globalisation that has become almost synonymous with neoliberalism. In the last few years a new kind of right-wing populism grew around figures like Donald Trump in the USA and Marine Le Pen's Rassemblement National in France, campaigning against the perceived 'elitism' of globalisation. Instead of globalisation, this view champions nationalism. It also indirectly encourages deep-seated attitudes of racism and xenophobia from predominantly white nationals of the countries. This right-wing xenophobia and racism have been demonstrated in events such as the Charlottesville riot in 2017, where neo-Nazis marched, the 2011 Norway killings, and the many anti-Muslim (and occasional anti-Semitic) demonstrations in Europe. Nationalism and populism also had a strong part to play in the Leave vote of the 2016 Brexit campaign in the UK.

My primary purpose in this book was to look at science fiction television in the Thatcher era and just before that change, and analyse the effects that neoliberalism and Thatcherite ideas had on its development. This included the external: its mode of production, and internal: its content. The effect was to enable the reader to understand the way that neoliberalism and Thatcherite rhetoric reshaped society and in a sense 'colonised' the public's thinking. What has now become so ingrained in our consciousness – the neoliberal system and its social narratives – that we seldom even consciously acknowledge it or the ways it is working through us and our experiences, was once an unknown reality. Britain before 1979 was a different country and did not operate on this logic.

I chose science fiction primarily because it is a genre of speculation (and a branch of it is sometimes called 'speculative fiction') wherein social changes in the empirical world of the series broadcast can be analysed in a context that is removed from that setting. Science fiction can project into the future, or the past – can involve other planets, aliens, different technology. Suvin (using Bloch) calls this mechanism the novum – an idea, technology, setting or time that is removed from its empirical reality. This creates an effect of what Suvin calls 'cognitive estrangement' – a way to remove us, the viewer, from our current milieu and enable us to view it as if from afar. Most science fiction uses this novum, this estrangement, to discuss and reflect on the political and social world of its immediate environment.

How much of this is deliberate? It is certainly true, as I discussed in the introduction, that a text – especially one with multiple authors – can produce meanings that were unintentional. Texts are always to an extent ambiguous, and there has been much media work on the ways that texts are 'encoded' and 'decoded' (starting from Hall, who originated the term). Within that, according to Hills and others, there are only a finite number of available readings. In some cases the creators' involvement with the world is obvious – Andrew Cartmel stated outright that he intended to encode *Doctor Who* of his era with anti-Thatcher sentiment, but even in this case there were unintended side effects – the Doctor became a more Thatcherite character than any of the writers intended, cutting against their intentions. Chris Boucher's *Star Cops* is quite obviously a series that comments on neoliberal turns in 1980s society, whereas *The Tripods* contains a narrative that is more open to speculation. I have attempted, in this book, to apply speculation where there is no recorded information about the effect of Thatcherism or neoliberalism, but my speculation has always been grounded in available discourses around television studies and cultural studies.

The science fiction television that appeared before the Thatcher era, mostly in the 1970s, was different in tone, and so I investigated the most salient of those differences. Pre-Thatcher series show a collective mentality, fidelity to duty, a faith in technological progress, and (most importantly) a deference to a certain authority: the authority of the white man in charge. Besides his ethnicity, the characteristics of this man are heroism, self-sacrifice, working within groups, a fidelity to moral duty and an absolute faith in science. Though there are differences between the BBC and ITV versions of this, they are similar in their privileging of the authority of the white man. Characters place an unspoken and axiomatic trust in him.

This all breaks down to a large extent in the three major series in the Thatcher era. In this era, we are thrust into a new world of duplicitous actions, Machiavellian behaviour, and use of Realpolitik solutions to problems. Faith in technology is often replaced by a dread of it, an indifference towards it, or a lament for its loss. Suddenly these characters – Steel, the Seventh Doctor, Avon – behave with selfish, Machiavellian intent, concealing their true motivations, sacrificing others for their own machinations.

Comparisons of major series: *Blake's 7*, *Sapphire & Steel* and *Doctor Who*

Thatcherite common sense – the clash between Victorian values and neoliberalism – is approached in various ways in the series studied. The series negotiate with the new myth of Thatcherism by approaching and critiquing ideas around authority, responsibility and freedom. The series negotiate with eschatological myth in various ways to reflect Thatcherism as a 'new beginning', as stated in the Conservative Party's 1979 manifesto. In this 'new world' of Thatcherism there is a strong sense that individualism and independence is becoming a more favoured strategy than working collectively (which was more prevalent in pre-Thatcher science fiction series) and resonates with the strongly individualistic approach that Thatcher herself promoted. These series also take a new perspective on authority. Whereas previously authority had been automatically connected to the main protagonist and seen as largely benign, in these series authority breaks down. The 'man in charge' is no longer fully trusted, and neither does he deserve the trust of those around him. He often operates in ways closer to authoritarianism, echoing the 'authoritarian populism' of Thatcherism. A Machiavellian style of operating is common across all three series, with the protagonists guilty of duplicitous actions that often reflect, in various ways, this new Thatcherite focus on individualism and personal wealth accumulation.

In *Sapphire & Steel* there is a clash between the old and the new, where neither one wins out. Rather, it is a series of empty signifiers: interchangeable signs that could belong to the past or the present. Wherever Sapphire and Steel are it is recognisably Britain, but its timeframe is unclear. Even when actual years are mentioned they are apparently interchangeable with others. But within that, *Sapphire & Steel* calls the past into being, and often when this 'past' intrudes into the nondescript present, it manifests as reminders of the times that Thatcher would in one way or another lionise as 'the best of British': the Second World War and the Victorian era. We are afforded glimpses of Victorians or soldiers at war, and they are always idealised portraits. *Sapphire & Steel* reflects the tensions of Thatcherite common sense, often recalling a twee version of the past intruding and imprinting on a blank, undefined present.

Blake's 7 does not focus on Victorian morality or recall the past in this way, but does hold in tension the concerns of the older consensus era in the person of Blake, and the new, Thatcherite world in the character of Avon. This becomes a clash between those two sets of values: collectivism and individualism, duty and pragmatism, Realpolitik decisions and those driven by moral duty. These tensions are all present in Thatcherite common sense too, though Thatcher often attempted to resolve them by using one (market economics) to describe the other (moral duty). She did this most clearly with the example of the Good Samaritan, who was only able to help because he had money. She used this to illustrate her belief that capitalist generation of wealth is a moral good in itself. Avon in *Blake's 7* does not subscribe to this, believing more cynically that wealth – accumulated by whatever means necessary – should merely liberate the wealthy: a view that many in the growing world of neoliberalism would recognise.

Doctor Who of the late Thatcher era is much more sceptical about the common sense of Thatcherism, seeing both the Victorian era and aspects of the modern era as lacking. In 'Ghost Light' (1988) the Victorian era is portrayed as a decaying archetype, a false veneer covering something alien. In 'The Greatest Show in the Galaxy' (1988) it reimagines the character of Captain Cook as an intergalactic traveller, but a contemptible character: cruel, cowardly and without redeeming characteristics. Where *Doctor Who* analyses the modern world of Thatcherism it finds it lacking too – 'The Greatest Show in the Galaxy' manages to hold both in tension: the Victorian buffoon Captain Cook, and the circus itself, mimicking modern consumerism: the relentless appetite for more stimulation, without ever being fully gratified, playing into Jameson's 'depthlessness' (1991: 6). *Doctor Who* also discusses themes like racism, xenophobia and nuclear war – all points of discussion in the Thatcher era – and takes a socially liberal stance on all of them. There is, however, a tension in the character of the Doctor himself, which mitigates against the liberal reading of the series.

From 1983 the character of the Doctor (particularly the Seventh Doctor), like Avon in *Blake's 7* and Steel in *Sapphire & Steel*, becomes a Machiavellian operator. Machiavellianism is a common theme in all three series. This, coupled with a Realpolitik strategy for solving problems, provides a loose template for describing how these three characters operate. When these two terms are used together, they describe a growing characteristic in Thatcherite Britain based on the spread of values associated with neoliberalism – like individualism, tax cuts for the rich and deregulation. Another aspect of the common sense of Thatcherism is that she used mythical language to evoke a sort of imaginary Britain constructed out of the ashes of Empire, and on the other hand she applied Realpolitik solutions. It would be inaccurate to describe her as Machiavellian herself, but the society she fostered normalised or even celebrated that kind of character.

All three protagonists from the three series exhibit characteristics of Machiavellianism. The Seventh Doctor's version behaves in an underhanded manner, concealing his true motives from everyone, including his companions. Steel in *Sapphire & Steel* is also a Machiavellian character who applies Realpolitik solutions, including the sacrifice of others without a second thought if the situation demands it. Steel, as his name suggests, is a cold, estranging character – aloof and inhuman. He is simply interested in the most expedient solution. Avon, too, is Machiavellian, once again in a different way. He is the most amoral operator of all, and basically the most selfish. His form of Machiavellianism is once again pragmatic in the extreme: allowing companions to die if need be, and behaving in a self-interested manner.

The series each approach the question of individualism and independence from different angles. The Thatcherite version of independence was narrow, evidenced by Thatcher's attempts to control the messaging around the BBC, to commercialise it and promote her own ministers and friends to the board. On the one hand she encouraged independence, on the other she kept a close eye on political messaging. Sapphire and Steel discover in their last assignment that they were betrayed by higher operators in their organisation. They comment to each other that these 'higher powers' resent the independence that they themselves have. Where the Thatcher government claimed to favour independence, this excluded independence of political messages that threatened its authority or credibility.

Blake's 7 echoes this tendency to an extent in Servalan. Just as Servalan allows the rebels to operate as long as it serves her interests, the characters in *Sapphire & Steel* are afforded the illusion of independence for as long as it serves their superiors, and no longer.

There is also a powerful strain of individualism in these series, largely absent from the consensus-era series. Avon in *Blake's 7* behaves in an almost entirely individualistic manner, putting his interests ahead of the common interests of the crew, and even threatening to kill crew members if they interfere with his plans. *Doctor Who* of the era also presents a very individualistic Doctor, both in the Sixth and Seventh incarnations of the character. The Sixth Doctor behaves in a way that comes close to madness, while the Seventh Doctor feels himself to be the ultimate authority.

The Doctor in this era takes authority onto himself in a way that his predecessors would not have recognised. Even though the series is 'liberal' on many topics, the character of the Doctor himself pulls against that. He operates according to his own rules, which he rarely discloses to anyone. He decides on who is 'good' and who is 'evil', and indeed who should live and die. Alongside *Doctor Who*, I claim that all the series in the Thatcher era contend with the 'authoritarian populism' that Thatcher herself preferred as a political strategy. Wright sees the characters in *Sapphire & Steel* as 'heroic figures, despite their misanthropy', who celebrate 'Margaret Thatcher's election as the triumph of conservative order over social chaos' (2006: 98). Sapphire and Steel, particularly Steel, often decide on the outcome of events and position themselves as the ultimate authority. They never pause to seek advice, and they have little interest in the collateral damage. Unlike the other two, *Blake's 7* does not present protagonists who take it on themselves to be authorities, with the possible exception of Blake's crusade, which posits him as a kind of revolutionary authority. In the main, the series shows an outright hatred of authoritarianism, and in this case the 'authority' is the Federation and Servalan, its commander, who is similar in some ways to Thatcher herself.

Duty is also treated differently – or disregarded entirely – in the Thatcher-era series. Before the Thatcher era, characters in science fiction television showed moral duty – often to military organisations, always with an unspoken allegiance to governmental hierarchies. This connection between duty and institutions ebbs away in the Thatcher-era series. *Sapphire & Steel* comes the closest to retaining this structure, but within that series it is clear that Sapphire and Steel work independently of their organisation. Steel does mention his duty to preserve the integrity of the timeline, but he carries out this duty as an independent operator, without the loyalty to the institution that his generic forebears would have shown. Blake in *Blake's 7* exhibits a loathing of the authorities, but has his own sense of duty to a cause, and that cause is revolution: destroying the Federation. However, Blake's actions are morally ambiguous, as they steer close to terrorism. Then when Avon takes over, he has no duty at all, and behaves entirely according to his own self-interest. The Sixth and Seventh Doctors still feel duty to some form of justice, but they carry it out very differently from their predecessors. They no longer work with others, or show the same amount of respect to their companions as they used to. The Sixth Doctor treats his companion Peri with some degree of contempt or indifference, and the Seventh Doctor views Ace, his companion, as merely a piece of the puzzle that he has to solve.

In both *Sapphire & Steel* and *Blake's 7* their world ends because, to some extent, their individualism has led them to a dead end. In the case of *Blake's 7* the individualistic tendencies of the protagonists lead to their demise – without cohesion and a common goal they are atomised, leading to misunderstandings, and ultimately death. In *Sapphire & Steel* it is similarly due to their independence – it seems they had always understood themselves as being able to operate independently, and had unwittingly displeased their superiors. Unlike *Blake's 7*, the protagonists of *Sapphire & Steel* are not saboteurs; rather they are simply 'independent of the state'. Just as Thatcher's government 'allowed' independence until it was no longer convenient, for instance at the BBC, so Sapphire and Steel are afforded the illusion of independence until their superiors decide on a new strategy.

The series also use the eschatological myths of the Book of Revelation and the Norse Ragnarök, analogous in their messaging to Thatcherism itself as a 'new beginning'. Both *Blake's 7* and *Sapphire & Steel* use the eschatological myths to depict an end to the status quo the characters inhabit. At the end of *Sapphire & Steel* the 'heroes' are betrayed by their own superiors and condemned to an eternal prison, echoing the fate of the 'Beast' in the Book of Revelation, while in *Blake's 7* the heroes are all killed, a scenario that moves closer to Ragnarök. *Doctor Who* references Norse myth overtly in 'The Curse of Fenric' to show how the world came to an end through Fenric, the evil being from the dawn of time, whose namesake is Fenrir, the wolf from Norse myth. These allusions to endings and new beginnings both reference the beginning of the new era of Thatcherism, and suggest another new beginning that destroys the status quo.

The shorter series

Much of the science fiction produced in the 1980s was unsuccessful. The reasons for this were embedded within the climate of television production at the time – more stringent market-based methods were applied to television, and a climate of distrust grew around science fiction because of its perceived inferiority to the American product. As such, only two series in the 1980s were written directly for the screen, and both failed. *Knights of God* imagined an England under the control of fascists. The series was deeply conservative, saturated with imagery of British superiority – the Union Jack, the Crown, the Church – and the Arthurian myth of the king who would return from exile to unite a nation. *Star Cops*, on the other hand, was a cynical take on neoliberalism, depicting space as privatised and outsourced. Bases on the moon and satellites around it were partly in private hands. The protagonist, Nathan Spring, adopted a cynical and ironic attitude to all this, reflecting some of the trends in the neoliberal workplace. Both series grappled with the Thatcherite landscape, but with very different outcomes. One mythologised and in doing so strongly advocated a conservative world view, complete with Christian devotion, to counter the effects of fascism, while the other more clearly reflected the many changes in society due to neoliberalism, but offered no solution for a more equitable existence.

The Day of the Triffids, adapted from John Wyndham's 1951 novel, made only subtle changes to the source material as it moved into the 1980s. In 1981 the world was still not yet feeling the effects of neoliberalism, and this television series offers us no direct (or even metaphorical) critique of the system. But it did show us the emergence of a new type of anti-hero, which British television elevated to a new level in the Thatcher era. Bill Masen, the protagonist of that story, spends a lot of time pondering whether his time is best spent helping the multitudes or helping certain select people who have a more realistic chance of survival. This somewhat utilitarian view is similar to Blake in *Blake's 7*, who ponders whether it's better to destroy Star One knowing that it will kill many millions of people but also destroy the Federation: or to not act. But Bill also shows some aspects of a prototypical Avon in emergence – his desire for self-preservation over altruism, his characterisation of people as sheep.

Much more well-adjusted for the Thatcher era is *The Tripods*, the adaptation of John Christopher's novels from the 1960s. The series expands on the books in many ways. It introduces the characters of the Black Guards – fascistic police who patrol the lands. It also introduces Machiavellian characters that the protagonists meet along the way. In the central conceit, or novum, of Capping, we see a kind of hegemony in action. *The Tripods* control the minds of their subjects to the point where humans love them and see them as their saviours. The series tends to universalise notions of authoritarianism. It operates within a world of Thatcherite authoritarianism, and constantly reinforces the theme of freedom, but this freedom is based not on economics but on the rights of the individual to his or her intellectual and creative autonomy. This theme is reinforced constantly, aligning itself to a 1960s sensibility, but also to the new Thatcherite landscape of individual self-interest. Mitigating against the Thatcherite world is the re-emergence of the theme of the illusion of independence. *The Tripods* appear to give people independence, but in fact exert a powerful control over the populace.

In America, shows like the rebooted *Battlestar Galactica* (2004–09), and more recently *Westworld* (2016–present) have made fascinating commentaries on their political moments. In the case of *Battlestar Galactica*, terrorism and religious fanaticism were discussed in allegorical form, connecting with 9/11 and fears around Islamic extremism. Westworld discusses the nature of consciousness and the moral dilemmas of violence within the context of a theme park containing human-like androids that guests are free to abuse and even kill. *Westworld* examines capitalism's tendency towards indulging base desires and instant gratification. *Black Mirror* (2011–present) has also proven itself to be prescient about political and cultural movements, including the rise of Trump and 'pig-gate'. There is more work to be done to compare science fiction television and film outside Britain to its political context. This book has focused only on the British context, and mainly within the Thatcher era. There is a body of scholarship that examines science fiction in terms of political contexts, to which this book will perhaps contribute, but further analysis along these lines will be a welcome addition to the study of science fiction as a means of political commentary.

Television programmes discussed

Black Mirror

'Fifteen Million Merits', produced by Charlie Brooker and Annabel Jones. Channel 4, 2013.
'Nosedive', produced by Charlie Brooker and Annabel Jones, Netflix, 2016.

Blake's 7

'Aftermath', produced by David Maloney, BBC, 7 January 1980.
'Blake', produced by Vere Lorrimer, BBC, 21 December 1981.
'Cygnus Alpha', produced by David Maloney, BBC, 16 January 1978.
'Orbit', produced by Vere Lorrimer, BBC, 12 October 1981.
'Space Fall', produced by David Maloney, BBC, 9 January 1978.
'Star One', produced by David Moloney, BBC, 3 April 1979.
'Terminal', produced by David Moloney, BBC, 31 March 1980.
'The Way Back', produced by David Moloney, BBC, 2 January 1978.

Doctor Who

'Battlefield', produced by John Nathan-Turner, BBC, 1989.
'Doctor Who and the Silurians', produced by Barry Letts, BBC, 1970.

'Earthshock', produced by John Nathan-Turner, BBC, 1981.
'Ghost Light', produced by John Nathan-Turner, BBC, 1989.
'Image of the Fendahl', produced by Graham Williams, BBC, 1977.
'Remembrance of the Daleks', produced by John Nathan-Turner, BBC, 1988.
'Terror of the Autons', directed & produced by Barry Letts, BBC, 1971.
'The Ambassadors of Death', directed by Michael Ferguson, produced by Barry Letts, BBC, 1970.
'The Curse of Fenric', produced by John Nathan-Turner, directed by Nicholas Mallett, BBC, October 1989.
'The Daemons', directed by Christopher Barry, produced by Barry Letts, BBC, 1971.
'The Greatest Show in the Galaxy', produced John Nathan-Turner, BBC, 1988.
'The Happiness Patrol', produced John Nathan-Turner, BBC, 1988.
'The Moonbase', produced by Innes Lloyd, BBC, 1967.
'The Sea Devils', directed by Michael E. Briant, produced by Barry Letts, BBC, 1972.
'The Talons of Weng-Chiang', produced by Philip Hinchcliffe, BBC, 1977.
'The Two Doctors', produced by John Nathan-Turner, BBC, 1986.
'World War Three', produced by Russell T. Davies, Julie Gardner and Mal Young, BBC, 2005.

Quatermass and the Pit

Directed and produced by Rudolph Cartier, BBC, 1958.

Sapphire & Steel

'A1', directed by Shaun O'Riordan, ITV, July 1979.
'A2', directed by David Foster, ITV, July, 1979.
'A3', directed by Shaun O'Riordan, ITV, January 1981.
'A4', directed by David Foster, ITV, January 1981.

'A5', directed by Shaun O'Riordan, ITV, August 1981.
'A6', directed by David Foster, ITV, August 1982.

Space: 1999

'Collision Course', directed by Ray Austin, produced by Gerry Anderson and Sylvia Anderson, ITV, 1975.

Star Cops

'An Instinct for Murder', produced by Evgeny Gridneff, BBC, 6 July, 1987.
'Intelligent Listening for Beginners', produced by Evgeny Gridneff, BBC, 20 July, 1987.
'Trivial Games and Paranoid Pursuits', produced by Evgeny Gridneff, BBC, 27 July 1987.

Survivors

Directed by Pennant Roberts, produced by Terence Dudley, BBC, 1975.

The Day of the Triffids

Directed by Ken Hannam, produced by David Moloney, BBC, 1981.

The Tripods

'Part 1: July 2089 – A Village in England', produced by Richard Bates, BBC, 1984.
'Part 6: July 2089 – Chateau Ricordeau, France', produced by Richard Bates, BBC, 1984.

'Part 7: July 2089 – Chateau Ricordeau, France', produced by Richard Bates, BBC, 1984.
'Part 8: August 2089 – Chateau Ricordeau, France', produced by Richard Bates, BBC, 1984.
'Part 11: October 2089 – France', produced by Richard Bates, BBC, 1984.

Time Shift

'The Kneale Tapes' Produced by Tom Ware, BBC, 2003.

UFO

'A Computer Affair', directed by David Lane, produced by Gerry Anderson and Reg Hill, ITV, 1971.
'A Question of Priorities', directed by David Lane, produced by Gerry Anderson and Reg Hill, ITV, 1970.

World in Action

'The Taming of the Beeb', produced by Ray Fitzwalter, Granada, 29 February 1988.

Bibliography

Adams, Stephen. 2010. 'Doctor Who had Anti-Thatcher Agenda.' *Telegraph*, 14 February, www.telegraph.co.uk/culture/tvandradio/doctor-who/7235547/Doctor-Who-had-anti-Thatcher-agenda.html (accessed 21 October 2022).
Adorno, Theodor W. 2004. *Negative Dialectics*, 3rd ed. Routledge.
Allen, Graham. 2003. *Roland Barthes*. Routledge.
'An Interview with Terry Nation.' 1987. Produced by Peter R. Baker. KTEH, www.youtube.com/watch?v=M35dCrNMMAw (accessed 21 October 2022).
Bahn, Christopher. 2012. '*Doctor Who* (Classic): "Vengeance On Varos".' *The AV Club*, 2 May, https://tv.avclub.com/doctor-who-classic-vengeance-on-varos-1798171410 (accessed 21 October 2022).
Barthes, Roland. 1989. *The Rustle of Language*. University of California Press.
Barthes, Roland. 1991. *Mythologies*, 25th ed. Noonday Press.
Bates, Stephen. 2000. 'Runcie's Parting Shot at Thatcher.' *Guardian*, 29 November, www.theguardian.com/uk/2000/nov/29/thatcher.politics (accessed 21 October 2022).
Beckett, Andy. 2015. *Promised You a Miracle: UK 80–82*. Penguin.
Berlin, Isaiah. 1969. *Four Essays on Liberty*. Oxford University Press.
Bignell, Jonathan. 2005. 'And the Rest is History: Lew Grade, Creation Narratives and Television Historiography.' *ITV Cultures: Independent Television over Fifty Years*, edited by Catherine Johnson and Rob Turnock. Open University Press, pp. 57–73.
Bignell, Jonathan and Andrew O'Day. 2004. *Terry Nation*. Manchester University Press.
Bloch, Ernst. 1995 [1954]. *The Principle of Hope*. MIT Press.
Booker, M. Keith. 2004. *Science Fiction Television: A History*. Praeger Publishers.

Bould, Mark. 2008. 'Science Fiction Television in the United Kingdom.' *The Essential Science Fiction Television Reader*, edited by J. P. Telotte. University Press of Kentucky, pp. 209–30.

Bould, Mark and China Mieville, editors. 2009. *Red Planets: Marxism and Science Fiction*. Pluto Press.

Bourdieu, Pierre. 1984. *Distinction: A Social Critique of the Judgement of Taste*. Routledge.

Bourne, J. 2013. '"May We Bring Harmony"? Thatcher's Legacy on "Race".' *Race & Class*, vol. 55, no. 1, pp. 87–91, http://journals.sagepub.com/doi/abs/10.1177/0306396813489247 (accessed 21 October 2022).

Briggs, A. 1961. *The Birth of Broadcasting: The History of Broadcasting in the United Kingdom*. Oxford University Press.

Britton, Piers D., and Simon J. Barker. 2003. *Reading Between Designs: Visual Imagery and the Generation of Meaning in The Avengers, The Prisoner, and Doctor Who*. University of Texas Press.

Brown, Maggie. 2009. 'Timeline: How ITV Got Where it is Today'. *Guardian*, 4 March, www.theguardian.com/media/2009/mar/04/how-itv-got-where-it-is-today (accessed 21 October 2022).

Brown, P. 2017. 'The American Western Mythology of *Breaking Bad*.' *Studies in Popular Culture*, vol. 40, no. 1, pp. 78–101.

Burns, J. H. 2005. 'Happiness and Utility: Jeremy Bentham's Equation.' *Utilitas*, vol. 17. Cambridge University Press.

Cartmel, Andrew. 2005. *Script Doctor: The Inside Story of Doctor Who, 1986–89*. Reynolds & Hearn Ltd.

Caughie, J. 2000. *Television Drama: Realism, Modernism, and British Culture*. Oxford University Press.

Central Board of Finance of the Church of England. 1985. *Faith in the City: A Call for Action by Church and Nation: The Report of the Archbishop of Canterbury's Commission of Urban Priority Areas*. Church House Publishing.

Charles, Alec. 2007. 'The Ideology of Anachronism: Television, History and the Nature of Time.' *Time and Relative Dissertations in Space: Critical Perspectives on 'Doctor Who'*, edited by David Butler. Manchester University Press, pp. 108–22.

Charteris-Black, Jonathan. 2011. *Politicians and Rhetoric: The Persuasive Power of Metaphor*, 2nd ed. Palgrave-Macmillan.

Christopher, John. 2014a. *The City of Gold and Lead*. Aladdin.

Christopher, John. 2014b. *The Pool of Fire*. Aladdin.

Christopher, John. 2014c. *The White Mountains*. Aladdin.

Christopher, John. 2014d. *When the Tripods Came*. Aladdin.

Clark, Phenderson Djèlí. 2013. 'Doctor Who(?)- Racey-Wacey-Timey-Wimey.' *The Musings of a Disgruntled Haradrim*, 3 June,

https://pdjeliclark.wordpress.com/2013/06/03/doctor-who-racey-wacey-timey-wimey/ (accessed 21 October 2022).
Clarke, Arthur C. 1972. *Profiles of the Future: An Enquiry into the Limits of the Possible*, 2nd ed. Gateway.
Cockerell, M. 1988. *Live from Number 10*. Faber & Faber.
Conservative Party. 1979. 'Conservative General Election Manifesto 1979.' *Margaret Thatcher Foundation*, 11 April, www.margaretthatcher.org/document/110858 (accessed 21 October 2022).
Cook, J. R. 2006. 'The Age of Aquarius: Utopia and Anti-Utopia in Late 1960s' and Early 1970s' British Science Fiction Television.' *British Science Fiction Television: A Hitchhiker's Guide*, edited by J. R. Cook and Peter Wright. IB Tauris, pp. 93–115.
Cooke, Lez. 2015. *British Television Drama: A History*. BFI Publishing.
Cornea, Christine. 2007. *Science Fiction Cinema: Between Fantasy and Reality*. Edinburgh University Press.
Cornea, Christine. 2011. 'British Science Fiction Television in the Discursive Context of Second Wave Feminism.' *Genders Online Journal*, no. 54, www.colorado.edu/gendersarchive1998-2013/2011/08/01/british-science-fiction-television-discursive-context-second-wave-feminism (accessed 21 October 2022).
Crisell, Andrew. 2002. *An Introductory History of British Broadcasting*. Routledge.
Cult of ... Star Cops. 2006. Directed by Tony Followell, BBC Scotland.
Denning, Darren J. 2010. 'In Pursuit of British Public Support for the Next War.' Master's thesis. Joint Forces Staff College, Washington, DC.
Downing, John D. H. 2001. *Radical Media: Rebellious Communication and Social Movements*. SAGE Publications.
Duckworth, Steven. 2010. '*Blake's 7*.' *The Essential Cult TV Reader*, edited by D. Lavery. University Press of Kentucky, pp. 51–60.
Durham, M. G. and D. Kellner. 2006. *Media and Cultural Studies*. Blackwell Publishing.
Eliot, T. S. 1963. *Collected Poems, 1909–1962*. Faber & Faber.
Ellis, J. 2007. 'Is it Possible to Construct a Canon of Television Programmes? Immanent Reading Versus Textual-Historicism.' *Re-Viewing Television History: Critical Issues in Television Historiography*, edited by Helen Wheatley. IB Tauris, pp. 15–27.
Engels, F. and Franz Mehring. 1968. 'Engels to Franz Mehring.' *Marx and Engels Correspondence*, translated by Donna Torr. International Publishers, www.marxists.org/archive/marx/works/1893/letters/93_07_14.htm (accessed 21 October 2022).
Filby, Eliza. 2015. *God and Mrs Thatcher*. Biteback Publishing.

Firing Line with William F. Buckley Jr. 1977. Directed by Warren Steibel, produced by Warren Steibel & Paul Sweeney, Community Television of Southern California.

Fisher, Mark. 2009. *Capitalist Realism: Is There No Alternative?* Zero Books.

Fisher, Mark. 2014. *Ghosts of My Life: Writings on Depression, Hauntology and Lost Futures.* Zero Books.

Fiske, John. 1980. *Television Culture.* Routledge.

Fiske, John. 2009. *Television Culture.* Taylor & Francis.

Forster, Laurel. 2009. 'Farmers, Feminists, and Dropouts: The Disguises of the Scientist in British Science Fiction Television in the 1970s.' *Channeling the Future: Essays on Science Fiction and Fantasy Television*, edited by Lincoln Geraghty. Scarecrow Press, pp. 75–93.

Friedman, Lester D., editor. 2006. *Fires Were Started: British Cinema and Thatcherism.* 2nd ed. Wallflower Press.

Geraghty, L. 2011. 'Visions of an English Dystopia: History, Technology and the Rural Landscape in *The Tripods*.' *British Science Fiction Film and Television: Critical Essays*, edited by Tobias Hochscherf and James Leggott. McFarland, pp. 104–14.

Giles, Paul. 2006. 'History with Holes: Channel Four Television Films of the 1980s.' *Fires Were Started: British Cinema and Thatcherism*, edited by Lester Friedman. Wallflower Press, pp. 58–77.

Goodwin, P. 1998. *Television Under the Tories: Broadcasting Policy, 1979–1997.* BFI Publishing.

Gottleib, Erika. 2001. *Dystopian Fiction East and West.* McGill-Queen's University Press.

Gould, Julius and Digby Anderson. 1987. 'Thatcherism and British Society.' *Thatcherism: Personality and Politics*, edited by Kenneth Minogue and Michael Biddiss. St Martin's Press, pp. 38–54.

Green, Earl. 2020. 'Who Took Up Arms Against "Knights Of God"?' *Pop Culture Retrorama*, 8 June, https://popcultureretrorama.wordpress.com/2020/06/08/who-took-up-arms-against-knights-of-god/ (accessed 14 November 2022).

Grieg, Mark. 2015. '*Sapphire and Steel* Series Review.' *Doux Reviews*, www.douxreviews.com/2015/09/sapphire-and-steel-series-review.html (accessed September 2018).

Haley, Guy. 2007. 'Steeling the Show: Q&A Peter J. Hammond.' *Haley's Comment*, https://guyhaley.wordpress.com/interviews-2/pj-hammond-2007/ (accessed October 2018).

Hall, Stuart. 1982. 'The Rediscovery of "Ideology"; Return of the Repressed in Media Studies.' *Culture, Society and the Media*, edited by Michael Gurevitch, Tony Bennett, James Curran and Janet Woollacott. Routledge, pp. 52–86.

Hall, Stuart. 1988. *The Hard Road to Renewal: Thatcherism and the Crisis of the Left.* Verso.

Hall, Stuart. 1998. 'Notes on Deconstructing the Popular.' *Cultural History and Popular Culture, A Reader*, 3rd ed., edited by John Stanley. Prentice Hall, pp. 477–88.

Hall, Stuart. 2005. 'Representation and the Media.' Media Education Foundation transcript, *cdeVision*, www.mediaed.org/transcripts/Stuart-Hall-Representation-and-the-Media-Transcript.pdf (accessed 14 November 2022).

Hall, Stuart. 2006. 'Encoding/Decoding.' *Media and Cultural Studies: Key Works*, edited by Douglas M. Kellner and M. G. Durham. Blackwell Publishing, pp. 163–74.

Hall, Stuart. 2011. 'The Neoliberal Revolution.' *Cultural Studies*, vol. 25, no. 6, pp. 705–28.

Hall, Stuart and Martin Jacques. 1983. *The Politics of Thatcherism.* Lawrence and Wishart.

Hanretty, Chris. 2011. *Public Broadcasting and Political Interference.* Routledge.

Harrison, Andrew. 2013. 'Is *Doctor Who* a Lefty?' *New Statesman America*, November, www.newstatesman.com/2013/11/spin-doctor (accessed 21 October 2022).

Harrison, Jackie. 2005. 'From Newsreels to a Theatre of News: The Growth and Development of Independent Television News.' *ITV Cultures: Independent Television over Fifty Years*, edited by Catherine Johnson and Rob Turnock. Open University Press, pp. 120–43.

Harvey, David. 2005. *A Brief History of Neoliberalism.* Oxford University Press.

Heffernan, Richard. 1997. 'Exploring Political Change: Thatcherism and the Remaking of the Labour Party 1979–1997.' PhD thesis, London School of Economics and Political Science, University of London.

Hills, M. 2018. 'How is Popular Television "Political"?: From the Texts of Steven Moffat's *Doctor Who* to Brand/Fan Politics'. *Journal of Popular Television*, vol. 6, no. 2, pp. 167–82.

Hoare, Quentin and Geoffrey Nowell-Smith, editors. 1999. *Selections from the Prison Notebooks of Antonio Gramsci.* Electric Book Company.

Hoffstadt, Christian and Dominic Shrey. 2011. 'Aftermaths: Post-Apocalyptic Imagery.' *British Science Fiction Film and Television: Critical Essays*, edited by Tobias Hochscherf, James Leggott and Donald E. Palumbo. McFarland & Company, pp. 28–39.

Howe, David J., Mark Stammers and Stephen James Walker. 1993. *Doctor Who: The Eighties.* Doctor Who Books.

Hutchings, Peter. 2011. 'Tracking *UFO*: Format, Text and Context.' *British Science Fiction Film and Television: Critical Essays*, edited by Tobias Hochscherf and James Leggott. McFarland, pp. 85–95.

Jameson, Fredric. 1991. *Postmodernism, or The Cultural Logic of Late Capitalism*. Duke University Press.

Jenkins, Peter. 1988. *Mrs Thatcher's Revolution: The Ending of the Socialist Era*. Harvard University Press.

John, Cindi. 2006. 'The Legacy of the Brixton Riots.' *BBC News*, 5 April, http://news.bbc.co.uk/2/hi/uk_news/4854556.stm (accessed 21 October 2022).

Johnson, Catherine and Rob Turnock, editors. 2005. *ITV Cultures: Independent Television over Fifty Years*. Open University Press.

Johnston, Derek. 2009. 'Genre, Taste and the BBC: The Origins of British Television Science Fiction.' PhD Thesis, University of East Anglia.

Jones, Daniel N. and Delroy L. Paulhus. 2009. 'Machiavellianism.' *Individual Differences in Social Behaviour*, edited by M. R. Leary and R. H. Hoyle. Guilford, pp. 93–108.

Jones, Steve. 2006. *Antonio Gramsci*. Routledge.

Kaltwasser, Cristobal Rovira and Cas Mulde. 2017. *Populism: A Very Short Introduction*, Very Short Introductions. Oxford University Press.

Koven, Mikel J. 2007. 'The Folklore Fallacy. A Folkloristic/Filmic Perspective on *The Wicker Man*.' *Fabula: Journal of Folktale Studies*, vol. 48, no. 3–4, pp. 270–80. https://doi.org/10.1515/FABL.2007.021

Kracauer, Siegfried. 1946. *From Caligari to Hitler: A Psychological History of the German Film*. Princeton University Press.

Kumar, Krishan. 1975, 'Holding the Middle Ground: The BBC, the Public and the Professional Broadcaster.' *Sociology*, vol. 9, no. 1, pp. 67–88.

Larsen, Kristine. 2017. 'Ape Man or Regular Guy? Depictions of Neanderthals and Neanderthal Culture in *Doctor Who*.' *Doctor Who and History: Critical Essays on Imagining the Past*, edited by Carey Fleiner and Dean October. McFarland & Company, pp. 148–68.

Le Jeune, Martin. 2009. *To Inform, Educate and Entertain?: British Broadcasting in the Twenty-First Century*. Centre for Policy Studies.

Lefkowitz, M. 1990. 'The Myth of Joseph Campbell.' *American Scholar*, vol. 59, no. 3, pp. 429–34.

Loza, Suzana. 2017. 'Remixing the Imperial Past: *Doctor Who*, British Slavery, and the White Saviour's Burden.' *Doctor Who and History: Critical Essays on Imagining the Past*, edited by Carey Fleiner and Dean October. McFarland & Company, pp. 47–61.

Mackenzie, Kelvin. 1982. '"Gotcha!": Our Lads Sink Gunboat and Hole Cruiser.' *Sun*, 4 May, p. 1.

Malnick, Edward. 2014. 'Margaret Thatcher Conducted Covert War Against BBC.' *Telegraph*, 30 December, www.telegraph.co.uk/news/

politics/margaret-thatcher/11313380/Margaret-Thatcher-conducted-covert-war-against-BBC.html (accessed 21 October 2022).
'Margaret Thatcher Considered Advertising on BBC.' *BBC News*, 30 December, www.bbc.co.uk/news/entertainment-arts-30622889 (accessed 21 October 2022).
McCormack, Una. 2006. 'Resist the Host: *Blake's 7* – A Very British Future.' *British Science Fiction Television: A Hitchhiker's Guide*, edited by J. R. Cook and P. Wright. IB Tauris Publishers, pp. 175–91.
McKee, Alan. 2001. 'Which is the Best Doctor Who Story? A Case Study in Value Judgements Outside the Academy.' *Intensities, the Journal of Cult Media*, no. 1 (Spring/Summer), pp. 1–54.
Metcalf, Stephen. 2017. 'Neoliberalism: The Idea that Swallowed the World.' *Guardian*, 18 August, www.theguardian.com/news/2017/aug/18/neoliberalism-the-idea-that-changed-the-world (accessed 21 October 2022).
Moffitt, Benjamin. 2016. *The Global Rise of Populism: Performance, Political Style and Representation*. Stanford University Press.
Monaghan, David. 1998. *The Falklands War: Myth and Countermyth*. Macmillan Press.
Moylan, Tom. 2000. *Scraps of the Untainted Sky: Science Fiction, Utopia, Dystopia*. Westview Press.
Muir, John Kenneth. 1999. *A Critical History of Doctor Who on Television*. McFarland & Company.
Muir, John Kenneth. 2012. *The Space: 1999 Equation*, Wordpress, 12 February 2012, https://johnkennethmuir.wordpress.com/2012/02/12/the-space-1999-equation/ (accessed 21 October 2022).
Munro, Tim. 1988. 'Review of *Knights of God*.' 625, http://www.625.org.uk/625/staraker/sb05kofg.htm (accessed 14 November 2022).
Nannicelli, Ted. 2017. *Appreciating the Art of Television: A Philosophical Perspective*. Taylor & Francis.
Neher, Andrew. 1990. *Paranormal and Transcendental Experience: A Psychological Examination*, 2nd ed. Dover Publications.
Newman, Sydney. 2010. 'Sydney Newman (1986).' *Doctor Who Interviews*, Wordpress, 25 October, https://drwhointerviews.wordpress.com/tag/sydney-newman/ (accessed 21 October 2022).
Ogland, Peter. 2014. *Space: 1999 – Episode by Episode*. Lulu Press.
Osgerby, Bill. 2000. '"Stand by for Action!" Gerry Anderson, Supermarionation and the "White Heat" of Sixties Modernity.' *Unruly Pleasures: The Cult Film and its Critics*, edited by Xavier Mendik and Graeme Harper. Fab Press, pp. 121–36.
O'Shaughnessy, Martin. 1996. 'The Lady Turns Back: The Thatcherite Discourse on Thatcherism.' *Atlantis*, vol. 18, no. 1. pp. 295–305.
Parry-Giles, Shawn J. 2015. 'Ronald Reagan, Address to the National Association of Evangelicals' ('Evil Empire Speech') (8 March 1983).

Voices of Democracy: A US Oratory Project, 23 November, http://voicesofdemocracy.umd.edu/reagan-evil-empire-speech-text/ (accessed 21 October 2022).

Petley, Julian. 1989. 'The Manxman.' *Monthly Film Bulletin*, March.

Philo, Greg. 1995. 'Television, Politics and the Rise of the New Right.' *Glasgow Media Group*, www.glasgowmediagroup.org/downloads/19-the-free-market-the-rise-of-the-new-right-social-mobility-education (accessed October 2018).

Philo, Greg, editor. 1995. *The Glasgow Media Group Reader, Vol II: Industry, Economy, War and Politics*. Routledge.

The Caretaker. 1963. Directed by Clive Donner, Caretaker Films.

Pippin, Robert B. 2010. *Hollywood Westerns and American Myth: The Importance of Howard Hawks and John Ford for Political Philosophy*. Yale University Press.

Potter, Dennis. 1994. *Without Walls: An Interview with Dennis Potter*, directed by Tom Poole, LWT.

Potter, Simon J. 2012. *Broadcasting Empire: The BBC and the British World, 1922–1970*. Oxford University Press.

Powell, Enoch. 2007. 'Enoch Powell's "Rivers of Blood" Speech.' *Telegraph*, 6 November, www.telegraph.co.uk/comment/3643823/Enoch-Powells-Rivers-of-Blood-speech.html (accessed 21 October 2022).

Priest, Christopher. 1979. 'British Science Fiction.' *Science Fiction: A Critical Guide*, edited by Patrick Parrinder. Longman.

Procter, James. 2004. *Stuart Hall*. Routledge.

Quart, Leonard. 2006. 'The Religion of the Market: Thatcherite Politics and the British Film of the 1980s.' *Fires Were Started: British Cinema and Thatcherism*, edited by Lester D. Friedman, 2nd ed. Wallflower Press, pp. 15–30.

'Revelation 20:10.' *BibleHub*, https://biblehub.com/revelation/20-10.htm (accessed 2 October 2018).

Rodman, Gilbert B. 2010. 'Cultural Studies is Ordinary.' *About Raymond Williams*, edited by Monika Seidl, Roman Horak and Lawrence Grossberg. Routledge, pp. 153–64.

Rollman, Hans. 2016. 'Personal Morality, Not Political Ideology: "Doctor Who" and the Cold War.' *Pop Matters*, May, www.popmatters.com/feature/personal-morality-not-political-ideology-doctor-who-and-the-cold-war (accessed 21 October 2022).

Ryan, Michael and Douglas Kellner. 1990. *Camera Politica: The Politics and Ideology of Contemporary Hollywood Film*. Indiana University Press.

Samuel, Raphael. 1992. 'Mrs Thatcher's Return to Victorian Values.' *Proceedings of the British Academy*, pp. 9–29, https://www.thebritishacademy.ac.uk/publishing/proceedings-british-academy/78/ (accessed 21 October 2022).

Sandvoss, Cornel. 2004. 'The Limits of Textuality: From Polysemy to Neutrosemy.' Research seminar at the University of Cardiff (Sociology). Library and Learning Services, Open Research, https://openresearch.surrey.ac.uk/esploro/outputs/conferencePresentation/The-Limits-of-Textuality-From-Polysemy-to-Neutrosemy/99512830002346 (accessed 14 November 2022).
'*Sapphire & Steel.*' *Counting Out Time.* 2007. Directed by Thomas Cock, Network Distributing.
Sapphire and Steel. The Sci Fi Freak Site, www.scififreaksite.com/sapphire.html (accessed September 2018).
Sawyer, Andy. 2006. 'Everyday Life in the Post-Catastrophe Future: Terry Nation's *Survivors.*' *British Science Fiction Television: A Hitchhiker's Guide*, edited by J. R. Cook and Peter Wright. IB Tauris, pp. 131–53.
Seaton, Jean. 2015. *'Pinkoes and Traitors': The BBC and the Nation, 1974–1987.* Profile Books.
Sexton, Max. 2016. '*The Tripods*: Distinction, Science Fiction and the BBC.' *Journal of British Cinema and Television*, vol. 13, no. 3. Edinburgh University Press, pp. 469–83.
Seymore, S. 2014. *Close Encounters of the Invasive Kind: Imperial History in Selected British Novels of Alien-Encounter Science Fiction After World War II.* Lit Verlag.
Sobchack, Vivian. 1987. *Screening Space: The American Science Fiction Film*, 3rd ed. Rutgers University Press.
Spencer, Keith A. 2018. 'Peak Superhero? Not Even Close: How One Movie Genre Became the Guiding Myth of Neoliberalism.' *Salon*, 28 April, www.salon.com/2018/04/28/how-superhero-films-became-the-guiding-myth-of-neoliberalism/ (accessed 21 October 2022).
Stalker, John. 2013. 'Margaret Thatcher Dead: Authoritarian Ruler Took Us to the Brink of Becoming a Police State.' *Mirror*, 10 April, www.mirror.co.uk/news/uk-news/margaret-thatcher-dead-authoritarian-ruler-1821699 (accessed 21 October 2022).
Stanley, Rob. 1993, 1996. 'P. J. Hammond Interview.' *Litost*, 1993, 1996, www.litost.org/SapphireAndSteel/hammond.html (accessed September 2018).
Stevens, Alan and Anthony Brown. 1992. 'Chris Boucher Interview.' *Kaldor City*, www.kaldorcity.com/people/cbinterview_1992.html (accessed 21 October 2022).
Stewart, Bruce. 2002. 'Writing Timeslip.' *The Official Timeslip Website*, www.timeslip.org.uk (accessed 14 November 2022).
Sutcliffe-Braithwaite, Florence. 2012. 'Neo-Liberalism and Morality in the Making of Thatcherite Social Policy.' *Historical Journal*, vol. 55, no. 2, pp. 497–520.

Sutcliffe-Braithwaite, Florence. 2013. 'Margaret Thatcher, Individualism and the Welfare State.' *History & Policy*, King's College, London, 15 April, www.historyandpolicy.org/opinion-articles/articles/margaret-thatcher-individualism-and-the-welfare-state (accessed 21 October 2022).

Suvin, Darko. 1979. *Metamorphoses of Science Fiction: On the Poetics and History of a Literary Genre.* Yale University Press.

Suvin, Darko. 2010. *Defined by a Hollow: Essays on Utopia, Science Fiction and Political Epistemology.* Peter Lang.

Suvin, Darko. 2014. 'Estrangement and Cognition.' *Strange Horizons*, 24 November, http://strangehorizons.com/non-fiction/articles/estrangement-and-cognition/#ps (accessed 21 October 2022).

Telotte, J. P. 2008. *The Essential Science Fiction Television Reader.* University Press Kentucky.

'Text of Statement Circulated in British Universities on Government Economic Policy (Letter of the 364 Economists to *The Times*)' [released 2013]. *Margaret Thatcher Foundation*, 30 March 1981, www.margaretthatcher.org/document/131671 (accessed 21 October 2022).

Tharoor, Ishaan. 2013. 'Margaret Thatcher's Foreign Policy: Was the Iron Lady on the Wrong Side of History?' *Time*, 8 April, http://world.time.com/2013/04/08/margaret-thatchers-foreign-policy-was-the-iron-lady-on-the-wrong-side-of-history/ (accessed 21 October 2022).

Thatcher, Margaret. 1967. 'Speech to Conservative Party Conference.' *Margaret Thatcher Foundation*, 20 October, www.margaretthatcher.org/document/101586 (accessed 21 October 2022).

Thatcher, Margaret. 1968. 'Conservative Political Centre (CPC) Lecture ("What's Wrong With Politics?").' *Margaret Thatcher Foundation*, 11 October, www.margaretthatcher.org/document/101632 (accessed 21 October 2022).

Thatcher, Margaret. 1975. 'Speech in Finchley (Conservative Leadership Election).' *Margaret Thatcher Foundation*, January, www.margaretthatcher.org/document/102605 (accessed 14 November 2022).

Thatcher, Margaret. 1977. 'Speech to Zurich Economic Society ("The New Renaissance").' *Margaret Thatcher Foundation*, 14 March, www.margaretthatcher.org/document/103336 (accessed 21 October 2022).

Thatcher, Margaret. 1978. 'TV Interview for Granada *World in Action* ("Rather Swamped").' *Margaret Thatcher Foundation*, 27 January, www.margaretthatcher.org/document/103485 (accessed 21 October 2022).

Thatcher, Margaret. 1979. 'Speech in Finchley.' *Margaret Thatcher Foundation*, 2 May, www.margaretthatcher.org/document/104072 (accessed 21 October 2022).

Thatcher, Margaret. 1980a. 'Airey Neave Memorial Lecture.' *Margaret Thatcher Foundation*, 3 March, www.margaretthatcher.org/document/104318 (accessed 21 October 2022).

Thatcher, Margaret. 1980b. 'TV Interview for London Weekend Television *Weekend World*.' *Margaret Thatcher Foundation*, 6 January, www.margaretthatcher.org/document/104210 (accessed 21 October 2022).

Thatcher, Margaret. 1981a. 'Interview for Sunday Times.' *Margaret Thatcher Foundation*, 1 May, www.margaretthatcher.org/document/104475 (accessed 14 November 2022).

Thatcher, Margaret. 1981b. 'Remarks Arriving at the White House.' *Margaret Thatcher Foundation*, 26 February, www.margaretthatcher.org/document/104576 (accessed 21 October 2022).

Thatcher, Margaret. 1981. 'Speech at Conservative Party Conference (Plus Address to Overflow Meeting).' 16 October, www.margaretthatcher.org/document/104717 (accessed 21 October 2022).

Thatcher, Margaret. 1982. 'TV Interview for ITN (Falklands).' *Margaret Thatcher Foundation*, 5 April, www.margaretthatcher.org/document/104913 (accessed 21 October 2022).

Thatcher, Margaret. 1983a. 'Speech to the Scottish Conservative Party Conference.' *Margaret Thatcher Foundation*, 13 May, www.margaretthatcher.org/document/105314 (accessed 21 October 2022).

Thatcher, Margaret. 1983b. 'TV Interview for LWT *Weekend World*.' *Margaret Thatcher Foundation*, 5 June, www.margaretthatcher.org/document/105098 (accessed 21 October 2022).

Thatcher, Margaret. 1984. 'TV Interview for ORF (Austrian TV) ("Vintage Thatcher").' *Margaret Thatcher Foundation*, 31 October, www.margaretthatcher.org/document/105579 (accessed 21 October 2022).

Thatcher, Margaret. 1985a. 'TV Interview for CBS *60 Minutes*.' *Margaret Thatcher Foundation*, 15 February, www.margaretthatcher.org/document/105964 (accessed 21 October 2022).

Thatcher, Margaret. 1985b. 'TV Interview for Yorkshire Television *Woman to Woman*.' *Margaret Thatcher Foundation*, 2 October, www.margaretthatcher.org/document/105830 (accessed 21 October 2022).

Thatcher, Margaret. 1987a. 'General Election Press Conference (Health and Social Security)', *Margaret Thatcher Foundation*, 4 June, www.margaretthatcher.org/document/106866 (accessed 21 October 2022).

Thatcher, Margaret. 1987b. 'Interview for *Woman's Own* ("No Such Thing as Society").' *Margaret Thatcher Foundation*, 23 September, www.margaretthatcher.org/document/106689 (accessed 21 October 2022).

Thatcher, Margaret. 1987c. 'Press Conference at Vancouver Commonwealth Summit'. *Margaret Thatcher Foundation*, October, www.margaretthatcher.org/document/106948 (accessed 21 October 2022).

Thatcher, Margaret. 1987d. 'Speech at Soviet Official Banquet.' *Margaret Thatcher Foundation,* 30 March, www.margaretthatcher.org/document/106776 (accessed 21 October 2022).

Thatcher, Margaret. 1988. 'TV Interview for ITN (Brussels NATO Summit).' *Margaret Thatcher Foundation,* 3 March, www.margaretthatcher.org/document/107185 (accessed 21 October 2022).

Thompson, Michael J. 2005. 'A Brief History of Neoliberalism by David Harvey.' *Dissent,* vol. 3, pp. 22–7, www.dissentmagazine.org/democratiya_issue/winter-2005 (accessed 21 October 2022).

Tomlinson, Claudia. 2013. 'What is Thatcher's Legacy to Black and Ethnic Minority People in the UK?' *HuffPost,* 11 June, www.huffingtonpost.co.uk/claudia-tomlinson/margaret-thatcher-legacy_b_3063611.html (accessed 21 October 2022).

Tracey, Michael. 2003. 'The BBC and the General Strike: May 1926.' *BBC and the Reporting of the General Strike.* Microform Academic Publishers.

Turnock, Rob. 2007. *Television and Consumer Culture: Britain and the Transformation of Modernity.* IB Tauris.

'Vengeance on Varos'. 2021. The *Doctor Who* transcripts, 18 August, www.chakoteya.net/DoctorWho/22-2.htm (accessed 14 November 2022).

Vint, Sherryl. 2013. 'Visualising the British Boom: British Science Fiction Film and Television.' *CR: The New Centennial Review,* vol. 13, no. 2, pp. 155–78.

Vohlidka, John. 2013. "With Proof, You Don't Have To Believe': *Doctor Who* and the Celestials.' *Time and Relative Dimensions in Faith: Religion and Doctor Who,* edited by Andrew Crome and James McGrath. Longman and Todd Ltd., pp. 118–31.

Von Dirke, Sabine. 2017. 'Neoliberalism's Reengineering of the Authoritarian Personality.' *Colloquia Germanica,* vol. 50, no. 3/4, pp. 327–38.

Watts, Paul. 2020. *Above the Law: The Unofficial Guide to Star Cops.* Miwk Publishing Ltd.

Wegner, Philip E. 2010. 'Preface: Emerging from the Flood in Which We Are Sinking: Or, Reading with Darko Suvin (Again).' *Defined by a Hollow: Essays on Utopia, Science Fiction and Political Epistemology,* by Darko Suvin. Peter Lang.

When Worlds Collide – Doctor Who and Politics. 2012. Produced and directed by Ed Stradling, 2entertain.

White, Mimi. 1992. 'Ideological Analysis and Television.' *Channels of Discourse, Reassembled,* edited by Robert C. Allen. University of North Carolina Press, pp. 161–202.

Willett, John. 1959. *The Theatre of Bertolt Brecht: A Study from Eight Aspects.* Methuen.

Willett, John. 1964. *Brecht on Theatre: The Development of an Aesthetic.* Methuen.

Williams, Linda Ruth. 2004. 'Dream Girls and Mechanic Panic: Dystopia and its Others in *Brazil* and *Nineteen Eighty-Four*.' *Liquid Metal: The Science Fiction Film Reader*, edited by Sean Redmond. Wallflower Press, pp. 64–75.

Woodhead, Linda. 2016. 'How the Church of England Lost the English People.' *Religion & Ethics*, 8 November, www.abc.net.au/religion/articles/2016/11/08/4571329.htm (accessed 21 October 2022).

Wright, Peter. 2005. 'British Science Fiction.' *A Companion to Science Fiction*, edited by David Seed. Blackwell, pp. 289–306.

Wright, Peter. 2006. 'Echoes of Discontent: Conservative Politics and *Sapphire & Steel*.' *British Science Fiction Television: A Hitchhiker's Guide*, edited by J. R. Cook and Peter Wright. IB Tauris Publishers, pp. 193–218.

Wright, Peter. 2009. 'Film and Television, 1960–1980.' *The Routledge Companion to Science Fiction*, edited by Mark Bould and Andrew M. Butler. Taylor & Francis Group, pp. 90–102.

Wright, Peter. 2011. 'Expatriate! Expatriate! *Doctor Who: The Movie* and Commercial Negotiation of a Multiple Text.' *British Science Fiction Film and Television: Critical Essays*, edited by Tobias Hochscherf and James Leggott. McFarland, pp. 128–43.

Wyndham, John. 2016. *The Day of the Triffids*. Gollancz.

Index

A-Team, The (TV series) 199
Adorno, Theodore 10
Americanisation 23–27
Anderson, Gerry and Sylvia 25, 27
authoritarian populism 60, 64, 92,
　120, 128, 132, 146, 160,
　209

Barthes, Roland 7–8, 12, 69, 115,
　156, 162–3, 192
　Mythologies 7–9, 119, 146,
　　156–7, 162, 192
　See also essential types
BBC 8–9, 12, 17, 22–3, 24, 27,
　34–5, 37, 41–2, 46, 50, 63,
　67, 79, 107, 147, 159, 161,
　175, 192–5, 208, 211, 213
Blake's 7 (TV series) 1, 2, 4, 9, 12,
　16–18, 28–9, 56, 57, 61,
　63–86, 92, 94, 96, 98, 100,
　107, 109, 111, 113, 115,
　118, 146, 147, 150, 156,
　167, 177, 178, 192, 195,
　198, 204, 205, 209–14, 215
Boucher, Chris 11, 68–9, 76, 78,
　80, 83, 86, 175, 192–3,
　194, 198, 208
Bould, Mark 4, 27, 38, 39, 42, 47,
　63, 148
Breaking Bad (TV series) 2, 71

Brecht, Bertolt 73–4, 77, 91, 99,
　141
　See also verfremdungseffekt
Burgess, Anthony
　A Clockwork Orange 165
Burke, Edmund 186

Campbell, Joseph 179–80, 205
　See also Hero's Journey, The
capitalism 15, 61, 102, 106, 109,
　125, 135, 136, 163, 164,
　166, 172, 185, 187, 200,
　201, 206
Cartmel, Andrew 11, 119–20, 126,
　127, 137, 139, 140, 144,
　208
Caughie, John 10, 35
Chase, David, 1
Christopher, John 148, 156, 163–5,
　173, 174
Church of England 26, 57, 113,
　176, 184–6, 191
Churchill, Winston 104, 139, 184,
　188, 190
Clarke, Arthur C
　Childhood's End 23, 39, 43,
　　150, 158, 164–5
cognitive estrangement 14, 54, 74,
　134, 207
　See also Suvin, Darko

Index

consensus politics 17, 18, 20, 23, 26, 32, 38, 39, 40, 41, 42, 43, 47, 56, 57, 61, 63, 64, 65, 67, 76, 77, 78, 84, 86, 89, 116, 118, 120, 145, 149, 153, 154, 155, 157, 187, 210, 212
Cooper, Richard 183, 184
critical dystopia (Moylan) 17, 65
Cromwell, Oliver 178
Cronenberg, David 164

Danger Man (TV series) 23
Day of the Triffids, The (TV series) 9, 18, 22, 51, 148–55, 214
Deadwood (TV series) 2
Death on the Rock 113
Demiurge 173
Dicks, Terrance 35, 48, 49, 117
Doctor Who (TV series) 2, 9, 11, 16, 17, 18, 22, 26, 29, 32, 35, 36, 38, 40–8, 55, 61, 84, 87, 88, 89, 92, 98, 113, 115, 116–46, 147, 150, 156, 165, 192, 208, 209–14
dystopia 3, 4, 15–17, 60, 64–5, 69, 122, 125, 132, 165, 177, 197
  See also critical dystopia (Moylan)

Eastwood, Clint 105
eschatology 57, 134
essential types (Barthes) 7, 42, 54, 110, 146, 162
Ever Decreasing Circles (TV series) 13

Falklands War 5, 73, 95, 107, 120, 134, 182, 188
Fargo (TV series) 2
Fascism 130, 173, 174, 183, 190, 214

Fellowes, Julian 177
Filby, Eliza 5, 161, 184, 185
Fisher, Mark 26, 90, 94, 95, 101, 106, 109, 111, 114, 120, 135, 141, 159, 170, 181, 194, 199, 200, 201, 204, 205, 206
Fiske, John 12, 23
Freiberger, Fred 27, 33

Galtieri, Leopoldo 188, 190, 191
Game of Thrones (TV series) 182
Geraghty, Lincoln 10, 147, 150, 151, 159, 160
Good Life, The (TV series) 13
Grade, Lew 17, 24, 87
Grade, Michael 117, 192
Gramsci, Antonio 6, 166, 172
  See also hegemony
Gridneff, Evgeny 193

Hall, Stuart 5, 6, 13, 30, 60, 66, 71
  See also authoritarian populism
Hammond, Peter J. 87, 88, 90, 95
Harvey, David 6, 166, 225, 232
Hayek, Friedrich 5
Hayward, Justin 175
hegemony, 11, 166, 172, 180, 215
Herbert, Frank 180
Hero's Journey, The 180, 181, 191
High-Rise (Ballard) 26
Hitler, Adolf 38, 188, 190
Holmes, Robert 150
Holmes, Sherlock 37, 106, 121
  Holmesian 105, 121
homosexuality 60, 162, 184
Hulke, Malcolm 35, 43, 44, 45, 117
Huxley, Aldous
  Brave New World 64, 69

Invisible Man, The (TV serial) 150
IRA 51, 79, 113, 122

ITV 17, 23–5, 35–7, 87, 88, 107, 113, 147, 175, 176, 187, 208
ATV 87, 88
Incorporated Television Company (ITC) 25, 27
Southern Television (TVS) 176

Jagger, Mick 161

Kneale, Nigel 35, 37, 38, 39, 49, 66
Knights of God (TV series) 2, 18, 50, 58, 137, 149, 175, 176–92, 205, 214

Letts, Barry 48, 49, 117
Lucas, George 180, 205

MacGyver (TV series) 202
Machiavellianism 1, 6, 9, 11, 18, 29, 54, 56, 59, 61, 64, 65, 66, 67, 73, 74, 75, 80, 86, 97, 98, 104, 106, 120, 139, 141, 145, 148, 149, 155, 159, 168, 169, 170, 171, 196, 197, 198, 205, 206, 208, 209, 211, 215
Mad Men (TV series) 2
Magnum, PI (TV series) 198, 202
Manicheanism 145, 179, 180, 183, 187, 202
Marxism 15, 71, 73, 74
Miami Vice (TV series) 199, 202
Milton, John
    Paradise Lost 113
Monaghan, David 188, 189
Moonbase-3 (TV series) 17, 48–50, 195
Moylan, Tom 16, 65
    See also critical dystopia

Nation, Terry 12, 35, 50, 53, 58, 67–9

neoliberalism, 3, 4, 5, 10, 19, 45, 61, 64, 86, 101, 104, 106, 138, 140, 148, 149, 150, 159, 164, 170–1, 176, 179, 186, 197, 201, 205, 206, 207–11, 214, 215
Newman, Sydney 117
NHS 204

O'Day, Andrew 4, 12, 16, 26, 45, 75, 85, 127, 132
Orwell, George
    Nineteen Eighty-Four 64

Powell, Enoch 29, 128
Powell, Jonathan 159, 192

Quatermass (TV serials) 9, 21, 36, 37, 38, 66, 89, 103, 104
    Quatermass and the Pit 37, 39, 40–1, 43, 164
    Quatermass Experiment, The 37
    Quatermass II 37

Ragnarök 56, 82, 119, 135, 213, 214
    Gods of Ragnarök 135
Reagan, Ronald 113, 143, 144, 145, 196, 202, 204
realpolitik 3, 9, 23, 57, 65, 67, 81, 97, 99, 100, 119, 121, 122, 124, 126, 138, 153, 154, 182, 208, 210, 211
Rees-Mogg, William 161
Revelation, Book of 56, 112, 113, 135, 182, 213, 214
Runcie, Robert 185–6
Russian Revolution 179

Saint, The (TV series) 24
Sapphire & Steel (TV series) 2, 4, 9, 16, 18, 26, 29, 55, 57, 61, 67, 73, 84, 87–115,

118, 120, 121, 124, 141, 147, 150, 165, 209, 210, 211, 212, 213
Second World War 20, 36, 38, 42, 46, 47, 88, 103, 137, 143, 189, 210
socialism 8, 15, 97, 106, 142, 185, 187
Sopranos, The (TV series) 1–2
Space: 1999 (TV series) 3, 17, 25, 27, 31–4, 66, 103, 104
Star Cops (TV series) 2, 18, 150, 175, 192–205, 208, 214
Survivors (TV series) 3, 12, 17, 32, 36, 50–9, 66, 71, 78, 99, 150, 151, 152, 156, 177, 182
Suvin, Darko 14–16, 30, 64, 69, 74, 81, 100, 197, 207
See also cognitive estrangement

Thatcher, Margaret 63, 93, 118, 132, 167, 212, 223, 226, 227, 229, 230, 231, 232, 233, 234
Thatcherism 4, 5, 6, 7, 9, 10, 11, 18, 38, 60, 61, 63, 64, 65, 67, 69, 71, 73, 75, 77, 79, 81, 83, 84, 85, 86, 89, 91, 92, 93, 95, 97, 99, 101, 103, 105, 106, 107, 109, 111, 113, 115, 116, 117, 118, 119, 120, 122, 125, 126, 127, 128, 132, 133, 136, 137, 138, 140, 145, 147, 150, 151, 153, 159, 161, 166, 176, 179, 182, 187, 189, 191, 197, 205, 208, 209, 210, 211, 213, 214
Time Machine, The 121
See also Wells, H. G.
Tripods, The (TV series) 2, 4, 10, 18, 50, 148–50, 156–74, 177, 183, 199, 208, 215

UFO (TV series) 3, 17, 21, 25, 27–31, 32, 33, 46, 48, 55, 59, 66, 78, 99, 103, 195

verfremdungseffekt (Brecht) 73–74, 77, 91, 99, 141
Victoria (Queen) 139, 189
Victorian 6, 7, 10, 47, 54, 91, 94, 95, 103, 104, 106, 111, 120, 122, 130, 131, 132, 133, 134, 135, 136, 137, 155, 177, 183, 189, 190, 191, 192, 206, 207, 210, 211

Wells, H. G. 22
  The Invisible Man 150
  The Time Machine 121
  The War of the Worlds 150, 156
  Wellsian fantasies 34
Whitehouse, Mary 184

Young Ones, The (TV series) 1

Zizek, Slavoj 181

EU authorised representative for GPSR:
Easy Access System Europe, Mustamäe tee 50,
10621 Tallinn, Estonia
gpsr.requests@easproject.com

www.ingramcontent.com/pod-product-compliance
Lightning Source LLC
Chambersburg PA
CBHW070346240426
43671CB00013BA/2420